Neural Networks

Proceedings of the-School on Neural Networks –
June 1967 in Ravello

Edited by E. R. Caianiello

With 80 Figures

Springer-Verlag New York Inc. 1968

ISBN 978-3-642-87598-4   ISBN 978-3-642-87596-0 (eBook)
DOI 10.1007/978-3-642-87596-0

Softcover reprint of the hardcover 1st edition 1968
Library of Congress Catalog Card Number 68-8783

Foreword

Sciences may be nowadays grouped into three classes, having as their subjects of study respectively Matter, Life and Intelligence. That "Intelligence" may be studied in a quantitative manner is a discovery of our age, not less significant in many ways than the 17th century realization that celestial phenomena are of one and the same nature as terrestrial and all other physical accidents. As the latter was accomplished through and accompanied by a major revolution in philosophy and method, so is now the scientific investigation of intelligent phenomena — although harely begun — already causing an unprecedented revolution in all our previous conceptions as mind and machine, society and organization. What electronic computers have already accomplished in disclosing perspectives to sciences and imposing new approaches to management is but a negligible change, if compared to those yet in store, which will closely follow the understanding of the many as yet unknown functional principles which make nervous systems act and react the way they do.

The study of Neural Networks is the key point in the systematic quantitative investigation of such phenomena. With patience and humility, neuroanatomists and physiologists try to connect structure with function in systems of neurons which are "simple" enough to be studied with the extant techniques, either because of the paucity of their elements or because of the high degree of symmetry these possess (e.g. some sensorial organs or the cerebellum); mathematicians and logicians produce models of individual neurons or aggregates of them and study their deterministic and probabilistic properties with all available techniques, from boolean and matrix algebra to statistical approaches; physicists, chemists and engineers develop new component parts to implement the hardware realization of such models, when their computer simulation is not deemed convenient. As is always the case, any answer which is found makes it necessary to pose more questions.

The most vivid aspect of these researches is perhaps their totally interdisciplinary character. The verification of a mathematical theory stemming from neuroanatomical and physiological considerations may be found, at times, only by observing the behavior of some piece of hardware; or, conversely, logical schemata do often suggest new physiological experiments. Moreover, once some principle is understood, even at only an approximate level, it becomes available for applications to instances of technological interest which are quite different from the natural ones: thus many devices, which perform useful tasks of pattern recognition, bear a resemblance to living neural systems which is often very loose, although the main inspiration originated from the study of the latter.

The lectures on Neuronal Networks which are collected in this Course, which was made possible by the generous assistance of the NATO Advanced Study Institute Programme, give a many-sided vies of the subject, as is required by its very nature. It was our luck that some of the most eminent people in the field kindly accepted to participate with original contributions; the timing of the Course was also very fortunate, because — as all those who shared that unusually exciting fortnight at Ravello unanimously acknowledged — it occurred that, together with the presentation of brilliant experimental researched and the formulation of challenging problems, also significant developments of mathematical techniques were discussed, such as to give hopes of being apt to handle concretely those very results and problems (to mention one of them: what language do neurons talk to each other? Some people are at present working on this problem with ideas which originated during our Course).

The individual contributions are not presented here in their primitive chronological order; it has seemed more advisable to group them so as to start from neuroanatomy and physiology, go then through logic, deterministic and probabilistic mathematical modeling, to end finally with more general approaches and considerations, which offer broad and diversified perspectives.

The Editor's task has been this time a very agreable one; it could be performed, for the most part, before the manuscripts were actually delivered, thanks to the generous collaboration of the Authors, who adjusted the nature and dimensions of their contributions to the wishes and interests of the audience, with a continued and harmonic process of feedback which, it is hoped, may make the reading of this Course as stimulating as it was the partaking in it.

Naples, August 1968   E. R. CAIANIELLO

Contents

List of Authors

Editor:

CAIANIELLO, E. R., Professor, Laboratorio di Cibernetica del CNR, 80072 Arco Felice, Napoli, Italia.

Contributors:

APLEVICH, J. D., Research Associate, Committee on Mathematical Biology, The University of Chicago, 5753 Drexel Avenue, Chicago, Ill. 60637, USA.

ARBIB, M., Assistant Professor of Electrical Engineering, ERL 233 B, Stanford, Calif. 94305, USA.

COWAN, J. D., Professor and Chairman, Committee on Mathematical Biology, University of Chicago, 5753 Drexel Avenue, Chicago, Ill. 60637, USA.

BRAITENBERG, V., Professor, Dr., Istituto di Fisica dell'Universita di Napoli, Napoli, Italia.

EVANS, E., F., Dr., Senior Research Fellow, Medical Research Council Group, Department of Communication, University of Keele, Staffordshire, England.

FRANKLIN, G. F., Professor of Electrical Engineering, Dr., Stanford University, Stanford, Calif. 94305, USA.

JOHANNESMA, P. I. M., Drs., Laboratory of Medical Physics, University of Nijmegen, Geert Grote Plein Noord 21, Nijmegen, The Netherlands.

KALMAN, R. E., Professor of Mathematical System Theory and Operations Research, Department of Operations Research, Stanford University, Stanford, Calif. 94305, USA.

LEVY, J.-CL., Ingénieur en Chef, Directeur de Recherches au CERA, 103 Boulevard de la Reine, 78 Versailles, France.

LUCA, A. DE, Research Associate of the Italian National Research Council, Laboratorio di Cibernetica del CNR, 80072 Arco Felice, Napoli, Italia.

McCULLOCH, W. S., Colonel, Institute of Technology, Rm 20 A-122, Massachusetts, Cambridge, Mass. 02139, USA.

MacKAY, D. M., Professor of Communication, Department of Communication, University of Keele, Staffordshire, England.

NAGASAWA, K., Research Fellow (Air Defence Force), Research Institute of Electrical Communication, Tohoku University, Sendai, Japan.

NILSSON, N. J. R., Senior Research Engineer, Stanford Research Institute, Menlo Park, California 94025, USA.

NOGUCHI, S., Professor, Research Institute of Electrical Communication, Tohoku University, Sendai, Japan.

OIZUMI, J., Professor, Research Institute of Electrical Communication, Tohoku University, Sendai, Japan.

RALL, W., Senior Research Physicist, Mathematical Research Branch, National Institute of Arthritis and Metabolic Diseases, National Institutes of Health, Bethesda, Maryland, USA.

RATLIFF, F., Professor, The Rockefeller University, New York, N.Y. 10021, USA.

RICCIARDI, L. M., Research Associate at the National Council of Researches, Laboratorio di Cibernetica del CNR, 80072 Arco Felice, Napoli, Italia.

STRASZAK, A., Professor, Institute for Automatic Control, Polish Academy of Sciences, ul KRN 55, Warsaw, Poland.

TOUSCHEK, B. F., Ph. D., Viale Pola 23, Rome, Italia.

Synaptic Activity at Dendritic Locations: Theory and Experiment

W. Rall

Mathematical Research Branch, National Institute of Arthritis and Metabolic Diseases,
National Institutes of Health, Bethesda, Maryland

Circumstances have prevented me from preparing a full report of the extemporaneous talks I gave at the summer school in Ravello. This is a brief statement and discussion of the theoretical and experimental material that was presented. Further details can be found in the several references listed.

The extensive dendritic branching of most neurons is an impressive anatomical fact that has been known for more than 50 years. During the past 10 years, it has become established that synapses are distributed in large numbers over the entire soma-dendritic surface of such neurons. Illustrations, quantitative estimates, and references to the literature can be found in several earlier papers [5, 6, 7]. The reason for emphasizing these anatomical facts is that models of neuronic networks have usually neglected them.

The development of a mathematical model of dendritic neurons was begun because of a need to combine biophysical models of nerve membrane with the anatomical facts of neuronal branching and with electrophysiological observations of whole neuron activity. At first, the need was to reinterpret electrophysiological observations where previous interpretations had neglected the dendrites. The theoretical results provided the basis for new methods of estimating such neuronal parameters as membrane resistivity, membrane time constant, the ratio of dendritic input conductance to soma membrane conductance, and later, also the effective length of the dendritic system. Once reasonable ranges of values were known for these parameters, it was possible to make theoretical predictions that could be subjected to experimental testing. Two different examples of such interaction between theory and experiment are presented below: one example involves synaptic potentials of motoneurons in cat spinal cord; the other involves functional interaction between the populations of mitral cells and granule cells in the olfactory bulb of rabbit. In both cases, certain non-trivial theoretical predictions have been confirmed by experiment.

The mathematical treatment of nerve membrane potential distributions in nerve cylinders has long been known to involve a partial differential equation of the form,

$$\frac{\partial^2 V}{\partial X^2} = V + \frac{\partial V}{\partial t}.$$

The fact that a class of interesting boundary value problems in dendritic trees can be transformed to problems in an equivalent cylinder was shown mathematically in 1961 [6]. Extension to a more general class of problems was achieved by using compartmental systems to represent dendritic trees; this is equivalent to replacing the partial differential equation with a system of ordinary differential equations that are linear and of first order [7]. With this compartmental approximation, it is possible to compute the effects of any specified spatio-temporal pattern of membrane conductance change distributed over any specified branching system. Many of the computations have been done with a chain of ten compartments, where the first compartment represents the neuron soma and the other compartments represent dendritic membrane divided into nine increments of increasing functional distance away from the soma.

Variety in Synaptic Potentials

Explicit theoretical predictions of different shapes of synaptic potentials for different soma-dendritic locations of synaptic input were made as early as 1962 [6, 7]; a more comprehensive exploration of such theoretical predictions has been published very recently [8]. The synaptic input was usually restricted to one compartment of the soma-dendritic chain of compartments. The synaptic potential was computed as the resulting transient membrane depolarization at the soma compartment. With a brief synaptic input, the effect of a somatic or proximal dendritic input location was to produce a synaptic potential characterized by a relatively sharp and early peak, as compared with the more rounded and delayed peak that results from a more distal dendritic input location.

By means of "shape index plots", where each synaptic potential shape is represented as a point in a plot of "half-width" versus "time to peak", it has been possible to compare the theoretical variety of shapes with the experimental variety obtained with stimulation of group I-A afferent fibers of cat motoneurons [1, 8, 9]. Careful consideration of this comparison between theoretical predictions and experimental results provides convincing support for the notion that different soma-dendritic distributions of synaptic input provide the most reasonable explanation of the experimentally observed variety. Additional support for this theoretical interpretation is provided by comparing theoretical predictions and observations made with polarizing currents [2, 8, 9] and impedance bridge techniques [13]. The slower synaptic potential shapes correlate with small effects of polarizing current and with failure to detect impedance transients, as would be expected theoretically for a predominantly distal dendritic input location. In contrast, the faster synaptic potential shapes correlate with large effects of polarizing current and with success in detecting an impedance transient, as would be expected theoretically for predominantly somatic and proximal dendritic synaptic input.

This interaction between theory and experiment has thus provided a satisfactory explanation of several findings that were previously regarded as paradoxical [1, 2, 8, 9, 13]. It has convinced us of the correctness of our hypothesis that dendritic synapses play a significant role even in the monosynaptic activation of cat motoneurons. This increases our conviction that dendritic synaptic input should be included in more realistic models of neuronic networks.

Electric Potentials in Olfactory Bulb

The experimental observations made upon the olfactory bulb of rabbit by PHILLIPS, POWELL and SHEPHERD [3, 4, 12] provided the starting point for this theoretical study. They observed, following a synchronous antidromic volley in the lateral olfactory tract, that the distribution of electric potential in the bulb is highly reproducible; it can be represented, essentially, as a function of two variables, time and depth in the bulbar layers. Dr. SHEPHERD then came to work with me at NIH; our aim was to develop a computational model, based upon the known anatomical organization of the olfactory bulb and upon generally accepted properties of nerve membrane, to reconstruct this experimentally observed distribution of electric potential. Full details of this theoretical model have not yet been published, but the essential results of these computations, their theoretical consequences, the prediction and anatomical discovery of dendro-dendritic synapses, and the wider implications of these findings have been published [10] and also reported at several symposia.

Briefly stated, the antidromic activation of a mitral cell was simulated by means of a compartmental model representing axon, soma and dendrites. Then, assuming synchronous activation of a population of mitral cells arranged in a spherical shell, the radial gradient of extracellular potential was computed as a function of (radial) depth and time. These computed radial gradients actually contain the essential results; however, in order to reconstruct the experimental recordings of potential relative to a distant electrode, it proved necessary to consider the consequences of the "punctured" spherical symmetry of the olfactory bulb. Although most of the electric current generated by the mitral cells remains confined within the bulb, there is an extra pathway for current to flow from the bulb surface, through the surrounding volume, and then through the "puncture" to the central region of the bulb; the distant electrode is located along this extra pathway and divides the potential drop in approximately the ratio, 1:4. When this potential divider effect is taken into account, the computed results show that the early portion (Periods I and II in reference 10) of the experimental recordings can be attributed primarily to synchronous antidromic activation of the mitral cell population.

The same quantitative considerations that led to the above result led also to the conclusion that the later portion (Period III in reference 10) of the experimental recordings could not be attributed to activity of the mitral cells. During period III, there is a large positivity centered deep in the granule layer of the bulb, together with a large negativity centered in the external plexiform layer. This implies a substantial flow of *extracellular* current from the depths of the granule layer radially outward into the external plexiform layer. The population of cells which generates this electric current must possess a substantial *intracellular* pathway for the return flow of current from the external plexiform layer, through the mitral body layer, into the depths of the granule layer. This requirement is quantitatively not met by the mitral cells which extend only thin axons into the granule layer. Furthermore, the large population of granule cells can satisfy this requirement, and there is no reasonable alternative to this choice. Our computations demonstrated that the potential distribution during Period III could be reconstructed by assuming that there is a strong membrane depolarization of the granule dendrites in the external plexiform layer, coupled with essentially passive membrane in their deeper processes and cell bodies.

Because this depolarization of granule dendrites would occur in the region of contact with many mitral dendrites, and at a time just after the mitral dendrites were depolarized, we postulated that the mitral secondary dendrites themselves deliver synaptic excitatory input directly to the granule dendrites. Furthermore, because Period III corresponds with the onset of mitral cell inhibition, the

1*

granule dendritic depolarization is both well timed and well placed to initiate synaptic inhibitory input to the mitral dendrites. Thus, the theoretical study led us to postulate two different kinds of dendro-dendritic synaptic actions: (i) mitral-to-granule synaptic excitation, and (ii) granule-to-mitral synaptic inhibition.

At the time we were led to this postulate, knowledge of such synaptic contacts was not available. Thus it was an exciting experience, when, several months later, the independent electron micrographic studies of REESE and BRIGHTMAN revealed two kinds of synaptic contacts, of opposite polarity, between the dendrites of granule cells and mitral cells. The polarity of these synaptic contacts was judged by the same criteria used elsewhere in the mammalian central nervous system. The remarkable finding of these pairs of oppositely oriented synapses fitted the requirements of our theoretical model so well that we agreed to report our findings and conclusions in a joint publication [10]. Further confirmatory anatomical results have been obtained by REESE [11].

This new dendrodendritic synaptic pathway has a number of unusual and interesting features. It provides a negative feedback with an anatomical distribution corresponding to a lateral inhibition which could contribute to sensory discrimination. This negative feedback can also provide sensory adaptation to a wide range of stimulus intensity. This hypothesis assigns an important function to neurons (the granule cells) which possess no axon, and suggests how they could function even without generating an action potential. It explains how such activity could account for the standing field potential of Period III. The various implications thus extend beyond the olfactory bulb.

The notion that dendrites can *send* as well as *receive* synaptically, and the notion that important interneuronal activity can be graded rather than an all-or-nothing event may be viewed by modelers in two different ways. These notions are a nuisance to anyone who prefers to work with oversimplified models; on the other hand, these notions provide additional degrees of freedom for the modeler. My conclusion here, and also with regard to implications of active versus passive dendritic membrane for information processing in the dendrites, is that I would be very much surprised if our nervous systems do not exploit these various degrees of freedom differently in different neuron types and in various portions of the nervous system.

Comment

Here I wish to comment briefly on a point that arose in a conversation with Drs. GERSTEIN and JOHANNESMA with regard to the feasibility of testing the predicted moments of Johannesma's theoretical interval distribution. It soon became apparent that a time series long enough to provide statistically reliable testing of these moments would usually be impractically long from the experimental point of view; it would be biologically unrealistic to assume stationary conditions for such a long time. This led me to comment that this very difficulty helps to strengthen the following conjecture: the information content of nervous activity should be sought not in the temporal sequence of impulses or bursts in one neuron, but rather, in the spatial ensemble of impulses or bursts in a set of neurons over a short time. The nervous system cannot wait around to analyse a long time series, it must convey information more quickly by means of spatial ensembles. Although this insight may seem all too obvious to some, nevertheless, it does imply that more theoretical and experimental effort should be devoted to spatial ensembles of neuronal activity. It should be added that considerable research on spatial ensembles has already been done, especially on visual systems, as represented in this School by Drs. RATLIFF, MacKAY and BRAITENBERG. Also, 1 week later in Pisa, I learned that Dr. MAFFEI had been thinking about the notion that a spatial ensemble can convey in a short time the information that requires a long time series with fewer units; he showed me unpublished results that demonstrate this for the case of sinusoidal modulation of light intensity to cat retina [14].

References

1. BURKE, R. E.: Composite nature of the monosynaptic excitatory postsynaptic potential. J. Neurophysiol. **30**, 1114—1137 (1967).
2. NELSON, P. G., and K. FRANK: Anomalous rectification in cat spinal motoneurons and the effect of polarizing currents on the excitatory postsynaptic potential. J. Neurophysiol. **30**, 1097—1113 (1967).
3. PHILLIPS, C. G., T. P. S. POWELL, and G. M. SHEPHERD: The mitral cell of the rabbit's olfactory bulb. J. Physiol. (Lond.) **156**, 26 P—27 P (1961).
4. — — — Responses of mitral cells to stimulation of the lateral olfactory tract in the rabbit. J. Physiol. (Lond.) **168**, 65—88 (1963).
5. RALL, W.: Branching dendritic trees and motoneuron membrane resistivity. Exp. Neurol. **1**, 491—527 (1959).
6. — Theory of physiological properties of dendrites. Ann. N.Y. Acad. Sci. **96**, 1071—1092 (1962).
7. — Theoretical significance of dendritic trees for neuronal input-output relations. In: Neural theory and modeling, pp. 73—79. Ed. by REISS, R. F. Stanford: Univ. press 1964.
8. — Distinguishing theoretical synaptic potentials computed for different soma-dendritic distributions of synaptic input. J. Neurophysiol. **30**, 1138—1168 (1967).
9. —, R. E. BURKE, T. G. SMITH, P. G. NELSON, and K. FRANK: Dendritic location of synapses and possible mechanisms for the monsynaptic EPSP in motoneurons. J. Neurophysiol. **30**, 1169—1193 (1967).
10. —, G. M. SHEPHERD, T. S. REESE, and M. W. BRIGHTMAN: Dendrodendritic synaptic pathway for inhibition in the olfactory bulb. Exp. Neurol. **14**, 44—56 (1966).
11. REESE, T. S.: Further studies on dendrodendritic synapses in the olfactory bulb. Anat. Rec. **154**, 408 (1966).
12. SHEPHERD, G. M.: Neuronal systems controlling mitral cell excitability. J. Physiol. (Lond.) **168**, 101—117 (1963).
13. SMITH, T. G., R. B. WUERKER, and K. FRANK: Membrane impedance changes during synaptic transmission in cat spinal motoneurons. J. Neurophysiol. **30**, 1072—1096 (1967).
14. MAFFEI, L.: Spatial and temporal averages in retinal channels. J. Neurophysiol. **31**, 283—287 (1968).

On Fields of Inhibitory Influence in a Neural Network

F. RATLIFF

The Rockefeller University, New York

I. Introduction

The aim of the research reported here is to reach an understanding of the complex dynamic behavior of a real neural network in terms of a few simple basic principles. The network is the retina of the compound eye of the horseshoe crab, *Limulus*. The basic principles are that fields of inhibitory influence surround points of excitation in the retina and that the ultimate response at any particular point is determined by the integration of the opposed excitatory and inhibitory influences at that point.

The spatial and temporal characteristics of these opposed influences and their integration are expressed in terms of a set of piece-wise linear simultaneous equations. Insofar as possible, all terms in the equations have physiological meaning. The validity of the equations and of the various terms contained in them is tested by comparing computed results with the results of experiments on the real neural network. To ensure rigorous tests, all constants are based on electrophysiological observations made in other independent experiments.

The fundamental principles that are elucidated in the study of this particular retinal network are expected to be relevant to the study of neural networks in general. Indeed, the three principal features of this retinal network, which provide the guidelines for the experimental analysis and quantitative theory, are common to many neutral networks:

1. The retina, as its name implies, contains extensive lateral interconnections by means of which a particular element may influence, or be influenced by, many other elements in an extensive *field* around it.

2. The response of any particular element in the network is determined by the *integration* of the opposed excitatory and inhibitory influences exerted on it.

3. Responses to transients are very pronounced; the network is a *dynamic* system.

The special functions of any particular neural network are determined primarily by the particular spatial and temporal configurations of the points and fields of opposed excitatory and inhibitory influences in that network. These special functions, of course, may differ greatly from one network to another, but — at the same time — may show many similarities. Practically all sensory networks, for example, share in common the special function of abstracting and transmitting information about stimulus *changes* in both time and space — often at the expense of accuracy of information about steady state conditions. There is good biological reason for this: the adjustments of an organism to the continual changes in its environment are undoubtedly more important for its survival than are adjustments to uniform conditions. Furthermore, it is far more economical for a nervous system to signal changes than it is to signal every bit of redundant information about steady states.

Several practical problems arise in the study of a real neural network: Where in the network to observe the properties of the fields of excitation and inhibition? What specific properties to record at these points? And how best to represent those properties in a quantitative description or mathematical theory?

Where to record data? The properties of a "field" can only be determined by making observations at more than one point in the system. Therefore, recordings from more than one neuron within the same field of excitation or inhibition are essential. In practice, recording from three points simultaneously seems to yield optimal results. There are many special situations, however, in which information from fewer points may be adequate or in which information from more points may be required. But, in general, multineuron observations of one kind or another are essential.

What is to be observed at these several points? For an understanding of the overall properties of a network of interconnected neurons, the most significant information is that which is transmitted from one part of the network to the other, that is, the information carried by the discrete propagated all-or-none impulses. The basic datum, therefore, is the time of occurence of an impulse.

Other data which can be recorded, such as the slow local excitatory and inhibitory potentials, are of interest also because they may either result from, or be the immediate precursors of, the information carrying impulses. Furthermore, it is by means of the local potentials that the excitatory and inhibitory influences are integrated.

How to analyze the basic recorded data? The times of occurrence of impulses can be analyzed in many different ways and represented in many different forms. "Instantaneous frequency" (reciprocals of the time intervals between succeeding impulses) is one of the most convenient and most meaningful forms, for it shows clearly, and in real time, such things as the mean frequency and the variations about the mean under steady state conditions, and the magnitude and duration of transient responses to changing conditions. Furthermore, no information is discarded in such a representation—each and every time of occurrence of an impulse is preserved and utilized.

More subtle analyses of the times of occurrence of nerve impulses—such as long term distributions of intervals about the mean interval—discard important information about how the intervals are distributed in real time. Furthermore, these distributions have not yet been shown to be significant carriers of information from one part of a network to another. Therefore, although they are of much interest to the physiologist because of their relation to underlying mechanisms, they need not be considered here.

In summary, it is the aim of this paper to outline a quantitative description of the steady state and dynamic behavior of a real neural network. The description will be couched in terms of the integration of opposed points of excitation and fields of inhibition. The data will consist mainly of times of occurrence of propagated impulses, recorded simultaneously from several neurons in the network and will be represented as an "instantaneous frequency". One special function of this particular network, it will be shown, is to abstract, enhance, and transmit information about spatial and temporal changes in the stimulus pattern on the receptor mosaic. Finally, the roles of fields of inhibitory influence in determining the special functions of other more complex retinal networks will be considered briefly.

II. Structure and Function of Individual "Receptor Units"

The compound lateral eye of *Limulus* contains approximately 1000 ommatidia (receptor units), arranged in a more or less hexagonal array. Each ommatidium contains about a dozen wedge shaped retinular cells arranged radially around the distal process of the eccentric cell—so called because although its distal process is in the center of the ommatidium, the cell body itself is eccentrically located. The retinular cells contain microvillous structures (the rhabdomeres) in which the photopigment is located. All of these rhabdomeres together form the rhabdom, which —in cross section—is shaped like the hub and spokes of a wheel centered on the distal process of the eccentric cell. The several retinular cells and the one eccentric cell each give rise to an axon. These are collected in small bundles that come together a few millimeters behind the eye to form the optic nerve. The optic nerve then travels several centimeters before entering the optic ganglion. Numerous fine branches arise from both the retinular cell axons and the eccentric cell axons. These fibers run laterally in small bundles and terminate in clumps of neuropile—generally around the axons of the eccentric cells—a short distance below the cell bodies. These lateral branches form an extensive network or *plexus* which mediates inhibitory influences. For anatomical details, see Miller (1957).

The optical properties of the lens-like structures of the individual ommatidia need not be considered here. In the experiments to be discussed, light was either guided into the individual ommatidia by means of special fiber-optics devices or else sharply focused on them by means of auxilliary lenses.

When an ommatidium is stimulated by light, the eccentric cell is depolarized (by an amount proportional to the logarithm of the intensity of illumination) and nerve impulses are discharged in its axon (the frequency of discharge being proportional to the amount of depolarization). Illumination of neighboring receptor units produces no impulses in the axon of this particular unit—instead it causes a hyperpolarization of the eccentric cell and a slowing of its discharge of nerve impulses. The hyperpolarization (and concomitant slowing of the discharge) is proportional to the number of neighboring receptor units activated and to their frequency of discharge. For details, see Purple and Dodge (1965).

In brief, each ommatidium may be regarded as a "receptor unit" in a large network of interconnected units. When stimulated by light, a receptor unit discharges nerve impulses in its eccentric cell axon. This activity produces inhibitory influences which are mediated by the plexus of interconnections and which slow the discharge of impulses in neighboring receptor units. Since each unit is also a neighbor of its neighbors, the inhibition is mutual. The frequency of discharge of impulses from each and every receptor unit in the network is determined by the sum of the opposed excitatory and inhibitory influences impinging upon it.

III. Excitation and Inhibition in the Steady State

The activity r of any particular receptor unit p is measured by the frequency of the discharge of impulses in its eccentric cell axon. This response is determined by the excitation e supplied by the external stimulus to the receptor unit. The excitation e_p of a particular receptor unit p is to be measured by its response r_p when the receptor unit is illuminated by itself. Measuring the excitation in this way lumps together the physical parameters of the stimulus and the characteristics of the photoexcitatory mechanism of the receptor. In short:

$$r_p = e_p$$

when the particular element p is illuminated alone. (Possible self inhibition will be considered later.)

The frequency of discharge of each of two neighboring receptor units is lower when illuminated together than when each is illuminated alone. Each inhibits the other. The magnitude of the inhibition (decrease in frequency) of each one has been shown to depend mainly upon the level of activity of the other. The activity of each is the resultant of the opposed excitatory and inhibitory influences from its respective light stimulus and the inhibitory influence exerted on it by its neighbor. Furthermore, it has been shown that, once a threshold has been reached, the inhibition exerted on each is a linear function of the level of activity of the other. See HARTLINE and RATLIFF (1957).

The responses to steady illumination of two receptor units that inhibit each other mutually (Fig. 1) may thus be described by two simultaneous linear equations that express concisely all of the above features of the interaction:

$$r_1 = e_1 - K_{1,\,2}\,(r_2 - r^0_{1,\,2})$$
$$r_2 = e_2 - K_{2,\,1}\,(r_1 - r^0_{2,\,1})$$

The response r of each receptor unit is determined by its excitation e diminished by the inhibitory influence exerted on it by its neighbor. The magnitude of this influence is expressed by the last term in each equation, which is written in accordance with the experimental findings as a simple linear expression. The threshold frequency that must be exceeded before a receptor unit can exert any inhibition on its neighbor is represented by r^0. It and the inhibitory coefficient K are labeled in each equation to identify the direction of the action: $r^0_{1,\,2}$ is the frequency of receptor 2 at which it begins to inhibit receptor 1; $r^0_{2,\,1}$ is the reverse. In the same way, $K_{1,\,2}$ is the coefficient of the inhibitory action of receptor 2 on receptor 1; $K_{2,\,1}$ the reverse. It is necessary to specify the direction of the action because the mutual influences are seldom identical, although they generally are similar.

To extend the description to more than two units it is necessary first to determine how the inhibitory influences from two different units combine when exerted on a third unit. We have found that they combine in a simple additive manner: the arithmetical sum of the inhibitory effect that each unit produces separately equals the physiological sum obtained when they act together see HARTLINE and RATLIFF (1958).

Consequently, the activity of n interacting receptors may be described by a set of simultaneous linear equations, each with $n-1$ inhibitory terms combined by simple addition.

$$r_p = e_p - \sum_{j=1}^{n} K_{p,\,j}\,(r_j - r^0_{p,\,j})$$

where p equals 1, 2, ..., n; and $j \neq p$. In other words, the total inhibitory influence exerted on a particular unit p is given by the simple summation of all the separate influences.

The separate influences, however, are those exerted when the units are simultaneously active—not those exerted when each unit is activated alone. That is, the inhibitory influences are simultaneous and mutual and must be expressed in terms of simultaneous equations. Each separate influence depends upon the response r of each element at the time the inhibition is exerted. In physiological terms the inhibition is *recurrent*. Impulses are not generated by excitation at one point and then abolished later by inhibition at another point. The excitatory and inhibitory influences act simultaneously at one common point—the site of impulse generation.

The above equations contain no explicit expressions for distance. None are required; the effects of distance are already implicit in the equations. In general, the threshold of inhibitory action increases with increasing distance between the units involved, and the coefficient of inhibitory action decreases. Thus, in the quantitative formulation, the changes in the inhibitory effect with distance may be ascribed to the combined effects of changing thresholds $(r^0_{p,j})$ and changing inhibitory coefficients $(K_{p,j})$ that accompany changes in the separation of the interacting units p and j. See Ratliff and Hartline (1957, 1959).

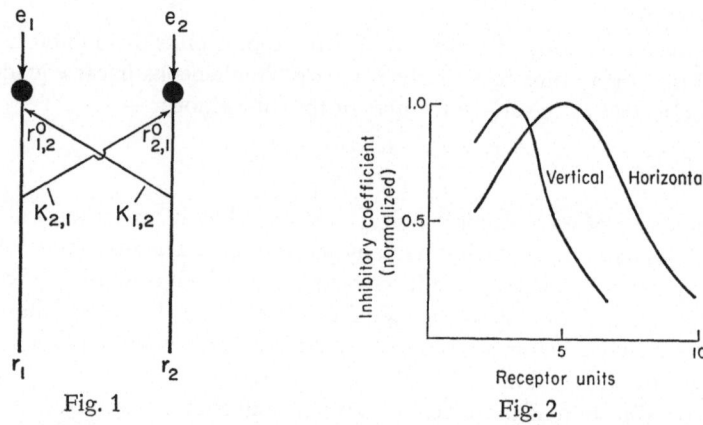

Fig. 1   Fig. 2

Fig. 1. Schema of mutual inhibitory interaction of two adjacent receptor units

Fig. 2. Dependence of inhibitory coefficient on separation of receptor units. Redrawn after R. B. Barlow (1967)

Early experiments suggested that the inhibition simply decreased monotonically with increasing distance. Recent experiments using an improved technique of illumination by means of fiber-optics and recording from as many as 20 fibers simultaneously, show that the maximum inhibitory effect is not immediately adjacent to the point of excitation producing it but is some distance removed (Fig. 2). The shape of the function can be nicely fitted by subtracting a narrow low amplitude gaussian curve from a broad high amplitude gaussian curve—both centered on the point of excitation. (The possible significance of the shape of the inhibitory field in space and of the shape of the inhibitory influence in time will be considered later.) The field is more or less elliptical. "Iso-inhibitory" contours roughly parallel the elliptical shape of the margin of the eye. See Barlow (1967).

Since the inhibition is recurrent and diminishes to zero with distance, the inhibitory effect produced by the combined action of several groups of receptors may be less than the sum of the inhibitory effects produced by each group acting alone. This can occur, because the inhibitory influence exerted by a receptor unit depends upon its own activity.

This can lead to peculiar effects. For example, when additional receptor units are illuminated in the vicinity of an interacting pair, too far from one to affect it directly but near enough to the second to inhibit it, the frequency of discharge of the first increases as it is partially released from the inhibition exerted on it by the second. Such "disinhibition" resembles facilitation: illumination of a distant region of the eye increases the level of activity of the test receptor. See HARTLINE and RATLIFF (1957).

Functional significance. The slope of the so-called characteristic curve (frequency of impulses plotted as a function of the logarithm of intensity) is reduced by lateral inhibition. See HARTLINE, RATLIFF, and MILLER (1961). This could be significant in

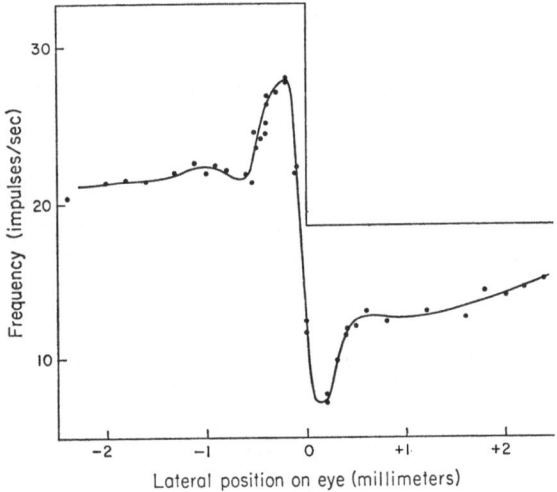

Fig. 3. Response to a step pattern of illumination. Upper curve shows response expected with no inhibition; lower curve shows response observed with inhibition. From R. B. BARLOW (1967)

at least two ways. First, if the impulse generating mechanism, rather than the receptor mechanism itself, sets the upper limit to the range of operation of the receptor unit, responding at generally lower frequencies would serve to extend this range. Second, coding the information in terms of lower frequencies is more economical for the system—requiring less energy to signal any particular level of intensity. The resolution provided by fewer impulses is poorer, of course.

One of the well known effects of lateral inhibition is the production of contrast effects. Border contrast, analogous to the border contrast in human vision that artists have known about for many centuries, occurs near the boundary between a dimly illuminated region and a brightly illuminated region of the retina. See RATLIFF and HARTLINE (1959), and RATLIFF (1965). A unit within the dimly illuminated region, but near this boundary, will be inhibited not only by dimly illuminated neighbors but also by brightly illuminated ones. The total inhibition exerted on such a unit will be greater, therefore, than exerted on other dimly illuminated elements that are farther from the boundary; consequently its frequency of response will be less than theirs. Similarly a unit within, but near the boundary of, the brightly illuminated field will have a higher frequency of discharge than other equally illuminated units that are located well within the bright field but are subject to stronger inhibition since all their immediate neighbors are also brightly illuminated. Maxima and minima therefore appear in the response of the receptor unit on either side of the boundary (Fig. 3). The discontinuity in the pattern of illumination is thus accentuated in the pattern of the neural response.

It might be argued that the inhibition is detrimental because it loses significant information that is retained in the uninhibited response pattern which more closely resembles the step in the pattern of illumination. The validity of any such argument depends entirely on how the neural information is processed at the next stage, and on what information is actually utilized by the organism. It may be that pronounced maxima and minima are much more effective and more economical carriers of information about a step or other discontinuity than are apparently more faithful reproductions of the step itself. Furthermore, as will be shown later, inhibition not only produces maxima and minima, it can actually amplify the difference between the maxima and minima in responses to stimulus changes in both space and time.

IV. The Dynamics of Excitation and Inhibition

Pronounced transient responses to temporal changes in the pattern of illumination on the retina are characteristic features of the neural activity of all well-developed visual systems. These transient responses may result from the separate or combined effects of many and diverse processes, including the photochemical process in the receptor itself, the electrochemical process underlying the generation of nerve impulses, and the interplay of excitatory and inhibitory influences among neighboring units in the retina.

A comprehensive experimental and theoretical analysis of the dynamics of lateral inhibition has been carried out recently (RATLIFF, HARTLINE, and MILLER, 1963; LANGE, 1965; LANGE, HARTLINE, and RATLIFF, 1966; and RATLIFF, HARTLINE, and LANGE, 1966). The essence of the theoretical formulation is the assumption that uniform amounts of an inhibitory transmitter substance are produced in a particular receptor unit by each nerve impulse in its neighbors. The transmitter is assumed to decay, or inactivate, along an exponential time course. The inhibitory potential is assumed to be linearly related to the transmitter concentration that exceeds a threshold value. This threshold is imposed locally (that is, there is no subliminal interaction among units or between self inhibition and lateral inhibition). It is assumed that the self inhibition has the same time constant as the lateral inhibition but that it has no threshold. The theory may be expressed as follows:

$$r_p(t) = e_p(t) - \sum_j^n K_{p,j} \left(\frac{1}{\tau} \int_0^t \exp\left[(t'-t)/\tau\right] r_j(t')\, dt' - r_{p,j}^0 \right)$$

when τ is the time constant of the exponential decay of the hypothetical transmitter and $K_{j,p}/\tau$ is the amplitude of the corresponding inhibitory potential in units of frequency change. Note that p is not excluded from the summation.

A simplification which seems to be justified is that $r_{p,j}^0 = C_p/K_{j,p}$. This makes the threshold term, when multiplied by the inhibitory constant, a function of p only. These dynamic integral equations reduce to the steady state equations when t approaches infinity and all frequencies become constant. In the case of no lateral inhibition (that is, when the summation includes only the pth term) the dynamic integral equation reduces to the equation for self-inhibition proposed by STEVENS (1964).

The transient responses to simple steps in illumination can be very complex. It is therefore necessary, at first, to simplify the situation — rather than to attempt to test the above formulation directly and immediately in terms of the complex actions and reactions such as those shown in Fig. 4.

To achieve better control over the activity of the optic nerve and the resulting inhibitory effects we have resorted to an electrical technique for stimulating the optic nerve proximal to the eye to provide trains of antidromic volleys. The advantage

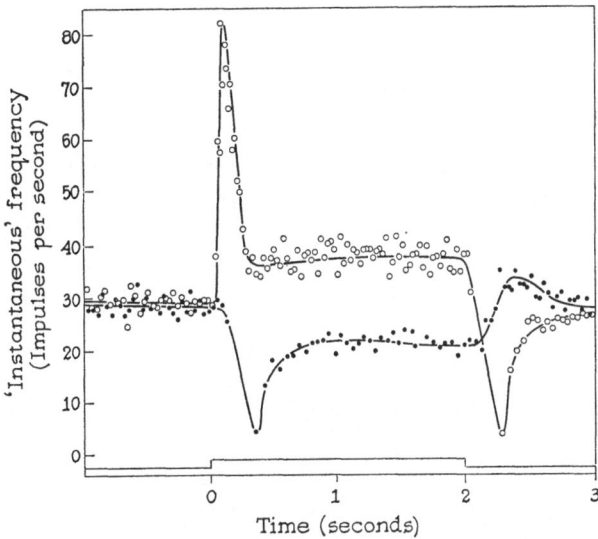

Fig. 4. Simultaneous excitatory and inhibitory transients in the responses of neighboring receptor units. The illumination was constant on one receptor unit (black filled circles). On neighboring receptor units (the response indicated by open circles) the illumination was first increased and then decreased abruptly, as indicated by the signal at the bottom of the graph. From RATLIFF (1961)

of this technique, of course, is that it allows for very precise control of the excitation of the optic nerve. Fortunately, the inhibition produced by antidromic stimulation —although admittedly unphysiological—seems to have essentially the same properties as the inhibition resulting from excitation of the same optic nerve fibers by stimulating the eye with light. The excitation of the test receptor is provided by light, as usual.

This experimental simplification brings both the experiment and the corresponding theory into a more manageable form. In effect, the group of antidromically driven units can be treated as a single unit which exerts strong inhibition on the test unit. The test unit, however, exerts no effective inhibition on the group, for it is being driven by externally controlled electrical stimulation. Under these conditions the lateral inhibition is, in effect, all one way. The dynamic equations above were expressed in this simpler form and written as a digital computer program. Writing the model in this form facilitated comparison of experimental and theoretical results, because input data generated during experiments, in which the computer was also used, could be used directly as input data for the model. For more detail see Lange, Hartline, and Ratliff (1966).

The model was written in cyclic form. Each basic "clock cycle" represented 1 millisec of time. In brief, a representation of the generator potential (g) in the test unit was formed from the excitatory term (e) minus the inhibitory terms (to be defined later). At each clock cycle of the program the generator (g) was added to a running sum (s). When this sum reached a critical value an "impulse" was recorded for the test unit and the summation was begun again. In short, this amounted to an integration of the generator and the production of an impulse frequency proportional to it.

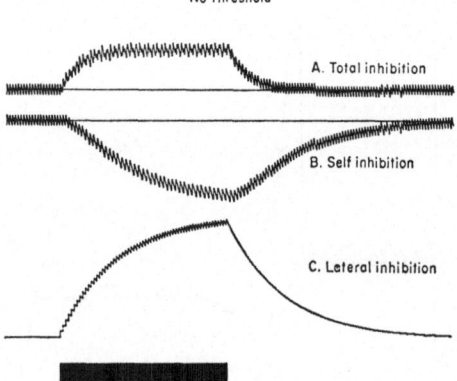

Fig. 5. Model inhibitory pools with no thresholds. Trace A shows the initial increase and subsequent decrease in the pool of lateral inhibition resulting from a uniform train of inhibitory pulses (indicated by the black bar). Trace B shows the concomitant decrease and increase in the pool of self-inhibition. Trace C shows the total effective inhibition (the sum of A and B). From Lange, Hartline, and Ratliff (1966)

The model was provided with self inhibition (I_s) which was set to zero at the beginning of the program. When an impulse was produced in the test unit, a quantity of inhibition (A_s) was added to the self inhibitory pool. At each cycle of the program a portion of this pool, proportional to its current value and to the reciprocal of the self inhibitory time constant (T_s) was subtracted from it. Thus there was formed an exponentially decaying inhibitory potential following each impulse generated. This leads to an exponential approach to the steady state frequency.

In the same way a pool of lateral inhibition (I_l) was formed with a quantity (A_l) added each time an antidromic pulse occured. At each cycle of the clock the pool diminishes, the decay being governed by the lateral inhibitory time constant (T_l). Thus, the impulse frequency of the test unit is governed by the generator which is simply the excitation minus the self inhibition and the lateral inhibition:

$$g = e - I_s - I_l .$$

The inhibition resulting from a uniform train of antidromic impulses is shown in Fig. 5. Note that the total inhibition curve has no latent period and that the onset and cessation are symmetrical. This does not conform to the results of the experiments.

Addition of a threshold to the lateral inhibitory pool corrects these defects and also yields a post-inhibitory rebound similar to that seen in the experiments. Furthermore it accounts for a facilitation of inhibition which had been observed. The threshold is entered in the program simply by subtracting a constant (C) from the lateral inhibition (I_l) leaving a remainder (I_r). If this resulted in a negative, I_r was set equal to zero. Now,

$$g = e - I_s - I_r .$$

Fig. 6 shows the self and lateral inhibition and the total inhibition resulting from a uniform train of antidromic impulses in this non-linear version of the model. Note

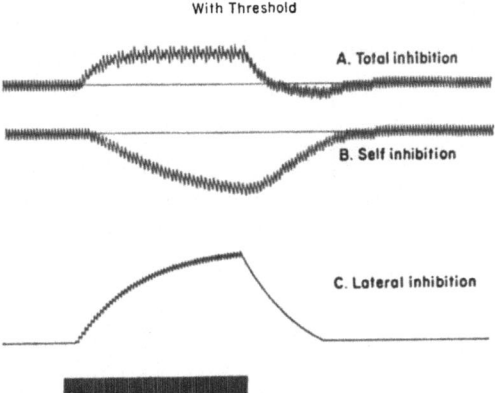

With Threshold

A. Total inhibition

B. Self inhibition

C. Lateral inhibition

Fig. 6. Model inhibitory pools with a threshold for the lateral inhibition. Note the delays in all three traces resulting from the time required for the lateral inhibition (trace C) to reach threshold. Note also the shortened decay of the lateral inhibition resulting from its dropping below threshold. Since there is no threshold for self inhibition (trace B), its decay is not shortened. As a result, the total effective inhibition (trace C) is reduced slightly following the cessation of the inhibitory pulses (black bar). This effect accounts for the "post-inhibitory-rebound". From LANGE, HARTLINE, and RATLIFF (1966)

the substantial time delay to the onset of the lateral inhibition and the asymmetry of the onset and cessation of the total inhibition.

Figs. 7 and 8 show sample comparisons of experimental and theoretical data. The facilitation of inhibition and post inhibitory rebound are fairly well accounted for, as are the changes in the delay to onset of inhibition which depend on the immediate past history of the inhibition. There are some important discrepancies between theory and experiment, however. These discrepancies are serving to guide further experiments which may lead to an improved theory and to further insights into the nature of the underlying mechanisms.

In Fig. 8, for example, the experiment shows a considerable delay before the step in antidromic frequency from 0 to 20 volleys per sec (dashed line) results in any appreciable inhibition. The model, however, shows an immediate inhibitory effect. This and other evidence indicates that there must be some time delay in the system in addition to those caused by the threshold. See HARTLINE, RATLIFF, and MILLER (1961); and RATLIFF, HARTLINE, and MILLER (1963).

It now appears that this additional delay results from the shape of the inhibitory potential. Rather than having an immediate onset with an exponential decay, it rises more gradually to its maximum and then decays slowly. The shape of the inhibitory potential in time is therefore quite similar to the shape of the inhibitory field along

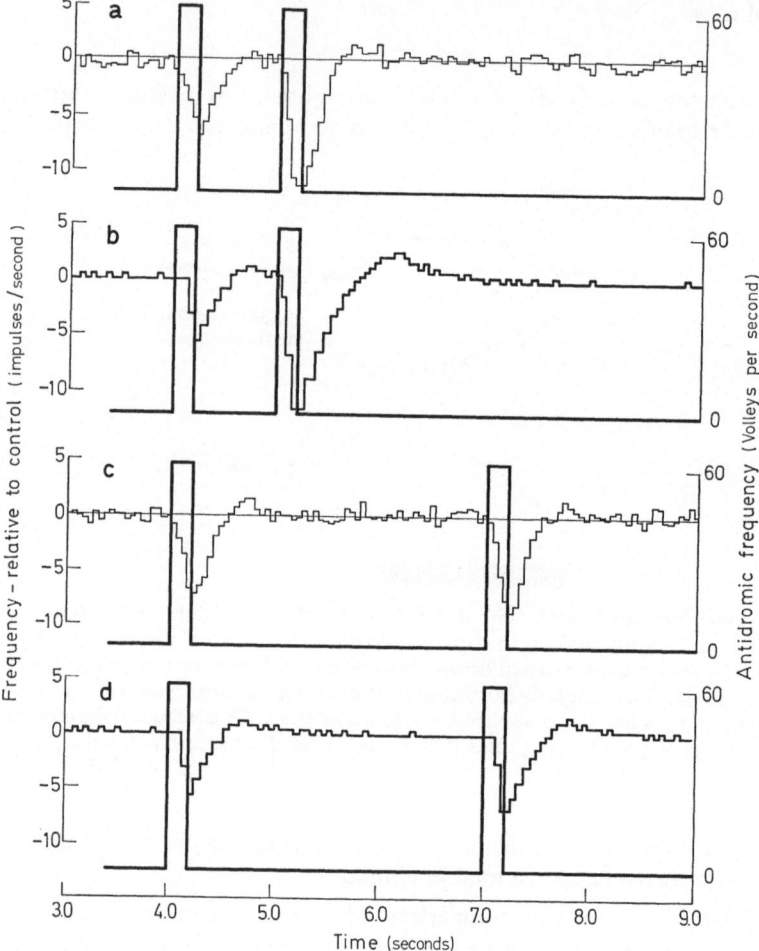

Fig. 7a—d. Facilitation of inhibition. A illustrates the facilitation of inhibition when a burst of inhibitory pulses is closely followed by another identical burst. C illustrates that the facilitation decreases with increasing time between bursts. The facilitation results from residual subthreshold lateral inhibition that follows the first burst and gradually decays. B and D illustrate the simulation of this experiment using the model described in the text. From Lange, Hartline, and Ratliff (1966)

one of its radii (illustrated in Fig. 2). We have not yet incorporated these particular spatial and temporal features of the lateral inhibition into our general model, but we have investigated their consequences in some special cases. The main consequence is that they result in a tuning of the system to, and an amplification of, certain spatial and temporal frequencies.

On tuning and amplification by lateral inhibition. It has been known, since Mach's work in 1865, that inhibitory interaction can produce maxima and minima in the neural response where there are no corresponding maxima or minima in the stimulus distribution—only steps or flections. See RATLIFF (1965). It has generally been assumed, however, that the peak-to-peak distance between maxima and minima such as those produced by a step cannot exceed the step that would appear in the response without inhibition. According to theory, however, lateral inhibition can actually

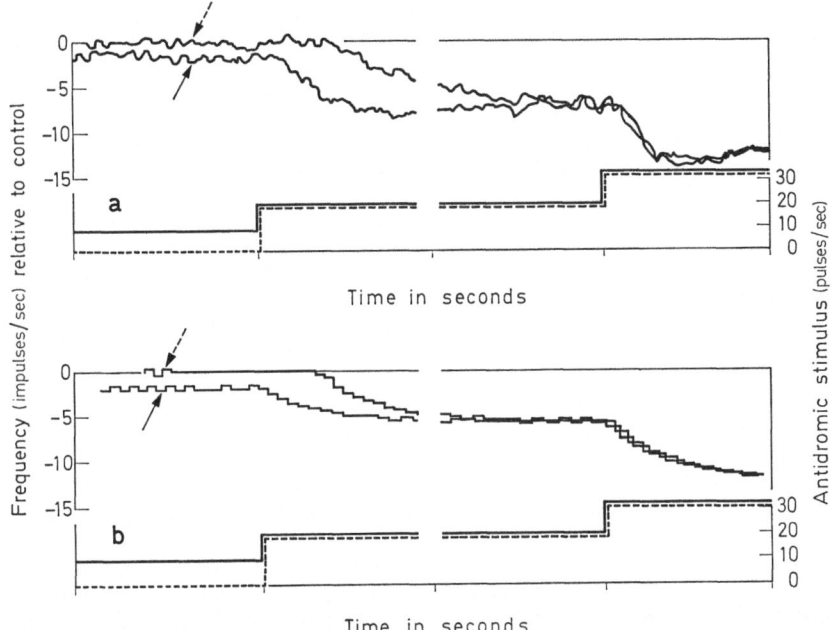

Fig. 8a and b. Effect of previous inhibition on the time of onset of an increment in inhibition. a Experimental results. b Simulation using the model described in the text. Traces marked by the dashed and solid arrows correspond to the antidromic stimuli represented by dashed and solid lines respectively. Note that when there is ongoing inhibition, the effect of the increment in the antidromic stimulus (solid line) appears almost immediately. When there is no ongoing inhibition, however, there is a substantial delay after the increment in the antidromic stimulus (dashed line) before the effect appears in the response. When the increments are identical (near the end of the graph) the responses are nearly identical. The delay when there is no ongoing inhibition is the time required for the inhibition to reach threshold.
From LANGE, HARTLINE, and RATLIFF (1966)

amplify the response so that the peak-to-peak distance with inhibition is greater than the comparable step in the response without inhibition. This kind of spatial amplification has been demonstrated in theoretical calculations by BEKESY (1967) for a sinusoidal spatial distribution, and by BARLOW and QUARLES (1967) for a step pattern of illumination. RATLIFF, KNIGHT, and GRAHAM (1968) have shown, in a more general theoretical treatment, that spatial amplification depends upon the shape of the distribution of the inhibitory field in space, and that analogous temporal amplification depends upon the shape of the inhibitory potential in time.

Spatial amplification has been demonstrated in theory only. Temporal amplification has been demonstrated in both theory and experiment. One set of experimental

results obtained by Ratliff, Knight, Toyoda, and Hartline (1967) are shown in
Fig. 9. The theory predicts essentially the same results; for a detailed comparison of
theory and experiment, see Ratliff, Knight, and Graham (1968).

The explanation of the amplification may be illustrated in terms of the effect that
inhibition has on the range of operation of a receptor unit. As Fig. 10 shows, any
modulation of the intensity of the stimulus will produce a much larger modulation
of the corresponding uninhibited response (solid line) than of the inhibited response
(dashed line). This is on the assumption that the modulation illustrated has such a
long wavelength with respect to the space constants of the inhibitory field or to the

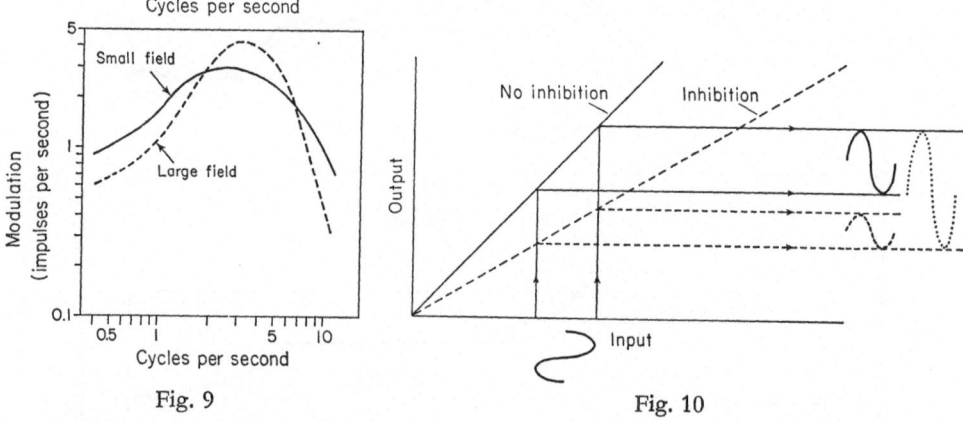

Fig. 9   Fig. 10

Fig. 9. Effect of inhibition on modulation of the response of a receptor unit (ordinate) by
various frequencies of sinusoidal modulation of the stimulus (abscissa). Solid line (small
field) shows effect of self-inhibition only. Dashed line (large field) shows effect of lateral
inhibition. Note "amplification" of response by lateral inhibition from about 2 to 7 cycles
per sec. From Ratliff, Knight, Toyoda, and Hartline (1967). Copyright 1967 by the
American Association for the Advancement of Science

Fig. 10. Input-output curves for a network with no inhibition (solid line) and with inhibition
(dashed line). In general, the two outputs for the input shown would not exceed the limits
indicated by the pair of solid lines (no inhibition) and the pair of dashed lines (inhibition).
If the inhibition could be turned completely off at the crest of the input and completely on
at the trough, the output would be "amplified" as indicated by the dotted curve. From
Ratliff, Knight, and Graham (1968)

time constants of the inhibitory potentials that the stimulus may be regarded as being
uniform in both space and time. That is, these are the general results that would be
obtained if the special properties of the spatial and temporal distributions of the
inhibitory influence in the network could be neglected.

Considering the above effects alone one might be led to believe that the inevitable
result of inhibition would be to reduce the amplitude of the response to any given
modulation of the signal. This is not the case, however. Indeed, if it were possible to
turn the inhibition completely off at the crest of the modulation and completely on at
the trough, the amplitude of the response could extend from the maximum uninhibited response to the minimum inhibited response (dotted line).

The inhibitory network can approach these theoretical limits. A considerable and
more or less constant time elapses between an impulse in one receptor and the maxi-

mum inhibitory potential produced by it in a neighboring unit. Therefore, at a certain frequency of modulation of the stimulus, the time between excitation and inhibition will be equal to one half the wavelength of the modulation. Impulses occurring at the crest of the response will produce their greatest inhibitory effect at the trough. Impulses occurring at the time of the trough will produce their greatest effect at the following peak. Thus, the inhibition will tend to "turn on" in the troughs (one half cycle after the high frequency impulses produced at the peak) and to "turn off" at the peaks (one half cycle after the low frequency impulses in the trough). The exact nature and extent of this "tuning" depends, of course, on the time constants of the inhibition. And only those frequencies to which the system is best "tuned" will be amplified. Furthermore, what the system gains in amplification of a particular frequency is paid for in attenuation of other frequencies and in a reduction of the mean level of the response.

The explanation of the theoretically predicted spatial amplification effects is similar to that outlined above. The spatial distribution of the inhibitory field will match half wavelengths of certain spatial frequencies. Responses at these spatial frequencies will be amplified, others will be attenuated, and the mean level of all will be reduced.

V. Toward a "Field" Theory of Vision

The conflict between Goethe's "holistic" or organic view of the nature of light and sight and the then prevailing analytic Newtonian view has its modern counterparts. The apparent conflict between Land's theory of color vision and the classical Young-Helmholtz theory is one example, and the apparent conflict between the Gestalt-like approach to visual perception and to the neurophysiology of vision and the more analytic quantitative methods used by most experimental psychologists and neurophysiologists is another. But, as in all such conflicts and controversies, both views are right, in part, and both are wrong, in part.

The fact of the matter is that there need not be any conflict between the analytic (or reductionistic) and the organic (or holistic) approaches to the study of vision, or to any other biological problem. The assertion that "the whole is more than the sum of its parts" is generally based on ignorance of the properties of the parts and of the laws that govern their integration. When these are understood, the mystery of the "emergence" of holistic phenomena often vanishes.

In support of this general view it is my aim to indicate, in the next few paragraphs, how a wide variety of special visual functions arising from the properties of the retina acting as a whole, may all be explained in terms of a few general laws governing the interplay of opposed excitatory and inhibitory influences over the network of interconnected individual photoreceptors and individual neurons. Indeed, there is now sufficient evidence, I think, for us to move toward a "field" theory of vision in which a few general principles will be sufficient to account for a large number of apparently diverse phenomena. I use the word "toward" advisedly, because we are still far from a comprehensive theory of vision. But, as far as I can tell, nothing has yet been discovered in the neurophysiology of vision that cannot be interpreted in terms of the relatively simple dynamics of interacting fields of opposed excitatory and inhibitory influences.

Transient response. The most striking features of the responses of single ganglion cells of the vertebrate retina are the vigorous discharges produced by changes in

2*

illumination. "On", "On-Off", and "Off" discharges, first noted by HARTLINE in his study of the frog retina in 1938, are common features of the neural activity—at one level or another—of all well developed visual systems. ADRIAN and MATTHEWS (1928), GRANIT (1933), and HARTLINE (1938) all attributed the complex transients seen in their respective studies of the whole optic nerve, the electroretinogram, and single fibers of the optic nerve, to the integration of excitatory and inhibitory influences. Support for this view has been provided by a number of later investigations. For example, RATLIFF and MUELLER (1957) synthesized "On-Off" and "Off" responses in the lateral eye of *Limulus* by properly timing and balancing the opposed excitatory and inhibitory influences. More recent quantitative work by BICKING (1965), and by BISHOP and RODIECK (1965), and RODIECK (1965), lends further support to this view.

The spatial organization of the receptive field. KUFFLER (1953) found that the organization of the receptive fields of the cat retina differed from that of the frog retina. The transient responses were similar to those of the frog, but all of the different types could often be observed in a single receptive field. For example, the center of the field might yield pure "On" responses, the periphery pure "Off" responses, and the intermediate zone "On-Off" responses. This organization has been attributed to a slight overlap of a central excitatory field and a surrounding annular inhibitory field. A more recent view is that the excitatory and inhibitory influences both extend over the whole of the field. See WAGNER, MACNICHOL, and WOLBARSHT (1963). Imbalance of the excitation and inhibition at some particular point in the field, rather than absence of one or the other, is supposed to determine the character of the response at that point. This view is based mainly on evidence from the experiments cited below on color coding in the retina.

Color coding. WAGNER, MACNICHOL, and WOLBARSHT (1960) found that in the gold fish retina the "On" and "Off" character of the responses of some ganglion cells depended on the wave length of illumination. The cells in one class that they found, for example, has "On" center "Off" surround responses to light near the middle of the visible spectrum. But the same cells were maximally excited by short wavelengths and maximally inhibited by long wavelengths. (In other classes these relations are reversed.)

Although it might appear that the center of these fields are purely excitatory, the surrounds purely inhibitory, and the intermediate zones a mixture of the two—this turns out not to be the case. Excitatory and inhibitory influences appear to extend over the whole of the receptive field, and the response at any point is governed by the relative amounts of the two influences. This they demonstrated by mapping the field first with short (excitatory) wavelengths and then with long (inhibitory) wavelengths.

Directional sensitivity. BARLOW and LEVICK (1965) describe ganglion cells in the retina of the rabbit that respond selectively to direction of movement, in addition to responding to changes in intensity of illumination. They attribute this directional sensitivity to asymmetrical inhibitory influences. Their experiments indicate that the asymmetry is such that with movement of the stimulus in one direction a wave of inhibition advances along with, or ahead of, the moving stimulus and cancels out responses to it. With movement in the opposite direction, the wave of inhibition lags behind the stimulus and responses to it are more or less unaffected. Thus the "preferred" direction and velocity are determined by the spatial and temporal properties of the inhibitory influence.

HUBEL and WIESEL (1962) describe elongated receptive fields of cells in the lateral geniculate and visual cortex that appear to respond preferentially to stimuli with their edges orientated parallel to the long axis of the field. Such elongated fields, they suggest, may be nothing more complex than the result of the integration of a row of simple circular retinal receptive fields.

Configuration. BARLOW (1953) noted that some frog retinal ganglion cells may respond preferentially to small stimuli. These he called "fly" detectors. It is clear from the work of TAYLOR (1956), REICHARDT and MACGINITIE (1962) and others that the output of an inhibitory network depends very much upon the configuration of the stimulus. In particular, since the inhibitory influences generally diminish with distance, the amount of interaction taking place will depend upon whether the stimulus exciting the interacting elements is compact or spread out. Such a mechanism may well play a role in shaping a preferential response to small stimuli.

A similar effect observed at the corners of areas of excitation in an inhibitory network also depends on the configuration of the stimulus. The points at the corners receive less inhibition than points near the center of the area of excitation, since those at the corners are only partially surrounded by other excited points while those in the center are completely surrounded. With the addition of a threshold, such a mechanism could easily account for the responses to sharp curvature or to corners observed by MATURANA, LETTVIN, McCULLOCH, and PITTS (1960) in ganglion cells of the frog retina.

Spatial and temporal filters. Numerous psychophysical and electrophysiological studies have been carried out on the spatial and temporal transfer functions of various visual systems. See, for example, KELLY (1965), and HUGHES and MAFFEI (1966). All visual systems studied thus far are similar in that they transmit low frequencies poorly, intermediate frequencies relatively well, and high frequencies poorly or not all. The forms of the functions are similar for both spatial and temporal frequencies.

The low frequency cut-off—in both spatial and temporal domains—has been attributed to the effects of lateral inhibition. See KELLY (1965), and RATLIFF (1965) for examples. Transmission of high frequencies in space cannot exceed the limits set by the high frequency cut off of the optical components of the system. See CAMPBELL and GUBISCH (1966). Transmission of high frequencies in time is probably limited by the impulse generating and impulse propagating mechanisms of the retina and optic nerve.

As was demonstrated above, amplification of responses to certain frequencies of modulation of stimuli (in both space and time) can result from this filtering or tuning. Spatial or temporal frequencies that have been filtered out entirely cannot be restored, of course, but those that have only been attenuated before they pass through the network can be either amplified or attenuated further when transmitted by it. Which will occur depends upon the space constants and time constants of the fields of inhibitory influence.

VI. Concluding Remarks

The simple Sherringtonian principle of the integration of fields of opposed excitatory and inhibitory influences is all that is required to account for the complex and diverse behavior of a number of different retinal networks. The various special properties of different networks do not appear to depend upon special or unique underlying neural mechanisms. Rather, they seem to depend on nothing more complicated than a few simple variations in the spatial and temporal configurations of the fields of excitation and inhibition. In my view, therefore, one of the most important areas of research for the neurophysiologist is to determine in detail the various spatial and temporal dimensions of these fields, and their functional significance, in whatever neural network he may be studying. Equally important, if not more so, will be the elucidation of the various underlying structures and mechanisms that determine the configurations of these fields of excitation and inhibition, and by way of which they may be modified during some process as simple as sensory adaptation, or as complex as memory or thought.

Acknowledgement. The research reported here was supported, in part, by a research grant (B 864) from the National Institute of Neurological Diseases and Blindness, Public Health Service, and by a research grant (GB-6540X) from the National Science Foundation.

References

ADRIAN, E. D., and R. MATTHEWS: The action of light on the eye. Part III. The interaction of retinal neurones. J. Physiol. (Lond.) **65**, 273—298 (1928).

BARLOW, H. B.: Summation and inhibition in the frog's retina. J. Physiol. (Lond.) **119**, 69—88 (1953).

BARLOW, R. B., JR.: Inhibitory fields in the Limulus lateral eye. Thesis, The Rockefeller University 1967.

—, and W. R. LEVICK: The mechanism of directionally selective units in the rabbit's retina. J. Physiol. (Lond.) **178**, 477—504 (1965).

— Inhibitory fields in the Limulus lateral eye. Thesis, The Rockefeller University 1967.

VON BEKESY, G.: Sensory inhibition. Princeton, N.J.; Princeton University Press 1967.

BICKING, L. A.: Some quantitative studies on retinal ganglion cells. Thesis, The Johns Hopkins University 1965.

BISHOP, P. O., and R. W. RODIECK: Discharge patterns of cat retina ganglion cells. Proceedings of the symposium on information processing in sight sensory systems, p. 116 to 127 (P. W. NYE, Ed.). Pasadena, Calif.: California Institute of Technology 1965.

CAMPBELL, F. W., and R. W. GUBICSH: Optical quality of the human eye. J. Physiol. (Lond.) **186**, 558—578 (1966).

GRANIT, R.: The components of the retinal action potential and their relation to the discharge in the optic nerve. J. Physiol. (Lond.) **77**, 207—240 (1933).

HARTLINE, H. K.: The response of single optic nerve fibers of the vertebrate eye to illumination of the retina. Amer. J. Physiol. **121**, 400—415 (1938).

— The receptive fields of optic nerve fibers. Amer. J. Physiol. **130**, 690—699 (1940).

—, and F. RATLIFF: Spatial summation of inhibitory influences in the eye of *Limulus*, and the mutual interaction of receptor units. J. Gen. Physiol. **41**, 1049—1066 (1958).

— — Inhibitory interaction of receptor units in the eye of *Limulus*. J. gen. Physiol. **40**, 357—376 (1957).

— —, and W. H. MILLER: Inhibitory interaction in the retina and its significance in vision. Nervous inhibition, p. 241—284 (E. FLOREY, Ed.) New York: Pergamon Press 1961.

HUBEL, D. H., and T. N. WIESEL: Receptive fields, binocular interaction and functional architecture in the cat's visual cortex. J. Physiol. (Lond.) **160**, 106—154 (1962).

HUGHES, G. W., and L. MAFFEI: Retinal ganglion cell response to sinusoidal light stimulation. J. Neurophysiol. (Lond.) **29**, 333—352 (1966).

KELLY, D. H.: Flicker thresholds. Proceedings of the symposium on information processing in sight sensory systems, p. 162—176 (P. W. NYE, Ed.). Pasadena, Calif.: California Institute of Technology 1965.

KUFFLER, S. W.: Discharge patterns and functional organization of mammalian retina. J. Neurophysiol. (Lond.) 16, 37—68 (1953).

LANGE, G. D.: Dynamics of inhibitory interaction in the eye of *Limulus*. Experimental and theoretical studies. Thesis, The Rockefeller University 1965.

—, H. K. HARTLINE, and F. RATLIFF: The dynamics of lateral inhibition in the compound eye of *Limulus*. II., The functional organization of the compound eye, p. 425—449 (C. G. BERNHARD, Ed.). Pergamon Press 1966.

— — — Inhibitory interaction in the retina: Techniques of experimental and theoretical analysis. Symposium on Advances in Biomedical Computer Applications. Ann. N.Y. Acad. Sci. 128, 955—971 (1966).

MATURANA, H. R., J. Y. LETTVIN, W. S. McCULLOCH, and W. H. PITTS: Anatomy and physiology of vision in the frog *(Rana pipiens)*. J. gen. Physiol. 43, (No. 6, Pt. 2), 129—175 (1960).

MILLER, W. H.: Morphology of the ommatidia of the compound eye of *Limulus*. J. biophys. biochem. Cytol. 3, 421—428 (1957).

PURPLE, R. L., and F. A. DODGE: Interaction of excitation and inhibition in the eccentric cell in the eye of *Limulus*. Cold Spring Harbor Symposia XXX, 529—537 (1965).

— — Self inhibition in the eye of *Limulus*, Functional organization of the compound eye, pp. 451—464 (C. G. BERNHARD, Ed.). Pergamon Press 1966.

RATLIFF, F.: Inhibitory interaction and the detection and enhancement of contours. Sensory communication, (W.A. ROSENBLITH, Ed.) p. 183—203. New York: MIT Press and John Wiley and Sons, 1961.

— Mach bands: Quantitative studies on neural networks in the retina. San Francisco: Holden-Day, 1965.

—, and H. K. HARTLINE: Fields of inhibitory influence of single receptor units in the lateral eye of *Limulus*. Science 126, 1234 (1957).

— — The responses of *Limulus* optic nerve fibers to patterns of illumination on the receptor mosaic. J. gen. Physiol. 42, 1241—1255 (1959).

—, and D. LANGE: The dynamics of lateral inhibition in the compound eye of *Limulus*, I., The functional organization of the compound eye, (C. G. BERNHARD, Ed.), pp. 399—424. Pergamon Press 1966.

— —, and W. H. MILLER: Spatial and temporal aspects of retinal inhibitory interaction. J. opt. Soc. Amer. 53, 110—120 (1963).

—, B. W. KNIGHT, and N. GRAHAM: On tuning and amplification by lateral inhibitory networks. In preparation. To be published in: Proc. nat. Acad. Sci. (Wash.) 1968.

— —, J. TOYODA, and H. K. HARTLINE: The enhancement of flicker by lateral inhibition. 158, 393—294 (1967).

—, and C. G. MUELLER: Synthesis of "On-Off" and "Off" responses in a visual-neural system. Science 126, 840—841 (1957).

REICHARDT, W., u. G. MACGINITIE: Zur Theorie der lateralen Inhibition. Kybernetik 1, 155—165 (1962).

RODIECK, R. W.: Quantitative analysis of cat retinal ganglion cell response to visual stimuli. Vision Res. 5, 583—601 (1965).

STEVENS, C. F.: A quantitative theory of neural interactions: Theoretical and experimental investigations. Thesis, The Rockefeller Institute 1964.

TAYLOR, W. K.: Electrical simulation of some nervous system functional activities. In: Information theory, (C. CHERRY, Ed.) pp. 314—328. New York: Academic Press 1956.

WAGNER, H. G., E. F. MACNICHOL Jr., and M. L. WOLBARSHT: The response properties of single ganglion cells in the goldfish retina. J. gen. Physiol. 43 (part 2), 45—62 (1960).

— — — Functional basis for "On"-center and "Off"-center receptive fields in the retina. J. opt. Soc. Amer. 53, 66—70 (1963).

Upper and Lower Levels of the Auditory System:
A Contrast of Structure and Function

E. F. Evans

Department of Communication, University of Keele, Staffordshire, England

This paper will attempt to illustrate some principles of sensory systems by contrasting features of the organization, and of the functional consequences of that organization, at upper and lower levels of the auditory pathway. For this purpose, the second order cell station or ventral cochlear nucleus (VCN), and the primary auditory cortex of the cat have been chosen for comparison. It will be pointed out that at the lower level a simple systematic organization leads to responses of individual neurones which are straightforward as a function of both static and dynamic stimulus parameters, whereas at the cortical level such as systematic organization is not found, and the neurones are particularly responsive to dynamic parameters of the stimulus. Many neurones in the auditory cortex in their responses emphasize certain features of the sound stimulus; they therefore appear to act in a manner analogous to neurones found in the visual cortex [1]; in the auditory case the abstraction is in terms of *temporal* features of a complex dynamic sound stimulus.

Experiments on the cochlear nucleus were performed with Dr. P. G. Nelson at the National Institutes of Health, Bethesda, Maryland (U.S.A.) [2, 3, 4] and on the cortex with Dr. I. C. Whitfield in the University of Birmingham, England [5, 6, 7]. Both sets of experiments were conducted mainly without anaesthesia: the former with the animal in the decerebrate state (some additional animals received pentobarbitone or chloralose anaesthesia); the latter entirely in the unanaesthetised, unrestrained state using an implanted micromanipulator [8]. A carefully calibrated free sound field in an anechoic chamber was employed in the cortical experiments and a substantially flat closed field for the experiments on the VCN. These precautions enabled the frequency of the sound to be changed independently of intensity, in the dynamic situation.

A. Ventral Cochlear Nucleus

In the cat, the cochlear nucleus is a protuberance of the brain stem surrounding the fibres of the auditory nerve as they emerge from the organ of hearing, the cochlea. These fibres enter the cochlear nucleus in an orderly sequence, bifurcate, and are distributed in an orderly fashion to the lower half of the cochlear nucleus, the ventral cochlear nucleus. There are a number of consequences of this systematic arrangement of input to the VCN. One is that the responses of the cells differ little from the responses of fibres of the auditory nerve [9, 10]. Each neurone responds to a band of frequencies, the width of which depends on the intensity of the stimulus. At threshold, only a single frequency (known as the characteristic frequency) or a narrow band of frequencies will excite the cell. At higher intensities, the effective band of frequencies becomes progressively wider Fig. 6d. In addition, the rate of firing of the neurone at any given frequency is a monotonic function of the intensity of the stimulating tone.

Another consequence of the systematic organization of input to the VCN is that the neurones are arranged in the nucleus according to the tone frequency to which they respond best. High frequencies are found dorsally and low frequencies ventrally. As a microelectrode penetrates the layers of cochlear nucleus in a dorsiventral direction, it encounters neurones with progressively lower characteristic frequencies. A plot of the characteristic frequency in octaves versus the position of the neurone along the electrode track is shown in Fig. 1. A tonotopic organization of the VCN is clearly shown, and it is remarkable how little deviation there is about the straight line.

With an on-line computer (LINC), the probability of firing of a neurone at any frequency can be determined in a systematic manner at a given intensity (Frequency Response Histogram). For this analysis, a train of tonal stimuli was produced whose frequency and intensity were controlled by the computer. The duration of the tones was 100 msec, their amplitude was constant, but their frequencies followed a pseudo-random-number sequence. By this means, the frequency range under consideration could be covered in a random but even manner in 1 to 2 min. At the same time, the computer counted the number of spike discharges evoked during the tone (the 'On'-count) and during the 100 msec following the tone (the 'Off'-count). At the end of the analysis, the plots were displayed on a c.r.t. face. Most neurones in the VCN produced roughly triangular-shaped plots, the peak usually corresponding to the characteristic frequency. Next, the time course of the response to a tone of any effective frequency

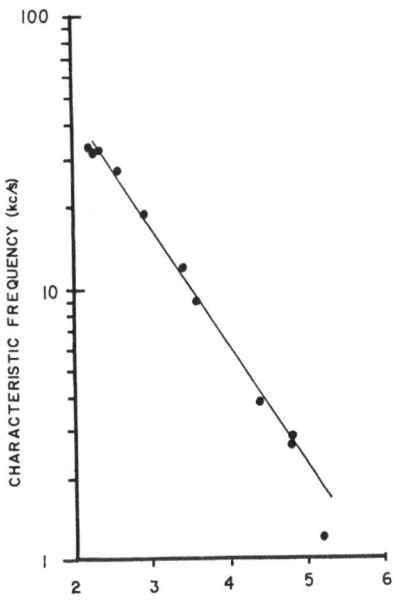

Fig. 1. Tonotopic organization in the ventral cochlear nucleus. The characteristic frequency of all the neurons encountered in a single track through the nucleus is plotted against the distance of the neurones from the dorsal surface of the cochlear nucleus. Electrode track in a sagittal dorsiventral direction

could be examined by using the computer to plot a 'time histogram', that is, the probability of firing before, during, and after a tone, averaged over a number of presentations. The simplest response was that of sustained excitation by a tone, followed by an immediate return to the spontaneous firing level. A more common situation was an excitatory response to the tone followed by inhibition when the tone was turned off. In time-course, this "off inhibition" was initially complete, followed by a gradual return of firing to the spontaneous level. "Off-inhibition" is not simply post-excitation depression of the neurone; the systematic examination of its frequency distribution, afforded by on-line computer control, indicated that it could occur at frequencies other than those exciting the neurone. This inhibition is functionally

similar to the recurrent inhibition of other systems and its consequences in the dynamic situation will discussed below.

In the non-steady stimulus situation, these neurones exhibited responses which
could be simply predicted on the basis of their behaviour to steady tones. Again, the
computer was used on-line to construct histograms of the firing distribution of the
neuronal responses to amplitude-and frequency-modulated tones, averaged over
many cycles of modulation with respect to the modulation cycle. Each histogram
could then be compared with that predicted from the Frequency Response and Time
Histograms previously obtained. To sinusoidal modulation of frequency, roughly
sinusoidal firing distributions were obtained when the frequency excursions extended
across the upper or lower slopes of the responsive region of the Frequency Response
Histogram. When the excursions of frequency extended across the entire bandwidth
of response of the neurone, a symmetrical double-humped distribution of firing was
obtained, as predicted. Sinusoidal amplitude modulation also evoked the predicted
sinusoidal firing distribution. Neurones having a Time Histogram which indicated
adaptation of response to a steady tone stimulus (i.e. progressive reduction in firing
rate from the onset of response) exhibited the predicted response to sinusoidal
modulation, namely a phase-advance of the response relative to the modulation
sinusoid.

These agreements with prediction could extend over a wide range of modulation
rates, from 0.1 c/s to 50 c/s, the upper frequency limit of the analytical system.
At higher rates of modulation (above 10 c/s), however, there often occurred distor-
tions of the appearance at low rates of modulation. Most significantly, the background
firing of the neurone was suppressed at the times when the excursions of frequency
or amplitude fell outside the response area. This appears to result from the process of
"off-inhibition", which becomes important at high rates of repetitive presentation
of an effective auditory stimulus. The effects of "off-inhibition" are therefore pro-
found in the dynamic, repetitive situation, and are analogous to the situation described
by Drs. Terzuolo and Ratliff in their papers. The mechanism would serve to
increase the signal-to-noise ratio or the dynamic range of the system, when dealing
with dynamic stimuli.

B. Primary Auditory Cortex

At this level of the auditory pathway there appears to exist quite a different
situation in terms of organization and neurone response.

In man, the auditory cortex is buried deep in fissures, but in the cat it is con-
veniently spread out over a wide surface of the brain. In contrast to the situation in
the cochlear nucleus, the input to the cells does not appear to be arranged in an
orderly manner. In fact, when the characteristic frequency of the neurones was plotted
as a function of their position along the surface of the auditory cortex, the situation
shown in Fig. 2 was obtained. Overall, there is a rough progression of characteristic
frequency from low to high as one moves forward over the cortex, but it is clear that
at any position one will encounter neurones ranging in characteristic frequency over
as much as four of the six octaves or so of the total hearing range of the cat. Indeed, in
a single puncture or electrode track in a cortex, one could find neurones with best
characteristic frequencies spanning the whole hearing range, for example, the neurones represented by the triangles at 12 mm.

Hitherto, in the literature, much stress has been laid on the principle of tonotopic organization of the auditory cortex and the functional consequences, for the discrimination of tone frequency, of such an arrangement. The conclusion drawn from this analysis of the organization of characteristic frequencies of single units in the unanaesthetised cortex, is that a tonotopic organization does not occur, or at least not in a manner that can have any functional significance [6].

No systematic arrangement of characteristic frequencies with depth of penetration normal to the cortical surface was found, apart from a tendency for neurones with

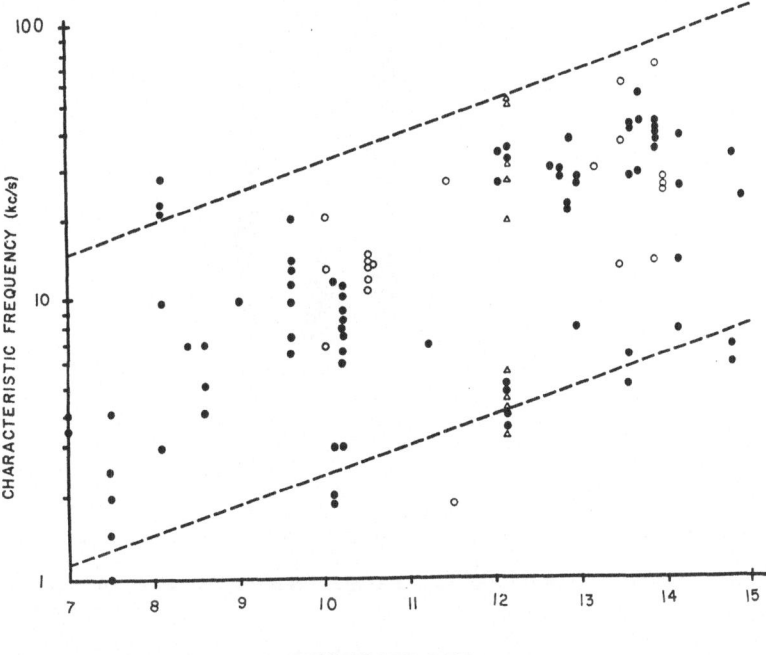

DISTANCE FROM PSSS (mm)

Fig. 2. Unanaesthetized primary auditory cortex. Plot of characteristic frequency of many neurones from several cats as a function of their position along the cortical surface. All measurements are from the posterior suprasylvian sulcus. Neurones indicated by the open symbols are from one cortex, with those indicated by open triangles (at 12 mm) from a single penetration normal to the surface of the cortex

similar characteristic frequencies to be grouped together. This may be related to a columnar organization of the cortex.

Fig. 3 indicates the kinds of stimuli to which cells in the auditory cortex would respond. It is surprising that a small number of cells would respond to moving visual stimuli and not to sounds. What these cells are doing in the auditory cortex is not at all clear. Most of the cells in the auditory cortex, however, did respond to some kind of sound. All of them responded to complex sounds such as fingerflicking, kissing noises, etc. Cortical cells are evidently very sensitive to such sounds, and about 20% of them would not respond to pure tones, that is, they responded only to these complex stimuli. Fig. 4 summarises the kinds of responses that may be shown by different cortical cells to static stimulation. In (a) the cell was excited by a tone in a sustained manner, analogous to that already described in the ventral cochlear nucleus. In (b), another cell was inhibited by tones. In (c), (d) and (e), cells are shown which were excited respectively at the onset, the termination and the beginning and end of the tone. These response types were not invariant. The response a neurone gave

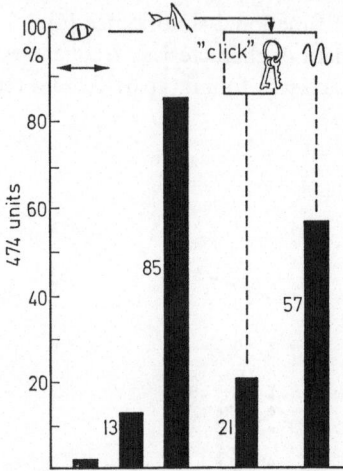

Fig. 3. Classification of neurones in primary auditory cortex according to the stimuli to which they would respond, respectively: visual only; no stimuli at all; to some kind of sound, subdivided into neurones responding only to complex sounds and not to tones, and neurones responding to both

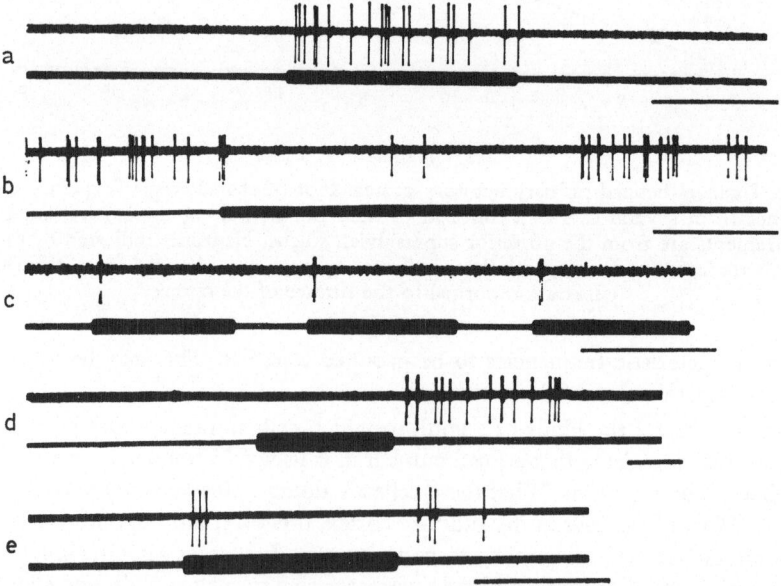

Fig. 4a—e. Auditory cortex. Examples of neuronal response to tones. Each record displays the neural spike discharge (upper trace) and the stimulating tone (thickening on lower trace). a Sustained excitation. b Sustained inhibition. c, d, e: Transient responses to onset, termination, and onset and termination of tone, respectively. Time bars: 0.5 sec

at any time was a function of many factors, including the frequency, intensity and repetition rate of the tone, and other factors as yet undefined. Many cells exhibited a lability of response, that is, they failed to give consistent responses under apparently identical conditions. This last property is as distressing for the experimenter as it must be important for normal cortical function. In spite of these factors, it is generally possible to classify neurones by the response which they give under most stimulus conditions. It is interesting that in contrast to neurones in the cochlear nucleus, about half of the cortical cells were silent in the absence of stimulation. Furthermore, the response of a cortical neurone was not necessarily a monotonic function of intensity; in many cases high intensity stimulation at a given frequency was inhibitory, whereas, low intensity stimulation at the same frequency was excitatory.

Dynamic stimuli, in this case modulation of frequency, produced in most cortical cells, very vigorous and consistent responses. In fact, there was a significant propor-

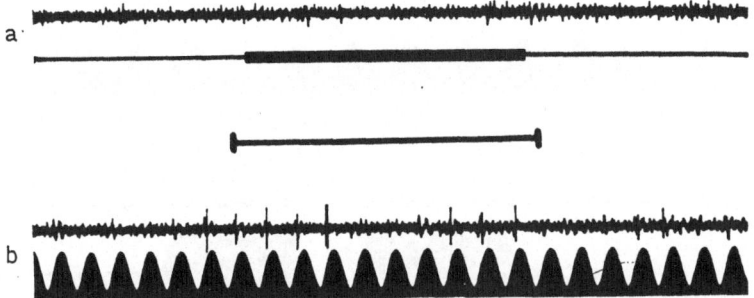

Fig. 5a and b. Auditory cortex. Neurone activated by modulated tone but not by any steady tone. a No response to tone of 2.5 Kc/s. (Tone indicated by thickening of lower line.) Time scale as (b). b Vigorous though intermittent response to a tone of the same frequency and intensity as that of (a), but whose frequency was modulated slightly (± 2.5%) at a rate of 10 c/s. Envelope of lower line represents excursions of frequency

tion of cells (10%) which would only respond to pure tones if the frequency was changing. Fig. 5 shows the responses of such a neurone. No steady tone was effective in exciting the cell (a), whereas it responded periodically (with intermissions) to changes in frequency as small as half a semitone on the musical scale (b). It will be noted that this neurone responded only to a particular direction of frequency change. This was a common property of cortical cells, and it appears to be analogous to that found in the visual system (e.g.: rabbit retina [11] and cat visual cortex [1]), where some cell responses are preferential to movement of the stimulus in a certain direction. This property is seen clearly in the unit of Fig. 6 where the response occurred only to upward frequency changes, whether of sinusoidal (a) or ramp (b) form. Some cortical cells responded to frequency changes only in the upward direction; others responded to downward frequency changes only; others to both upward and downward frequency changes. The responses to frequency change occurred over a wide range of sinusoidal modulation rates, but in contrast to the situation in the cochlear nucleus, the range was restricted to within about 2 and about 15 c/s. This is illustrated in Fig. 7. This neurone responded to downward frequency changes of both sinusoidal and ramp form. There was an infrequent response at 1 c/s (a), a consistent response at 2 and 7 c/s (b and c), and almost no response at 20 c/s sinusoidal modulation (d). The elimination of the response at high modulation rates appeared to be the result of the high rate of repetition of the stimulus rather than rapid frequency change *per se*, for if intermittent frequency ramps of the same order of rate of change of frequency were used, then the response still occurred (d: lower trace). I suspect that the curve obtained by Dr. RATLIFF, of response as a function of modulation rate, would not turn downward at higher modulation rates if intermittent ramp changes in light intensity were used instead of repetitive sinusoidal modulation.

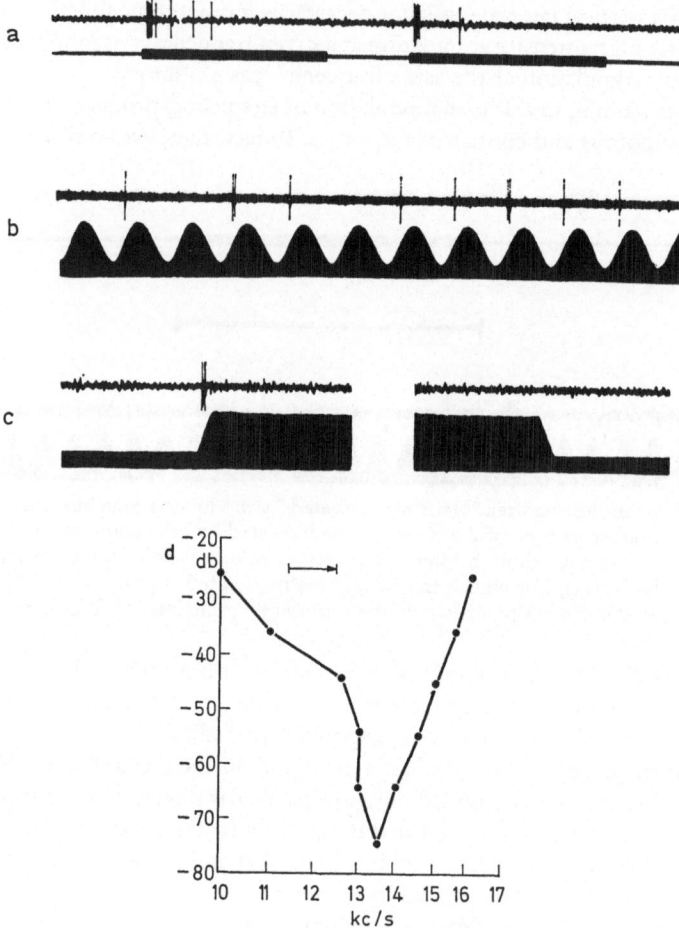

Fig. 6a—d. Auditory cortex. Neurone sensitive to direction of frequency change. a Responses to steady tone stimuli at frequency and intensity indicated by the centre of the arrow in (d). [Time-scale as for (c)]. b Sinusoidal modulation of frequency of ± 5% at a rate of 2 c/s. Note response to changes of frequency in upward direction only. c Intermittent ramp modulations of frequency in upward and downward directions. Ramp duration: 50 msec; depth of modulation as in (b). d Intensity threshold of the neurone's response to steady tones, as a function of tone frequency. Intensity in decibels relative to 100 db SPL; increasing intensity upwards. The area within the curve represents the frequency-intensity "response area" over which a tone is effective in eliciting a response. The horizontal arrow indicates the tone intensity and the excursions in frequency involved in (b) and (c); they are well within the response area of the neurone

In the case of the auditory system, the ineffectiveness of high rates of sinusoidal modulation is very probably due to the off-inhibition previously discussed.

There is evidence that the preference of response for certain directions of frequency change is due to a time-delayed inhibition of a collateral or recurrent nature, but in

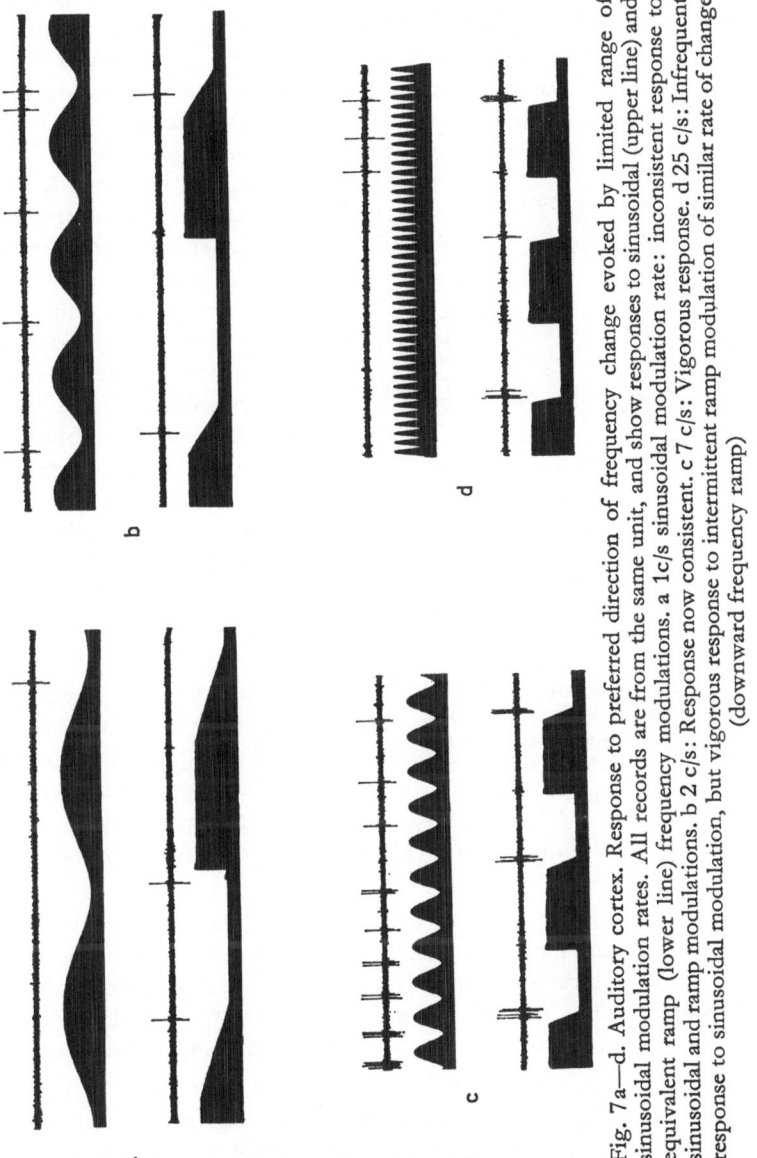

Fig. 7a—d. Auditory cortex. Response to preferred direction of frequency change evoked by limited range of sinusoidal modulation rates. All records are from the same unit, and show responses to sinusoidal (upper line) and equivalent ramp (lower line) frequency modulations. a 1c/s sinusoidal modulation rate: inconsistent response to sinusoidal and ramp modulations. b 2 c/s: Response now consistent. c 7 c/s: Vigorous response. d 25 c/s: Infrequent response to sinusoidal modulation, but vigorous response to intermittent ramp modulation of similar rate of change (downward frequency ramp)

which the inhibitory projection is asymmetrically distributed with respect to frequency. Such distributions are found plentifully in the dorsal portion of the cochlear nucleus. This subdivision of the cochlear nucleus is a cortical-like structure, in contrast to the more simple, homogeneous architecture of the ventral division. It is probably not a second order nucleus [12], and unlike the ventral division exhibits responses to tones predominantly inhibitory in nature with complex time course, which responses are very sensitive to barbiturate anaesthesia [4].

A circuit model that might be drawn for an organization producing responses preferential to direction of frequency change, utilising this property of asymmetrically distributed delayed inhibition, is shown in Fig. 8. It is identical in principle to that postulated by BARLOW and LEVICK [11] for neurones in the rabbit's retina which were sensitive to direction of movements in the visual field. Consider an array of neurones organized tonotopically, as found in the cochlear nucleus. Each neurone receives an excitatory input, and also an inhibitory (probably collateral afferent) input from its neighbour on one side only. In this case, higher frequency neurones project in an inhibitory manner on their lower frequency neighbours. This model would predict: (a) an asymmetric distribution of delayed inhibition to static tones, that is, sideband inhibition; (b) preferential sensitivity to upward frequency changes: downward frequency changes would produce inhibition of the cells. A converse arrangement of inhibition would produce an array of cells responding preferentially to downward changes of frequency.

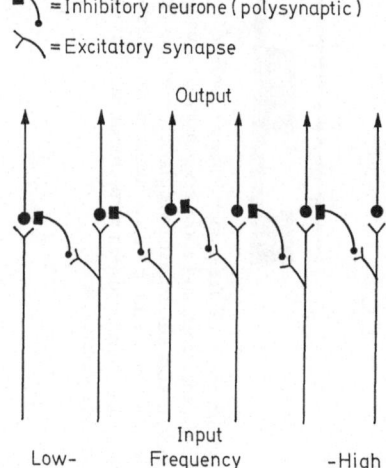

= Inhibitory neurone (polysynaptic)

= Excitatory synapse

Output

Input
Low-   Frequency   -High

Fig. 8a and b. Model of neural organization which would predict: a High frequency "sideband" inhibition and delayed inhibition to steady tones. b Preferential excitation by upward frequency sweeps

In summary, therefore, an attempt has been made to show that at low levels of the auditory system one has: an orderly arrangement of cells and inputs which presumably allows interaction to occur on the basis of frequency of tone; spontaneous activity in the absence of stimulation, and sustained responses to tones; monotonic relationships between firing rate and intensity of stimulus; relatively uncomplicated responses to dynamic stimuli.

In the cortex, however, one has by contrast to the above: an apparently disorderly arrangement of cells and inputs, in other words, the arrangement is not tonotopic; in most cells there is little or no spontaneous activity, but sustained and transient responses to static tones (i.e. on, off, on-off responses); dynamic responses are vigorous and show preference for changing frequencies and certain directions of frequency change.

The information of a sound stimulus at higher levels of the auditory system therefore appears to be presented as a mass of *abstractions* of features of the stimulus, and the system appears to be asking the questions: is the tone on or off? Is the frequency changing? If so, by how much and in what direction? How often is the stimulus changing? Is the stimulus change repetitive? Presumably it is the sum of this mass of abstractions which eliminates the ambiguities which would otherwise be presented to the decision-making elements of the system.

References

1. HUBEL, D. H., and T. N. WIESEL: J. Physiol. (Lond.) **148**, 574—591 (1959).
2. EVANS, E. F., and P. G. NELSON: Fed. Proc. **25**, 463 (1966).
3. — — J. acoust. soc. Amer. **40**, 1275—1276 (1966).
4. — — In preparation.
5. —, and I. C. WHITFIELD: J. Physiol. (Lond.) **171**, 476—493 (1964).
6. —, H. F. Ross, and I. C. WHITFIELD: J. Physiol. (Lond.) **179**, 238—247 (1965).
7. WHITFIELD, I. C., and E. F. EVANS: J. Neurophysiol. **28**, 655—672 (1965).
8. HUBEL, D. H.: J. Physiol. (Lond.) **147**, 226—238 (1959).
9. KIANG, N. Y-s: Acta oto-laryngol. (Stockh.) **59**, 186—200 (1965).
10. PFEIFFER, R. R.: Science **154**, 667—668 (1966).
11. BARLOW, H. B., and W. R. LEVICK: J. Physiol. (Lond.) **178**, 477—504 (1965).
12. EVANS, E. F., and P. G. NELSON: J. Physiol. (Lond.) **196,** 76—78 (1968).

On Chiasms

V. Braitenberg

Gruppo Nazionale di Cibernetica del C.N.R., Napoli

In many instances we find information reaching the brain from the sense organs again displayed in geometrical order in some space which has one or more coordinates easily identifiable with coordinates of the sensory space represented. This is trivially true for the visual and tactile maps, more interestingly true for the representation of frequencies in the auditory system. Here the metrics of the internal representation, on a space coordinate representing the logarithm of frequency, corresponds even to the subjective metrics of pitch perception and therefore to the metrics of a piano keyboard, as was shown again at this meeting by Evans in the case of the cochlear nucleus. Only for the chemical senses, olfaction and taste, we have no clue yet as to the meaning of the coordinates of their spatial display within the brain.

With this role of spatial coordinates of the brain tissue indicating positions or properties of the outside, it is not surprising that we should find orderly systems of parallel fibers providing projection from one such internal region onto another, and occasionally twisted or crossed or braided bundles of fibers, chiasms, decussations as they are called in neuroanatomy, doing what mirrors, prisms or lenses would do in an optical analogy. I shall consider three particularly striking instances of such fiber-crossings, one in vertebrate and two in insect brains and attempt a functional explanation in each case.

The Crossed Representation of the World in the Brain

In vertebrate brains, an overall rule governs the mapping of the visual, tactile, proprioceptive and motor-target-coordinates within the brain. Electrical effects of sensory stimulation provided on one side of the median plane of the animal are more easily observed on the opposite side of the brain, and electrical stimulation of one side of the brain will have its most direct effects on the opposite side of the body. There are exceptions to this rule, and in some parts of the brain (the cerebellum) the coordinate system is even inverted with respect to this general plan. But in the cerebral cortex, where, in higher vertebrates, the layout according to sensory categories and to position in the individual sensory field is most spectacular, the impression of a rotation of the outside coordinates is most compelling, since even the vertical coordinate appears to conform to it, the motor and sensory homunculus as well as the visual map being *upside down*. To this inversion of the internal coordinates corresponds, of course, the crossing of all the couples of nerves coming from or going to the paired sensory or motor organs. In the optic nerves of man an arrangement is well known, by which only those fibers of each eye cross the midline on their way to the brain, which carry information from retinal elements looking out toward the same side of visual field (supposing the eyes locked in a forward gaze), while those fibers which stem from elements in the retina looking toward the opposite side, i.e. from the lateral region of each retina, proceed uncrossed. Thus the rule of the crossed representation clearly refers to positions in the outside world and is not explainable by invoking merely some trick in the internal construction of the apparatus. In various animals with varying degrees of overlap of the visual fields of the two eyes, from no overlap, as in the rabbit (Fig. 1a), to almost complete overlap, as in man, (Fig. 1c) the proportion of uncrossed to crossed fibers seems to correspond quite well to the percentage of visual field of each eye which reaches beyond the midline of the animal (Fig. 1b) (TANSLEY, 1950).

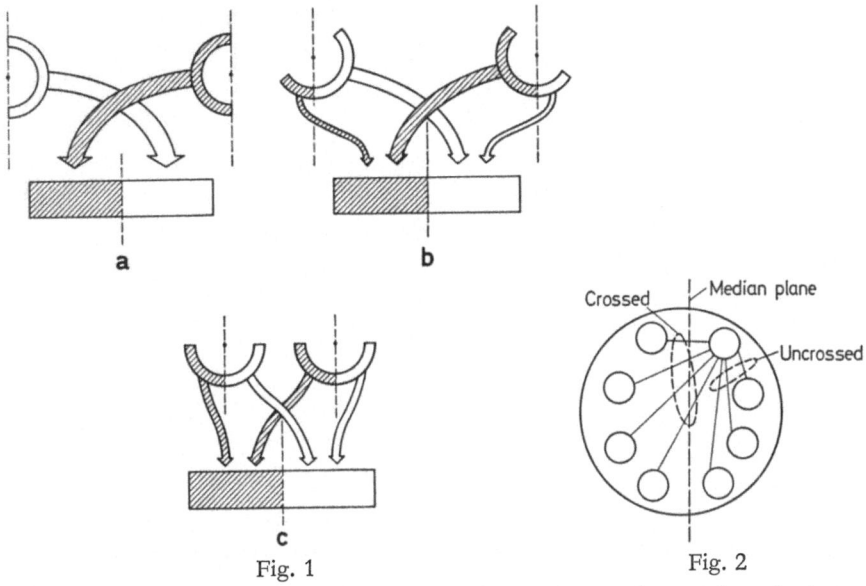

Fig. 1

Fig. 2

Fig. 1. Diagram of the optic chiasm in three cases with different degree of overlap between the two visual fields. a: no overlap, b: some overlap, c: complete superposition. Shaded: portions of retina, optic nerve, and brain pertaining to the right half of the world. Otherwise self-explanatory

Fig. 2. To illustrate W. S. McCulloch's explanation of the crossing of most fiber tracts. See text

This curious crossed relation between the environment and the brain has of course been the object of various explanations. It has been pointed out that the crossing of many fiber tracts within the brain may make the brain mechanically more stable, weaving it more thoroughly, as it were, and this advantage may be important enough to favour the crossed scheme over the uncrossed one, other things being equal. Another very simple and therefore appealing explanation is due to W. S. McCULLOCH (personal communication). Assuming that the vertebrate phylum descends from ancestors with spherical or radial symmetry, having a diffuse nerve net, once a median plane is defined in the transition to a bilaterally symmetrical animal, from any one point of the nerve net there will be emanating more fibers which cross the median plane than uncrossed fibers. This may be a sufficient bias in further evolution to produce the striking scheme of recent vertebrates (Fig. 2).

3*

But it was Ramon y Cajal's idea that was received with the greatest favor as an explanation of the crossed projection. He thought that the reason may well lie in the camera type eyes of the vertebrate which provide inverted pictures on both retinas. Were we to imagine a vertebrate ancester with non overlapping visual fields of the two eyes, and were his two optic nerves to reach a common receiving apparatus, uncrossed and untwisted, the image of an object directly ahead of the animal, and therefore perceived half with the right eye and half with the left eye, would be projected into something quite different from the image of the same object in the lateral position, when it is seen with one eye only (Fig. 3). The crossing of the optic nerve recon-

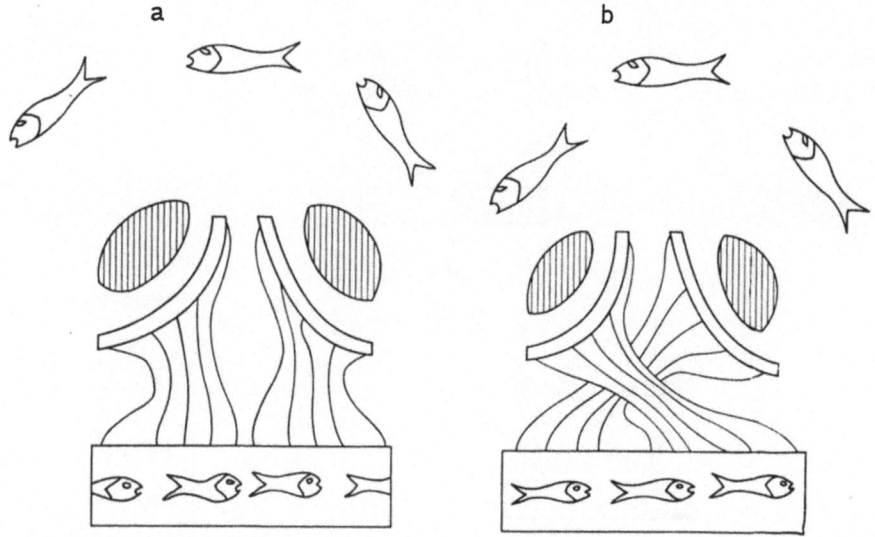

Fig. 3a and b. To illustrate Ramon y Cajal's explanation of the optic chiasm. See text

stitutes the continuity of the visual field, even if inverted. It is interesting that Cajal's argument contains implicitly an idea which has been in the foreground of attention lately in many discussions about a mechanism of form perception. In fact there would be no advantage in having an object represented by the same spatial distribution of excitation independently of its position in the visual field, unless the preceiving apparatus were of such a nature as to give the same response to a local constellation of activity, invariant to translations. Apart from the fact that we do not know yet whether the central nerve nets responsible for visual perception actually have this property, there are some other arguments I have collected once (Braitenberg, 1965) which can be advanced against Cajal's explanation. Among other things a twist of 180 degrees in each optic nerve or a detour of the optic nerve around the optic tectum to enter it from the back would effect quite the same correction of the optical inversion.

One idea which we may certainly accept from Cajal's argument is that it is, sufficient to find an explanation for the crossing in one of the (visual, tactile, motor, proprioceptive) projection system in order to explain the crossing in all the rest of them, since it is obviously advantageous to let the various internal representations share common coordinates in some way.

I want to propose another explanation even if in a tentative way, starting from a sensory projection which appears to be at least preponderately *uncrossed*: the olfactory projection onto the primary and secondary olfactory centers. There is no question about the fact that the telencephalic hemispheres are closely connected in their development to the olfactory centers; in a somewhat romantic view of the older comparative neuroanatomy it was even customary to say that they *grow out of* the central olfactory representation. From the telencephalon to the motor organs the pathways are crossed as is well known. Thus effectively the global input-output pathway is crossed for the olfactory system while the double crossing makes the input-output relation effectively homolateral (uncrossed) for the visual and the tactile system. It is interesting to speculate on the possible advantage of controlateral motor responses to unilateral sensory input. At this point we will have to make a few rather arbitrary assumptions, mainly that the ancestral vertebrate in which these relations were first established had paired olfactory organs with the ability to des-

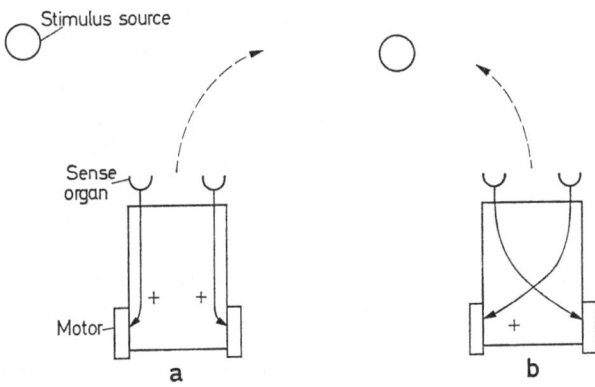

Fig. 4a and b. Diagram to show how paired sense organs activating paired motors will produce positive taxis with crossed connections, negative taxis with uncrossed connections

criminate gradients of concentration between right and left nostril and that its motor organs were of such a nature that activation on one side only would make the animal deviate to the opposite side. We may think of a propulsion by means of a pair of jets or a pair of oar-like appendages such as fins. Let us consider such an animal with uncrossed sensory-motor connections, moving under the influence of gradients of some substance in its environment which will be perceived by the olfactory organs which in turn will activate the motor organs in a graded fashion, the more strongly, the higher the concentration. We may say that the animal has a positive kinesis for that substance. However, when the animal lies obliquely in the gradient, the stronger stimulation coming through one nostril, driving the motor on the same side more strongly, will give the animal negative taxis, i.e. the animal will tend to avert himself from the origin of the stimulus (Fig. 4a). On the contrary, if the sensory motor connections are crossed, positive taxis will correspond to positive kinesis (Fig. 4b) and negative taxis to negative kinesis. The advantage of having taxis and kinesis of the same sign is not absolutly apparent, but it is plausible that the same mechanism which alerts an animal to the presence of a stimulus should also orient it toward the source. I shall turn this problem over the ethologists who may well be able to establish whether chemical taxis and kinesis tend to be of the same sign or of opposite signs as a general rule in vertebrates and particularly in those which we may repute to be close to the roots of the vertebrate genealogical tree. If the answer is that actually opposite signs seem to be favored ,(it would not surprise me if a scheme which would make an animal spend more time near the sources of stimulation — negative kinesis — to which it orients itself — positive taxis — would be more widespread) the argument would still be valid in its general form, but would make us change our supposition of an oar-like propulsion into the kind of propulsion by waves of contraction travelling along the animal such as have been so well described by GRAY (1933) for fishes. In this case the animal turns toward the side of the stronger contraction. Most recent fishes most of the time seem to move according to this second mode. So much remaining open in my argument, as in other arguments based on the likelihood of evolutionary selective advantages belonging to the remote past, I should perhaps restate my point more carefully proposing that an explanation for the crossed representation may be found in the crossed olfactory motor pathway in its relation to extremely primitive, and therefore general, mechanisms of orientation and alerting.

The Crossed Projection of the Ommatidia onto the First Visual Ganglion in the Fly

I shall present the curious chiasms occuring at the base of the retina of the fly between neighboring units only in summary here since I have recently published a paper with the pictorial evidence and with a detailed hypothesis on their function (BRAITENBERG, 1967). Each of the two compound eyes of a fly is composed of about 3200 ommatidia, i.e. roughly identical units, each consisting in a lens and some additional dioptric apparatus, a set of eight sensory cells (retinular cells) with their axons, besides shielding pigment and supporting tissue. In close proximity to the retina lies the first ganglion, the lamina ganglionaris with a neat periodic structure essentially defined by as many synaptic structures (the optical cartridges) as there are ommatidia in the retina. While two of the axons of the retinular cells in each ommatidium seem to proceed toward stations farther inward, the remaining six end in the lamina ganglionaris making synaptic contacts with the second order fibers which arise there. The fine structure of these synaptic contacts has been described in detail by TRUJILLO-CENOZ (1965). The curious thing is that these six fibres reach cartridges in the lamina arranged in a constant asymmetrical array around the cartridge whose

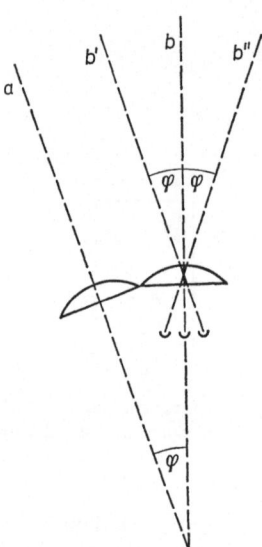

Fig. 5. Diagram of an ommatidium of the fly with a lens projecting an image onto the "retinula" composed of seven sensory elements. Fibers leaving the ommatidium are distributed on the first optic ganglion according to the same pattern as that of the seven lines of sight corresponding to the seven sensory elements

position corresponds to the ommatidium in question. Depending on the direction of the cut, an histological section through the retina and the lamina will therefore show various patterns of criss-crossing of the fibres projecting from one to the other. Here the explanation of the crossing as a correction of the inversion occuring in camera type eyes seems to be entirely correct, even if previously we had found some arguments to doubt this explanation as proposed by CAJAL for the optic chiasm of vertebrates. Recently AUTRUM and WIEDEMANN (1962), WIEDEMANN (1965), KIRSCHFELD (1967) have shown conclusively that the dioptric apparatus of each ommatidium acts as a camera-lens type optical system which projects an inverted image of a small section of the optical environment onto the retinula, the set of seven retinular cells (the eighth retinular cell is nothing but a continuation of the

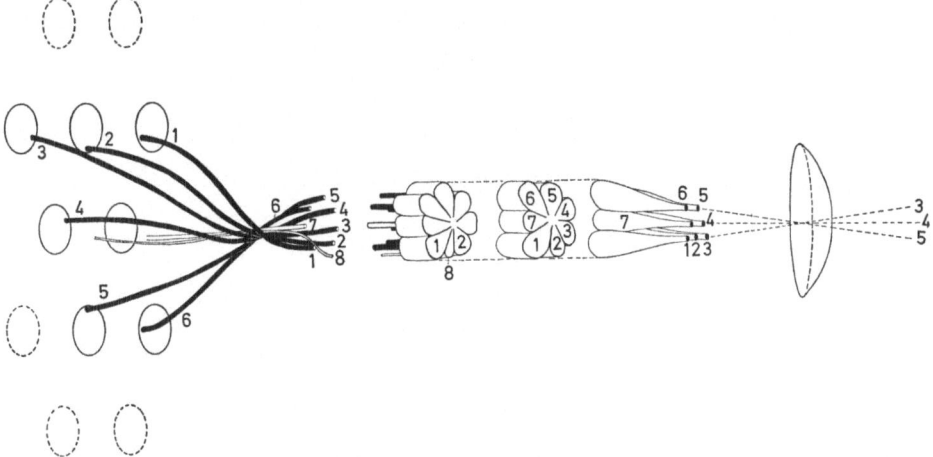

Fig. 6. Equivalence of the interommatidial angle φ with the angle between two neighbouring lines of sight in one ommatidium of the fly

seventh) whose upper delimination lies in the focal plane of the optical system. It so happens that six of the rhabdomeres (the photosensitive portions of the retinular cells) are arranged around the seventh in the retinula according to quite the same asymmetrical pattern which we have seen characterizes the arrangement of those cartridges in the lamina which are reached by the fibres of a single ommatidium, only with an orientation rotated 180 degrees with respect to this latter arrangement. The explanation is obvious, simply invoking the superposition of the non-inverting optics of the compound eye as a whole and the inverting optics of each individual ommatidium. If the small inverted portions of the optical environment seen by the retinulas of all the ommatidia are to be aligned with the projection of the environment afforded by the compound eye as a whole, the fibre bundle between the ommatidium and the ganglion has to be twisted around 180 degrees and this is in fact the case. Moreover if the projection of the optical environment on to the lamina is to be metrically correct, the angles between the lines of sight of the seven elements of each retinula will determine the distance on the lamina of the points reached by the corresponding fibres. The result is the pattern already described. The whole situation is greatly simplified if the period of the non inverting macro-projection of the array

of ommatidia matches that of the inverting micro-system of each individual ommatidium. This was found to be the case by Kirschfeld (1967) who found the angles
between the axes of neighboring ommatidia to be the same as the angles between
the lines of sight of neighboring elements of one retinula (Fig. 5). The whole system
is summarized in Fig. 6.

The Chiasm between the First and the Second Visual Ganglion of the Fly

As we have seen in the preceding section, the optical environment is represented
on the lamina with preservation of continuity and orientation and to a good approximation also with preservation of angular distance. The output of the lamina is again
a bundle of fibers — actually a bundle of small fiber bundles, one for each cartridge —
projecting one to one onto the input units of the second visual ganglion, the *medulla,*
which has again a neatly periodic structure with as many units as there are ommatidia
in the retina and cartridges in the lamina ganglionaris. But this bundle is twisted or

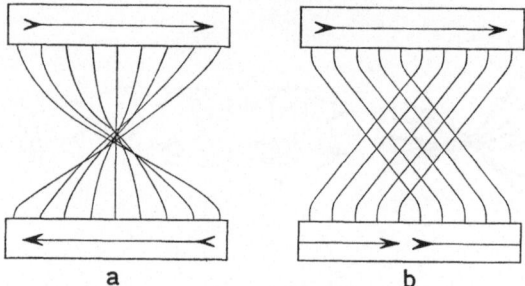

Fig. 7. a) twisted chiasm, b) braided chiasm

crossed or braided in a curious way, forming what is usually called the *external
chiasm* between the first and second visual ganglion. This chiasm is an extremely
widespread feature in arthropod brains, having been described in insects, crustaceans,
isopods as a constant adjunct of the compound eye. All descriptions seem to agree to
the extent that the fiber crossing in the external chiasm is such as to make the more
forward portions of the lamina and therefore of the eye project onto the posterior
portions of the medulla and viceversa. (In order to avoid misunderstanding, it is
perhaps not superfluous to add that there is a separate chiasm on each side of the
animal, there are no fibers crossing the midline as in the optic chiasm of vertebrates
illustrated in the first section of this paper!) For many species a second or internal
chiasm has been described between the second and third visual ganglion (sometimes
called medulla externa and medulla interna) arranged at right angles to the first
chiasm, i.e. projecting from the upper portions of the second ganglion to the lower
portions of the third ganglion and viceversa, but I shall limit myself to the external
chiasm of the fly here.

The illustrations of the external chiasm which are to be found in the literature are
of two types (Fig. 7a and 7b), which we may distinguish as (a) twisting and (b)
braiding. Thinking in terms of optical projections, the effect of the two types of
crossing are quite different. The twisting chiasm exchanges right and left in the
projection, leaving the continuity of the picture intact. On the contrary, the braiding

chiasm disrupts the image by exchanging the right and left half of the image without inverting the two halves. In terms of information processing, the twisting chiasm could be understood only by invoking the superposition of the optical image onto some other frame of reference, since internally, within the visual system, obviously any operation which is performed after the twist might as well work with the untwisted projection. On the other hand, the disruption of the image which occurs in the braided chiasm effects a sort of geometrical inside-out transformation which may have functional significance.

We are currently trying to determine which kind of chiasm occurs in the fly. Our own material up to now was sufficient to exclude the pattern of (b), since fibers running from the middle of the lamina to the middle of the medulla could be clearly observed and the entire bundle starting from the anterior portions of the lamina appears to be twisted. The twist of the posterior bundle, which would make the pattern (a) complete, remained, however, uncertain on our preparations. Indeed CAJAL and SANCHEZ (1915, Table 1 and Fig. 15 for the bee, Table 2 for the fly) present

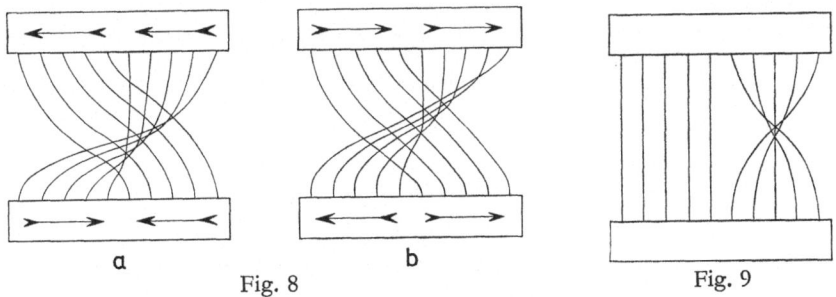

Fig. 8   Fig. 9

Fig. 8a and b. Asymmetrical chiasm illustrated by CAJAL and SANCHEZ (1915)

Fig. 9. See text

some drawings based on GOLGI studies in which yet another pattern of fiber crossing in the external chiasm is recognizable. It is illustrated diagrammatically in Fig. 8 here. The effect of this strangely asymmetrical chiasm would be the following. Suppose a pattern moves in a backward direction through the visual field of the fly. This will turn out to be a movement of a pattern of excitation converging toward a vertical line somewhere within the medulla (Fig. 8a). Suppose on the contrary that the same pattern moves in the opposite direction through the visual field (Fig. 8b). It will produce divergent movement of excitation in the ganglion. To a fly obviously the perception of movement backward, corresponding to the fly proceeding forward, is an entirely different situation from the perception of movement forward through its visual field. It may be advantageous to have the two situations represented as the two very different happenings within the ganglion, convergent and divergent excitation respectively. Considering RALL's dendritic models (RALL, this meeting) it is easy to imagine neurons within the ganglion so connected that they would respond only to one or to the other type of stimulation.

I should add however, that this cannot be taken as an *explanation* of the chiasm, even if it may certainly be an important consequence of this type of fiber crossing. As a matter of fact, if the anterior half of the fibers were twisted and the posterior half untwisted, without the crossing of the two bundles (Fig. 9), motion in the two directions would still be transformed into convergent and divergent motion in the ganglion. We must admit that something escapes us in the interpretation of these structures. It may be a reason connected with ontogenetic mechanisms, in which case it would be idle to speculate on functional advantages. It may be, on the other hand, that the full understanding of one partial system even in the fly cannot be obtained without a thorough knowledge of the rest of the brain, and this, especially in the fly, lies in the far future.

References

AUTRUM, H. J., u. I. WIEDEMANN: Versuche über den Strahlengang im Insektenauge (Appositionsauge). Z. Naturforsch. **17b**, 480—482 (1962).

BRAITENBERG, V.: Taxis, kinesis and decussation. In: Cybernetics of the nervous system. WIENER, N., and P. J. SCHADE Eds. Progress in Brain Research, Vol. 17. Amsterdam: Elsevier 1965.

—, Patterns of projection in the visual system of the fly. I. Retina-Lamina projections. Exp. Brain Res. **3**, 271 298 (1967).

CAJAL, S. RAMON y: Histologie du système nerveux de l'homme et des vertèbres. Paris: Maloine 1911.

—, y D. SANCHEZ: Contribución al conocimento de los centros nerviosos de los insectos. Trab. Lab. Invest. biol. Univ. Madrid **13**, 1—164 (1915).

GRAY, J.: Directional control of fish movement. Proc. roy. Soc. B. **113**, 115—125 (1933).

KIRSCHFELD, K.: Die Beziehung zwischen dem Raster der Ommatidien und dem Raster der Rhabdomere im Komplexauge von Musca. Exp. Brain Res. **3**, 248—270 (1967).

TANSLEY, K.: Vision. In: Physiological mechanisms in animal behaviour. Cambridge Symposium. Cambridge: University Press 1950.

TRUJILLO-CENÓZ, O.: Some aspects of the structural organization of the intermediate retina of dipterans. J. Ultrastruct. Res. **13**, 1—33 (1965).

WIEDEMANN, I.: Versuche über den Strahlengang im Insektenauge (Appositionsauge). Z. vergl. Physiol. **49**, 526—542 (1965).

Some Ideas on Information Processing in the Cerebellum *

M. A. Arbib**, G. F. Franklin**, and N. Nilsson***

Introduction

Other papers presented at this conference tend to deal either with extremely formalised models of neural networks, or with peripheral processing. Therefore, it may be a useful reminder of how much further such studies have to go if we present here some ideas on information processing in the cerebellum, to emphasize how complicated real neuronic interactions can be, and to emphasize how ignorant we are of "the language of neurons" when we move away from the periphery. Here we attempt to formulate questions rather than provide answers — our hope being that we may remind the theorist of a vast range of exacting problems, and stimulate the biologist to learn new types of experimental questions. Our models are not yet in predictive form, not least because much crucial experimental data is lacking — we hope that experimentalists, reading between the lines, will be prompted to carry out new experiments, and then confront the theorists with the task of appropriately refining our approach. We clearly have a long way to go before we can be satisfied with any models of complex neural structures which are not located in the mainstream of the input and output systems.

In the first section, we attempt to clarify the processes of complex motor control in biological mechanisms by inquiring how one might design a robot to perform tasks requiring the coordination of various actions. We do not imply that the engineering solution will be identical to the biological one, but certainly an engineering analysis of the problems will provide a useful framework in which to discuss various hypotheses about biological functions.

In the second section, we entertain some speculations as to how these processes might be parcelled out between the cerebellum and the cerebrum in a real nervous system. We also try to make some sense out of the spatial arrangements of the cerebellar cortex, and suggest how learning might be incorporated in such a system. We would mention two points which are not always sufficiently emphasized: (a) Extremely sophisticated processing takes place in the pyramidal and extrapyramidal systems, whether the cerebellum is there or not. We can find no evidence of a clear understanding of the relative role of these systems; (b) The interfaces of the

* An early version of this paper was prepared for discussion at the workshop on "Information Processing in the Cerebellum", sponsored by the Neurosciences Research Program, and held at Salishan Lodge, Oregon, May 15 to 17, 1967. The authors are grateful for that opportunity to learn more of the relations, and the divergences, between current studies in neurophysiology and neuroanatomy, and their own fields of automata theory, computer science, and control engineering. This research was supported in part by the U.S. Air Force Office of Scientific Research (Information Sciences Directorate) under Grant No. AF-AFOSR-1198-67.

** Electrical Engineering Department, Stanford University, Stanford, California (U.S.A.).
*** Stanford Research Institute, Menlo Park, California (U.S.A.).

cerebellum with the rest of the CNS, e.g., the inferior olive, are themselves systems of subtle circuitry which must serve to modify rather than simply channel the cerebellar information-flow. It is thus our clear impression that no one really knows precisely what the cerebellum does, or what information its input and output convey, so that our modelling is but loosely constrained by the data. However, we believe that our models will prove useful, even if some of the functions we now ascribe to the cerebellum should later migrate to other parts of the CNS. We also note that a precise model explaining the actuator characteristics of muscle has been obtained, and suggest a control-theoretic approach to experiments on the cerebellum.

I. Problems of Motor Control in the Design of a Robot [1]

Without discussing the details of its tasks or the actual mechanics, we can say a great deal about the types of problem facing the designer of a robot which is able to get around in its environment and use sophisticated manipulators requiring more or less delicate control and coordination. Let us begin our discussion by observing that the tasks to be performed can be analyzed into a sequence of basic actions. For example, locomotion from place to place is accomplished by a sequence of acts such as:

1. Forward one foot,
2. Turn left 30°,
3. Forward until wall is bumped,
4. Turn right 90°,
5. Forward three feet,
6. Extend right arm straight ahead.

Since all tasks can be broken down into a list of readily accomplished basic actions, we could say that the robot problem in its most fundamental terms involves composing and executing the basic component actions necessary to accomplish a task. We shall attempt to elaborate from an engineering viewpoint the problems raised by Lashley (1951): "What ... determines the order (of language or coordinated motor behavior)? It seems that the mechanism which determines the serial activation of the motor units is relatively independent, both of the motor units and of the thought structure. The readiness with which the form or expression of an idea can be changed, the facility with which different word orders may be utilized to express the same thought, are further evidence that ... syntax is not inherent in the words employed or in the idea to be expressed. It is a generalized pattern imposed upon the specific acts as they occur."

First we should clarify what is meant by a *sequence* of actions. Sequences may be quite complex. They may involve, for example, the simultaneous execution of a group of several actions at once as well as the serial ordering of these groups. Such sequences therefore are not so simple as single links in a chain but are more accurately portrayed as intertwined and overlapping fibres making up a long thread. Thus, we might modify the simple serial chain of six basic actions given in our example above by performing actions five and six at the same time. Not always can actions be combined, however. For example, actions one through four must be executed in

---

[1] Two papers describing the preliminary design of robots have been written by Nilsson and Raphael (1967), and by Rosen and Nilsson (1967). In Fig. 1 we present a tentative diagram for the information-processing requirements for a brain, be it of man or robot, taken from Arbib (1967).

serial order. The types of action sequence that our robot must perform pose two important problems: coordination and phasing. Simultaneous actions must be coordinated, and serial groups of actions must be smoothly phased so that the beginning of one action group is appropriately timed to the ending of the previous one.

Our example with the six serial actions also reveals that there are two basic types of actions. We shall call these two types *open-loop* and *closed-loop*. Action 3 is an example of a closed-loop action, while the others are open-loop. Action 3 is called "closed-loop" because it *requires* that an action continue until some external condition verified by sensory information (bumping into the wall) is met. The robot could perform such an act without sensing until the last moment how far away the wall might be. The

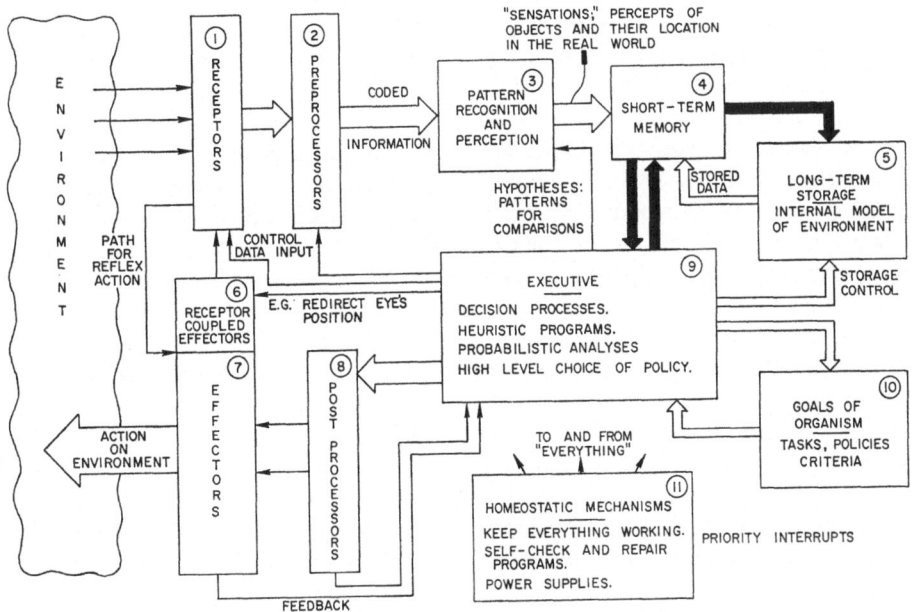

Fig. 1. Functional Block Diagram of a Cybernetic Brain

other actions are called *open-loop* because they could be executed as *discrete* steps without monitoring the robot's sensors. There is evidence that both types of actions will be useful in composing useful sequences. Sometimes the robot has a choice and must decide which type of action to employ in a situation where either might seem to suffice.

The problems of composing and executing action sequences are made easier if we combine frequently used sequences into higher order *routines* and then combine these into still higher order *procedures*, and so on. Thus a task would first be analyzed into a sequence of procedures, say, and then each procedure into a sequence of routines, and so on until the basic actions were finally established. Once the decision is made to organize robot actions in such a hierarchy, the problem still remains of the most efficient organizational form for such a hierarchy.

As we turn now to the problem of composing and executing sequences — be they at the level of basic actions or of higher order routines — we will do well to remember some further remarks of LASHLEY (1951):

"The finger strokes of a musician may reach 16 per second in passages which call for a definite and changing order of successive finger movements. The succession of movements is too quick even for visual reaction time. In rapid sight reading it is impossible to read the individual notes of an arpeggio. The notes must be seen in groups. Sensory control of movement seems to be ruled out in such acts. They require the postulation of some central nervous mechanism which fires with predetermined intensity and duration or activates different muscles in predetermined order.

"For a number of animals from the centipede to the dog, the removal of one or more legs results in a spontaneous change in the order of stepping ... (and) patterns of coordinated movement may often be transferred directly to other motor systems than the one practised."

There is a spectrum of approaches toward composing and executing sequences. At one end of this spectrum a task is performed by first composing long sequences of actions adequate to accomplish the task. The process by which these sequences are composed we shall call planning. After the whole sequence is known, the steps of the plan are executed. Planning and execution are thus carried out separately. Intermediate in the spectrum, planning and execution are much more interwoven. A short sequence is composed and then executed before another short sequence is composed and executed, etc. At the other end of the spectrum, actions are executed with what might be called no planning at all. Such actions could be considered automatic and direct responses to certain external and internal stimuli.

The advantage of planning the entire sequence before beginning its execution is that the appropriate acts at the beginning may depend on crucial details near termination of the task. On the other hand, there are situations in which remote future details are irrelevant or unknowable and one might as well plan only a few steps ahead and execute a few actions to see what happens ("playing it by ear", as the saying goes). Often repeated sequences that might be performed rapidly and accurately under rather stereotyped environmental conditions might be accomplished best at the stimulus-response end of the spectrum. Since these sequences are not composed, they must be stored in internal memory. Various stimulus-response nets have been suggested for efficient storage of these sequences. A particularly interesting storage scheme has been suggested by Friedman (1967).

For efficient operation, the robot should probably have some ability to decide in any given situation where on this spectrum it should operate: whether it should plan its whole task in elaborate detail or begin execution after only a modest amount of planning. One possible way of incorporating this feature might be to design the robot as a stimulus-response device one of whose responses is the "planning" response. Thus we reject any notion that responses are purely external. Under the appropriate set of internal and external conditions (stimulus) the response is to plan a sequence. As the sequence of planned basic actions grows, the internal conditions change and the response switches to the execution of an action, for example the first action on the list of planned ones. Whatever degree of planning is used in composing sequences, we need a strategy for this planning. The robot cannot invent out of thin air a sequence of actions to accomplish a task. It must have a model of its world in which significant objects, causal laws, and relationships are represented. Using this model, various techniques that do not really concern us here can be suggested to accomplish planning. In essence, the robot conducts a "thought experiment" in which it tries out various possible action sequences and selects one of them thought to be capable of accomplishing the task.

Let us leave the subject of composing or planning sequences of actions and turn to the matter of their execution. Executing strings of open loop actions presents no serious problems, but let us consider this simple case for a moment anyway. If a string of open loop actions is planned based on an inaccurate model, its execution will soon lead the robot into unanticipated situations, perhaps far off the track of efficient execution of the task. Clearly, the robot must be prepared to detect such straying as a signal to update the plan. As each action is executed the internal model of the world must be updated to the version that would apply after execution. This updated model should then be checked against sensory inputs to detect possible contradictions. Large discrepancies should signal a correction of the model and the need for replanning of the task.

We may relate this to Lashley's emphasis on the existence of systems of space coordinates in the animal nervous system — the postural system based on excitations from proprioceptors and involving cerebellar effects, the system imposed by distance receptors, and the vestibular, or gravitational, system (which acts as do the gyros of a man-made control system to provide a stabilised reference with respect to which things can be measured): "Their influences pervade the motor system so that every gross movement of limbs or body is made with reference to the space system. The perceptions from the distance receptors, vision, hearing and touch are also constantly modified and referred to the same space coordinates. The stimulus is *there*, in a definite place; it has definite relation to the position of the body, and it shifts with respect to the sense organ, but not with respect to the general orientation, with changes in body posture."

If strings of closed-loop actions are being executed, then, besides the need for confirming the updated model of the world, we have more acute coordination and phasing problems. The stopping-condition for a certain closed-loop action may depend on the status of other closed-loop actions in a most complex way. Another requirement of closed-loop actions is that there must be adequate communication channels from sensors associated with the action back to higher centers. Coordination demands communication and closed-loop acts require feedback.

We now turn to the important organizational problem of "flow of control". We can imagine that the robot is controlled by a computer program (permitting a large amount of parallel processing) with ultimate control vested in some sort of executive program. This executive program might in turn call various planning, stimulus-response or action-executing subprograms temporarily relinquishing control to one of them. These subprograms may in turn call each other or additional subprograms in order to accomplish the task assigned. The question is under what conditions should a program relinquish control to another and, when it does relinquish control, which program should take over.

There are at least two ways in which this question could be answered. The most straightforward approach is to have a called program relinquish control to its calling program as soon as the former has completed its assignment. Even with this simple strategy, various contingencies must be anticipated such as the inability of the called program to continue functioning. A disadvantage of this strategy is that the called program may have effects on the external world that render its further functioning inappropriate to the task. The called program may have no way of knowing about this futility; such knowledge may be available only in quiescent higher levels.

An organizational form that avoids this difficulty would have all programs at all levels always functioning in parallel. When a subprogram is called, the calling program continues to monitor performance so that control may be regained whenever appropriate. Friedman's (1967) hierarchial structure implements such a strategy, although he simulated the parallel action of all programs on a conventional, non-parallel computer. Friedman speculated that the nervous system of animals employed a similar hierarchial collection of programs running in parallel on a biological computer. The flow of control descended down a "tree" reaching to all called programs with each calling program able to regain control from its descendants.

There are many other organizational problems that a robot designer must face to increase the efficiency of the system. We shall not treat all of these here, but will close our discussion with the subject of action sequence storage. Suppose a task is given to the robot and a sequence of actions is composed by the planning programs and then successfully executed. The question arises, should this successfull sequence be stored away somewhere in anticipation of the occasion in which the robot is asked to perform the same task again? The answer to this question depends solely on the relation between the cost of storage and rapid retrieval of the sequence and the cost of recomputing it. If storage space is limited, it should be used mainly for storing often-repeated sequences. Other sequences should be recomputed.

For those sequences important enough to store there is the further organizational question of efficient storage and retrieval methods. If the robot has m basic actions it can take, there are m^n different sequences of these actions each n actions long. Certainly the robot does not have to provide storage space for all of these; some are impossible, and most are improbable. What is needed is an efficient way to store the important sequences and a powerful indexing scheme that relates the sequence to the particular task to which it applies. The stimulus-response methods of composing and executing actions solve this problem by depending on the regular properties of the environment to ease the storage burden. One action causes changes in the environment which trigger the next action, and so on. When whole sequences must be stored, various "hash-coding" techniques may provide the needed efficiency. Another interesting approach toward storing sequences has been proposed by Rosenblatt (1967).

The above discussion of robot design has covered many of the more important conceptual problems that must be solved in any successful complex task-performing device whether biological or mechanical. As robot designers accumulate more experience in meeting and solving these kinds of problem it is hoped that a framework will thus be developed that will be found useful by those trying to understand and describe complex motor control processes in biology. In the next section we shall speculate on the ways in which phasing may be shared between cerebrum and cerebellum in the neural control of human movements.

II. The Cerebellum in an Adaptive Control System

Our first model for the role of the cerebellum in the control of human movement is presented as a crude block diagram based on the gross data of ataxia and decomposition of movement. Consider the task of moving a hand to touch an object. We dissect out three main components and present them serially, but emphasize in reality they proceed in parallel with mutual interaction. We ignore local feedback to concentrate on the external loop (see Fig. 2):

1. Given that the present goal of the system is to grab a moving object, the cerebrum analyses the recent history of movement of the object to formulate a strategy for catching it, e.g. chase it — if it's moving directly away; versus await its return — if it's moving in a circle.

2. The *cerebellum*, knowing the strategy via its cerebral input, adjusts the "timing parameters" such as gain for smooth swift executing of strategy. (Perhaps input from the reticular formation can adjust the gain.)

3. The strategy is executed, using feedback which undoubtedly has both cerebellar and cerebral components. Delay times in the various loops play a crucial role here—facilitation may bias them. Strategy is then to provide a control function for positioning the hand, depending on the position of the object, the position of hand (and its velocity), and timing parameters. Cerebellar lesions could damage the

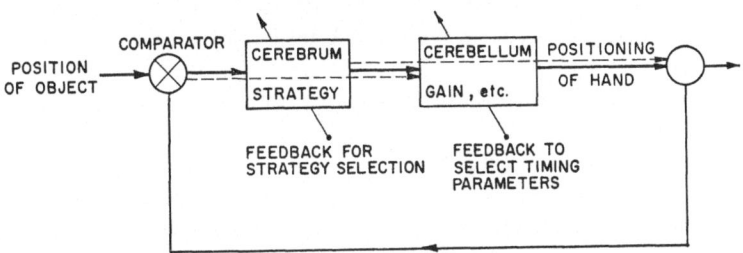

Fig. 2. An adaptive Feedback Loop in which it is posited that the Cerebrum controls the strategy of Motion, whereas the Cerebellum controls fine timing parameters

strategy by supplying false timing parameters, or by corrupting the sample of the hand's velocity.

The cerebrum may formulate a strategy requiring sequential execution of components. The whole sequence may be "conscious" (i.e., we immediately know that "get suitcase out of trunk" involves "walk to car, get keys out of pocket, select trunk key, insert in lock and turn, etc.") but only one component is to be executed at a time.

A cerebral loop can handle "component n executed, next execute component $n + 1$". At a lower level, however, the cerebellum seems to be involved in smooth phasing. Testing the phase to optimize parameters for sequential execution, the cerebrum gives gross values, and the cerebellum refines the values. The sequence we refer to is of acts, such as presented at the beginning of section 1. In terms of actual implementation, we would expect activity to be initiated in opposing force generators in an overlapping time sequence; indeed, both members of each pair may be continuously active.

While control theory has good algorithms for "go optimally from A to B", it seems to be a new question—and one most relevant to a study of the cerebellum—to ask for algorithms "go optimally from A to C via B, while smoothing the transition at B between the two sub-sequences" (cf. Fig. 3).

We now give a very simple specialization of this model which is tractable to careful analysis. Two interesting topics in systems theory present themselves for deeper consideration — (i) effects of changing delay times of loops on the stability of control systems, and (ii) the study of trade-off between time and space in complexity of computation by automata.

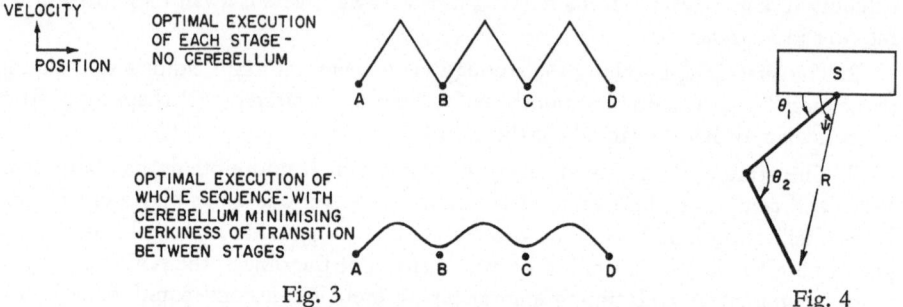

Fig. 3   Fig. 4

Fig. 3. Emphasising the need for smooth phasing in sequential execution

Fig. 4. A system S whose effector is a jointed arm

Consider a system S which has for effector a jointed arm, whose control parameters are θ_1, θ_2, but whose external receptors only monitor the polar coordinators (ψ, R) of the end of the arm (Fig. 4).

We imagine the control centers of system S to be partitioned into two subsystems, which we call the cerebrum$_S$ and the cerebellum$_S$, with the control and information paths shown in Fig. 5.

The cerebrum$_S$, on the basis of strategic formulations, issues to the cerebellum$_S$ the information that a desired change, or sequence of changes, of (ψ, R) is desired,

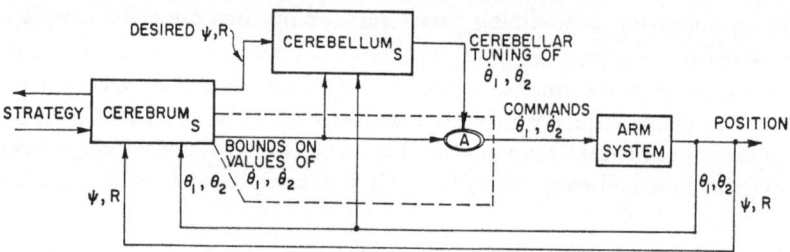

Fig. 5. A posited cerebrum-cerebellum control system for the control of the system S of Fig. 4

and at the same time issues to the arm system a command, monitored by the cerebellum$_S$ as to maximal velocities for executing the strategy. The cerebellum$_S$ then computes, as part of a (θ_1, θ_2) feedback loop, the optimal values of $(\dot{\theta}_1, \dot{\theta}_2)$ and uses these to modulate the $(\dot{\theta}_1, \dot{\theta}_2)$ commands to the arm system. We see that the cerebellum$_S$ inhibits maximal acceleration and deceleration to smooth the action. The cerebrum$_S$ uses (ψ, R) feedback to check that the cerebellum$_S$ is suitably implementing the strategy — and if this is so, it ignores the θ_1, θ_2 inputs. If the cerebellum$_S$ is damaged in some way, the cerebrum$_S$ diverts computation time to rough tuning of its $(\dot{\theta}_1, \dot{\theta}_2)$ output. Since the cerebrum$_S$ has other tasks, it cannot devote as much time to the (θ_1, θ_2) computation as the cerebellum$_S$ can (we might regard the cerebrum $_S$ = executive as time-shared, not normally needing to allocate time to tasks usually executed by the cerebellum$_S$). We thus get either delays in computation, or less accurate computation. In either case, we get a less finely tuned control system, and the resultant instabilities may approximate those seen in a patient with cerebellar lesions.

We should note that our diagram may serve well for older sections of the cerebellum which exert their influence on the spinal pathways. For neocerebellum, the same logic may well suffice, but with the site A of interaction in Fig. 5 located within the cerebrum itself—as suggested by the dotted lines.

This discussion suggests the comparison of "normals" with patients with cerebellar lesions in normal tracking tasks in which normal feedback can be delayed by variable intervals.

Our model relates to McCulloch's "redundancy of potential command" notion. We imagine two pilots of a ship faced with a (ψ, R) knob and a (θ_1, θ_2) knob—one

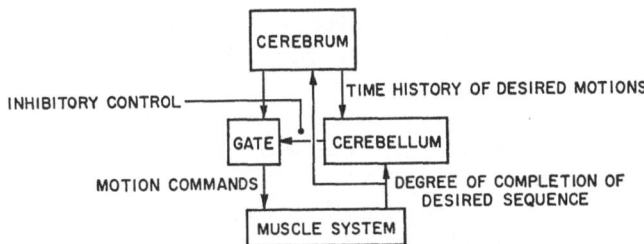

Fig. 6. Sequential Computation in a cerebrum-cerebellum System

normally sets (ψ, R) at the bridge, and leaves the corresponding (θ_1, θ_2) settings to the other, who can do it better; but in case one learns something that enables him to do it better, he sets (θ_1, θ_2) himself, albeit at the cost of impaired performance of that and other duties (see, e. g., McCulloch and Brodey, 1967). We would emphasize that the control loops here do seem to add something new to those well-known ones of Merton which we shall discuss below.

The phasing is not just serial, of course—picking up a pencil involves smooth coordination of parallel action of many muscles, pronation, elbow, shoulder and even body movement, as well as grasping, etc. To elaborate the model, we will have to further explore the literature, and perhaps learn of new data on such questions as: What is the communication between muscle sets? Where are the post-processors for the motor system? Are they in the spinal cord? Who coordinates the coordinators? Can coordination between arms and legs be handled only at the cerebral level, with the smoothing within each subsystem being handled by the cerebellum?

We have emphasized the importance of smooth transitions between different phases of a sequence. The cerebral input to cerebellum must then present the instructions for at least two steps of the sequence to permit the computation of the appropriate transition (Fig. 6). Note, here, the importance of register of the cerebellar or cerebral somatopic maps. If, as some have suggested, the cerebellar cortex is essentially a "dead-beat" system—all input is transferred to inhibition in one or two steps – precluding a short-term reverberatory memory, it would seem that extra-cortical loops must play a vital role in this sequencing.

If we actually wish to experiment on the role of the cerebellum in the control of movement from the point of view of control theory, it is first of all necessary to limit the range of study to the simplest possible functions in order to identify the specific characteristics of this role. It is clear that among functions, the cerebellum is involved in maintaining posture and tonic activity, and in making voluntary move-ments. There are extensive connections between the cerebellum and other parts of the nervous system, and the evidence is strong that some connections are quite specific so that in the neocerebellum there are areas of highly organized somatotopic maps of both efferent and afferent fibers. It would seem that there are at least two approaches to the concentration of study on cerebellar role. One of these would direct attention downwards in complexity to the simplest most basic functions and backwards in time, phylogenetically, to the earliest instances of development of an identifiable cerebellum. A second possibility for detailed functional study of control is to consider the cerebellar role in specialized, skilled, voluntary movements in animals with a highly developed cerebellum such as man, primates, or cats. From a brief look at present knowledge, it would appear that sufficient information is available to make the second approach a useful exercise. Many authors have sug-gested in a more or less gross way the important interconnections involved in the cerebellum when fine, voluntary movement is effected. From the point of view of coordinated control, the objective needs to be to identify as specifically as possible the pathways over which flow the information relating only to the move in question. It is assumed that the move takes place against an extensive background of nervous activity stimulated by sensory inputs and causing postural and tonic muscle activity of many types. These are not of concern here. Furthermore, it may be assumed that the voluntary motion is effected through and past many connections and organs which, in other circumstances, may strongly influence the muscles concerned. These too are for the present purpose ignored. A great deal of complexity remains.

MERTON (1951) was apparently the first to explicitly hypothesise servo-control in the alpha-gamma-system of the muscle – a general hypothesis still accepted in its broad outlines, though modified in detail by recent work on the separate role of primary and secondary afferents of muscle spindles and on the Renshaw cells, or inhibitory interneurons (MATTHEWS, 1964, and MILSUM, 1966). The hypothesis may be summarised as follows (see Fig. 7): The muscle-spindles are arranged in parallel with the main muscle and so respond to changes in length rather than in tension. The gamma-system serves to cause the muscle-spindles to contract, the spindle afferents then respond to the incongruity in length between the spindle and the main muscle and excite the alpha-neurons which cause the main muscle to contact, until congruity is attained. He hypothesised that higher centres activate the gamma-neurons for ordinary movements, but that the alpha-neurons may be activated directly for initiating urgent movements.

If a muscle should be pulled externally, feedback would thus act to reduce the resultant incongruity between muscle and spindle and so restore the muscle to its original length. MERTON hypothesised that this same servo-mechanism underlies the maintenance of posture in normal life, and reminded us of Sherrington's observation that movement takes place against a background of posture: (i) movement of one limb requires postural adjustments by the body and other limbs to keep a steady balance, and (ii) in the active muscles themselves, movements are in some way blended into preexisting posture. It seems to us that local feedbacks could well help account for (ii), but that (i) must require integration via higher centres.

As we stated above, there are two possible routes, the alpha and the gamma, from the brainstem to the muscle, indicated very schematically in Fig. 7. GRANIT, HOLMGREN and MERTON (1955) studied the relative degree of usage of the two routes before and after anterior cerebellectomy. They feel that it is probable that posture would mainly employ the gamma-route, and that rapid movements with minimum reaction time go through the alpha-route. Their experiments suggested that the

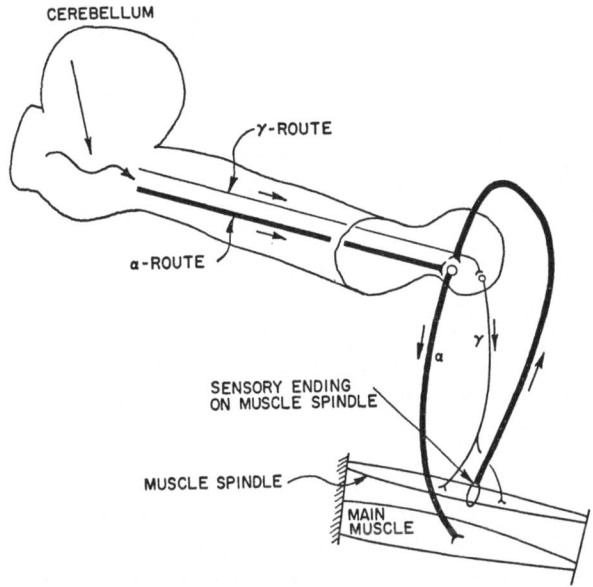

Fig. 7. Merton's model of the α—γ system of muscle

cerebellum serves to adjust activity quickly between one route and the other — cerebellectomy caused gamma-paralysis, but not muscle paralysis, suggesting that more excitation was being directed to the alpha-motoneurons. While recalling these results, we would reject the authors' "simplest interpretation" of their data: "that the cerebellum controlled a neutral switch (sketched in Fig. 7) which directed excitation, originating elswhere, into either the alpha- or the gamma-route. The data requires that the same movement be brought about by a different mode of excitation, not an entirely different movement produced". But what would be the role of such a switch —and, if the cerebellum is but a switch, why is it so elaborate? We would at most allow that the cerebellum functions as a two-dimensional array of micro-switches functioning in concert to orchestrate spatio-temporal shifts in emphasis between the alpha- and gamma-systems.

Despite these last strictures, we now turn to a rather simple control-loop model which ignores the spatial complexities of the cerebellum, in an effort to show how one might derive formulae amenable to experimental testing. A first attempt to

sketch a path of information flow around the control function for voluntary movement is given in Fig. 8. We concentrate on skilled voluntary movement, and *assume
it to be a useful simplification if the ancient parts of the cerebellum are completely omitted.*
The figure is distinguished perhaps more by what is omitted than by what is included,
but represents a short but serious attempt by an amateur to collect the important
pathways involved in skilled voluntary movement from the material in Bell and
Dow (1967), and Truex and Carpenter (1964). As is seen, the assumption is made
that such movements are effected through the pyramidal tract from the motor cortex
to the alpha- and the gamma-efferents. All extrapyramidal systems are omitted.
Otherwise, the pathways indicated are those which seem most likely to be involved
in skilled voluntary movements. Even so, evidence points toward at least one other
strong pathway to the dentate nucleus with excitatory endings. The indication for
this is that the cerebellar output from the Purkinje cells is inhibitory and in the

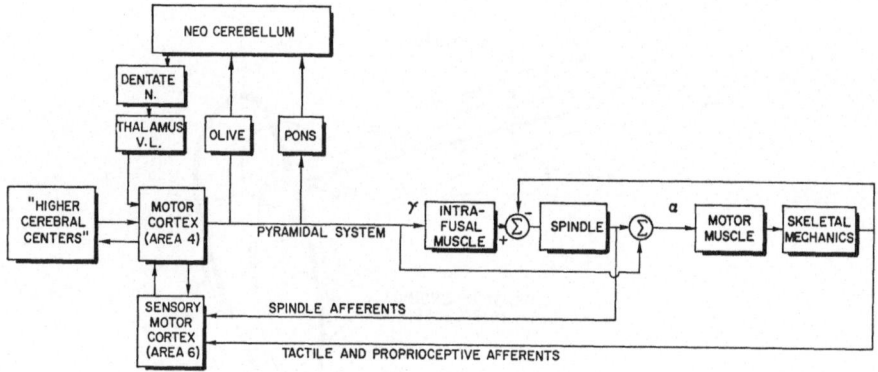

Fig. 8. A Simplified Diagram of Brain Systems involved in the
Control of Voluntary Movement

dentate nucleus there must be a pathway to inhibit. In fact, research by Ito and his
colleagues [summarised in Chapter XIII of Eccles, Ito and Szentagothai (1967)]
has shown that climbing fibres, en route to the Purkinje cells, send off collaterals
which excite the cells of the dentate (lateral) nucleus. A similar situation appears to
hold with respect to the mossy fibres. In view of these data, we feel that Eccles, Ito
and Szentagothai (1967, p. 257) may be premature when they state that "there is
no doubt (our italics) that specific patterns are formed in the cerebellar cortex owing
to its elaborate neuronal arrangement while at most the excitatory synaptic inputs
would provide *subsidiary* (our italics) organized pattern within the subcortical
nuclei" — while this may be true, it seems that further experiments are needed before
we can exclude the possibility that the nuclei are the sites of the "real" computations,
with the cerebellar cortex serving "only" to give a delayed and partially averaged,
although still spatio-temporally arranged, reference level.

We make explicit four assumptions that have guided our construction of Fig. 8.

1. We assume, first, that the action of interest is mediated mainly by the cerebellar
hemispheres. Therefore, those projections which do not go principally to the hemispheres, such as the spino-cerebellar tract which project essentially to the vermis
[Bell and Dow, 1967 (Fig. 24)], are omitted.

2. We assume that the volition to move is initiated in the cerebral cortex *and* *initially* transmitted to the motor cortex in area 4 of BRODMANN.

3. The cerebral-cortical projection from the sensori-motor area on the neo-cerebellum is anteriorly via mossy fibres from the pons and posteriorly via climbing fibers from the inferior olive. The projection back is via the dentate nucleus and thalamus.

4. The dorsal spino-cerebellar tract seems to project *medially* on the cerebellar cortex and, as a first approximation, is omitted.

The purpose of constructing such simplified structures as given in Fig. 8 is to focus attention on a simplest possible model capable of explaining the experimental evidence concerning the functions in question. The first step toward such an explanation is the construction of adequate models of the parts of the simplified system. For the spinal and muscular portions of the figure, this is now being done for simple agonist-antagonist systems, including reciprocal inhibition at the spinal level. Based on the properties of the muscle spindle as reported by MATTHEWS (1964) and using experimental evidence of skilled pilots, a model explaining the actuator characteristics of muscle has been obtained (MCRUER, 1966). MCRUER did a linearized analysis of Hill's equation (HILL, 1938) for a two-muscle agonist-antagonist system. From this he obtained a describing-function relating small limb rotation angles θ to gammaneuron firing frequency change Δf as

$$\frac{\theta}{\Delta f} = \frac{a_o}{s^2 + b_1 s + b_2}$$

where s is the Laplace transform variable and a_o, b_1, b_2 are constants under the particular conditions assumed. Using experiments with pilots and tedious but simple sinusoidal testing methods, he measured mean values for the constants and estimates on their variation under a variety tasks. His numerical values are not inconsistent with known properties of muscle and nerve. The construction of such detailed models is especially important since, as T. C. RUCH (1951) comments: "One may question the value of likening neural systems to servo systems. Such analogues, *devoid of mathematical treatment* are essentially allegorical, somewhat akin to FREUDian psychology. Whether a mathematical treatment will lead to predictions capable of experimental verification remains to be seen. Otherwise, we have added little since 1826 to BELL's circle of nerves."

It should be possible to infer the roles of the cerebellum and the cerebral cortex in voluntary movement from the nature of the information flow and its transformation during external experiments in which such movements are initiated and monitored. The aim of the experiments would be to compute transfer functions or other expressions of the information processing which can be attributed to them. The contribution of control theory to the process can only be to provide a language and an experience with similar mechanisms requiring equivalent transformations. For example, the construction of a mathematical model of coordinated motion about two joints designed according to optimal control theory may give an interesting system for comparison with the life system. Once such a mathematical model is constructed, its parameters can be chosen to fit most closely the observed performance of the life system and from this a plausible model of central processing in voluntary movement obtained. With such a model in hand of the essential nature of the information processing in the cerebellum, one can proceed to examine the cellular components of the cerebellar cortex to discover how this function might be computed by the elements at hand. Work by Franklin and his colleagues at the Stanford Medical School is now underway to change these vague prescriptions into specific formulae and experiments.

Eccles, Ito and Szenthagothai (1967) point out that since we envisage the cerebellum as playing a major role in the performance of all skilled actions, we would expect it to learn from experience. They suggest (p. 314) that growth of spines and formation of secondary spines in Purkinje dendrites might provide for this learning. It is in this context that we would recall that MacKay (1964) suggested that stable changes in the conduction-time of axonal or dendritic pathways (say by alteration in diameter of fibres) might be an important way of storing information in the nervous system [see also MacKay (1962, pp. 41—47) for further details]. Synaptic changes would not, of course, be ruled out. They might well have a major part to play in short-term retention, for which changes of conduction-time would certainly be too sluggish. Both the coupling and the timing of impulses reaching a given element could be varied. The total configuration of couplings and time-delays would thus come to serve as an implicit representation of the structure of the field of action, as encountered by the system. We would suggest that this seems like a good bet for learning in the cerebellum, with the possibility of varying the relations of 100,000 to 200,000 parallel fiber inputs to each Purkinje cell.

Eccles (1967), in discussing circuits in the cerebellar control of movement, suggests that the role of the cerebellar cortex is best understood in feedback loops which combine many diverse subsets of information to control movement, but insists that integration of the various local computations of the cerebellar sheet takes place in the evolving movements, by dint of the mechanical unity of a limb in the bones and joints. We would ascribe such integration to higher levels since it seems that if the limbs could really smooth their own actions, then the cerebellum is not needed at all! While Eccles' hypotheses are expressed in diagrams which elucidate the pathways involved, we feel that they lack the functional viewpoint we have tried to present here—even though in so doing we may have revealed a certain ingenuousness with respect to the neuroscientific literature.

We should make some attempt to reconcile these general questions with the highly regular geometry of the cerebellar cortex. Although some differences have been noted in the fine details of mossy fibre connections in different parts of the cortex, it still seems that the cardinal question to ask is: "What is the (almost? or not very?) uniform function computed by the cerebellar sheet — albeit fed by different preprocessors, and feeding different postprocessors". As a simple aid to further clarification, consider the motion of a purely hypothetical row of particles in the vertical direction, as shown in Fig. 9a. Suppose we wish to change the configuration $\{x_n\}$ to a new configuration $\{\hat{x}_n\}$ and that the control law is

$$\dot{x}_n = -\,(x_n - \hat{x}_n)^\star$$

but, due to the necessity of avoiding strain of the interconnecting strips, we have a constraint

$$|x_n - x_{n+1}| < 2\,\delta^\star$$

---

* These details have no physiological relatum, and are chosen simply to aid exposition.

To satisfy this, if $x_n > x_{n+1} > 0$ and $y_n = \frac{1}{2}(x_n + x_{n+1})$ and $\hat{x}_n = \hat{x}_{n+1} = 0$ we could take

$$\dot{x}_n = - \min(x_n, y_n + \delta)$$
$$\dot{x}_{n+1} = - \max(x_{n+1}, y_n - \delta)$$

so that taking the $x_n - x_{n-1}$ consideration into account, we end up with our velocities being computed by an iterative array of the form shown in Fig. 9b. The boxes are to be compared to patches of tissue rather than single Purkinje cells, but we find tantalising the suggestion of two input systems, one output system and a series of parallel fibres.

Thus, we feel that part of the function of the cerebellar sheet is involved in smoothing or filtering to give a smooth envelope of output firing. The cerebellar

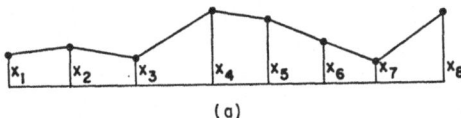

(a)

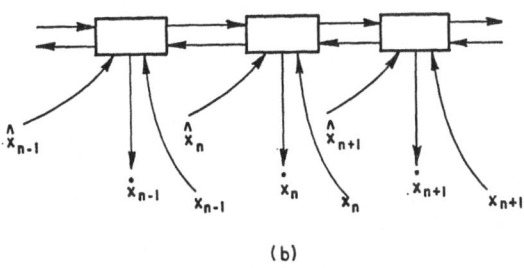

(b)

Fig. 9a and b. The iterative array in b serves to coordinate the motion of the particles in a

geometry aids local muscular coordination by iterated overlap to give a smooth envelope of output firing with much cross-coupling between different parameters. Local computation gives local optima — the surround serves to smooth this in relation to neighboring activity. This discussion should point up the relevance of study of computation in two-dimensional iterative arrays to cerebellar theorists — but with a shift of emphasis, since, as BRAITENBERG has repeatedly stressed, the timing around the multiple loops must play a crucial role in cerebellar function. We stress that the nice loops diagrammed by the physiologists are somewhat misleading since their multiplicity is not apparent. We do not yet know how to analyze multiple loops. Perhaps hardware work is needed to give us suitable structures in which to simulate timings on highly multiple loops — serial computers are highly inefficient for simulation of highly parallel nets. We close our paper with five questions that condition our ideas about information-processing in the cerebellum:

1. Can we make a real systems approach to cerebellar function without modelling the whole motor system?

2. What is the real information entering and leaving the cerebellum?

3. Are the nuclei the real computers rather than the cerebellar cortex?

4. How uniform is the cerebellar cortex? What are the best questions to ask of the neuro-numerologists?

5. What can the cerebellum learn?

References

Arbib, M. A.: Theoretical concepts of nervous system function. Suplementary lecture notes for the course "Brains, machines and mathematics". Stanford University 1967.

Bell, C.: On the nervous circle which connects the voluntary muscles with the brain. Phil. Trans. Pt. 2, 163—173 (1826).

—, and S. Dow: Cerebellar circuitry. Bulletin of the Neurosciences Research Program 5, 2, April 1, 1967, MIT.

Denny-Brown, D.: The cerebral control of movement: The Sherrington lectures VIII. Springfield, Ill.: Charles C. Thomas 1966.

Dow, R. S., and G. Moruzzi: The physiology and the pathology of the cerebellum. Minneapolis: University of Minnesota Press 1958.

Eccles, J. C.: Circuits in the cerebellar control of movement. Proc. Nat. Acad. Sci. 58, 336—343 (1967).

—, M. Ito, and J. Szentagothai: The cerebellum as a neuronal machine. Berlin-Heidelberg-New York: Springer 1967.

Friedman, L.: Instinctive behavior and its computer synthesis. Behav. Sci. 12 (1967).

Granit, R., B. Holmgren, and P. A. Merton: The two routes for excitation of muscle and their subservience to the cerebellum. J. Physiol. (Lond.) 130, 213—224 (1955).

Hill, A. V.: The heat of shortening and the dynamic constants of muscle. Proc. Roy. Soc. 126 B, 136 (1938).

Lashley, K. S.: The problem of serial order in behavior. In: Cerebral mechanisms in behavior: The Hixon Symposium, pp. 112—136 (L. A. Jeffress, Ed.). Wiley 1951.(Discussion 136—146), reprinted in Readings in Physiological Psychology: The bodily basis of behavior. (T. L. Landauer, Ed.). New York: McGraw-Hill Book Company 1967.

MacKay, D. M.: Self organization in the time domain. In: Self-organizing systems 1962, pp. 37—48 (Yovits, Jacobi, and Goldstein, Eds.). Washington: Spartan Press 1962.

— Synthese 9, 182—198 (1954).

Matthews, P. B. C.: Muscle spindles and their motor control. Physiol. Rev. 44, 219—288 (1964).

McCulloch, W. S., and W. Brodey: The biological sciences. Encyclopaedia Brittanica 1967. Review of the Biological Sciences, p. 326.

McRuer, D. T.: The human pilot neuromuscular system as an actuator. Technical report of Systems Technology, Inc., Hawthorne, California, August 1966.

Merton, P. A.: Speculations on the servo-control of movement. In: The spinal cord. A CIBA Foundation Symposium, pp. 247—255 (Discussion 255—260). London:

Milsum, J. H.: Biological control system analysis. McGraw-Hill London 1966. See especially Sec. J. and A. Churchill Ltd. 1953. 12.4: The skeletal muscle servo-mechanism.

Nilsson, N. J., and B. Raphael: Preliminary design of an intelligent robot. Computer and Information Sciences II (J. T. Tou, Ed.). New York: Academic Press 1967.

Paillard, J.: The patterning of skilled movements. In: Handbook of Physiology, Section I. Neurophysiology 3, 1679—1708 (1960).

Rosen, C. A., and N. J. Nilsson: An intelligent automaton, IEEE International Convention Record 15, Part 9 (1967).

Rosenblatt, F.: Recent work on theoretical models of biological memory. Computer and Information Sciences II (J. T. Tou, Ed.). New York: Academic Press 1967.

Ruch, T. C.: Motor systems. In: Handbook of Experimental Psychology, pp. 154—208 (S. S. Stevens, Ed.). Wiley 1951.

Truex, R. C., and M. B. Carpenter: Strong and Elwyn's Human Neuroanatomy. Baltimore: Williams and Wilkins 1964.

The Importance of 'Landmarks' for Visual Perception

D. M. MacKay

Department of Communication, University of Keele, Staffordshire, England

A theoretical model of a conventional mosaic-type television system would naturally take as its starting point the distribution of light as a function of the coordinates of the photo-sensitive array. Since the retina is composed of discrete and well-separated elements with massive parallel connections to the brain, the visual system seems *prima facie* to invite a similar approach; and for many purposes this is justified. Not only have we the growing evidence from single-unit recording referred to by Dr. RATLIFF, that some cortical neurones have definable 'receptive fields' in the retinal coordinate frame, but we also know that small visual-cortical lesions can produce 'blind spots' quite narrowly defined in that same coordinate system; and visual anatomy demonstrates at least a general preservation of retinal topography in the primary cortical 'map'.

Despite all this, I want in the present paper to draw attention to a number of facts which point in a different direction. They are mainly concerned with the ways in which visual perception can be affected by the presence and nature of *landmarks* in the visual field; or, to put it otherwise, with the surprising ease with which reference-contours in the visual field can influence the perceived form and motion of the contents. It may be taken for granted that at a sufficiently 'atomic' level of analysis all these phenomena must have a basis in the excitation and interaction of elements that are stationary in some anatomical coordinate-frame, which we may assume to be at rest relative to the retinal array. My question is whether for many purposes of understanding and prediction we may not have to go to a level at which the coordinates and activity of individual neural elements are as irrelevant as those of the individual air-molecules in a sound wave; in short, to a field-type model in which interactions occur by wave-like propagation through the neuronal population, and the operative coordinate-framework is supplied mainly by whatever determines the boundary conditions. I do not intend to present such a model in any detail, but rather to concentrate on samples of the relevant evidence, some of it familiar, some of it fresh, and none of it more than suggestive of further experimental questions.

A caution should perhaps be entered as to the dangers of misusing psychophysical evidence of the kind we shall consider. Logically, subjective experience is (at best) a *correlate* of physiological activity: it must never be misconstrued as a *description* of it [1]. Once this is realized, however, psychological evidence can have three valuable functions for the neural investigator:

a) It can help to identify the *dimensions* in terms of which information is represented neurally.

b) It offers a sensitive indicator of changes produced by specific stimuli in the information-processing mechanism.

c) It helps to set constraints on model-making, by eliminating models that cannot find room for phenomena (such as illusions) indicated by subjective observation.

1. Perceived Brightness

Lateral inhibitory mechanisms, as Dr. Ratliff has shown, can well account for normal 'brightness contrast', whereby areas of the same physical intensity are seen to have different subjective brightnesses when surrounded by areas of contrasting intensity. It has long been known, however, that with stimuli such as Fig. 1 the subjective brightness of an area near the mid-line can be changed by superimposing a fine reference-line. If for example a thread is stretched along the mid-line and moved to left or right, it seems to enhance and 'draw with it' the brightness-boundary bet-

Fig. 1. The effect of a boundary on induced contrast can be seen by drawing a black thread over the midline of this figure, moving it laterally, and observing the changes in apparent brightness of the annules near the mid-line

ween the left and right halves of the annulus, so that the region on the mid-line can be made to adopt the subjective brightness of the right or left half respectively. The landmark offered by the thread apparently divides some level of the neural population stimulated by the annulus into two regions, which are thus rendered sufficiently independent to assume *as a whole* states corresponding to different subjective brightnesses. I am far from suggesting that this must occur at the same neural levels at which Ratliff's lateral inhibition is found; but any neural theory of perceived brightness must account for the phenomenon. The generalizing process here may be related to that in the illusion demonstrated by Ratliff (p. 6), in which some kind of spatial integration at a circular boundary of non-uniform intensity results in the perception of a uniform brightness over the whole of the enclosed circle.

2. Perception of Contour

Stabilized retinal images, as Ratliff showed, tend to disappear. It is tempting to put this down to adaptation of receptors or neural links due to the unvarying condition of stimulation; but an observation made some years ago [2] suggests a complication.

If an object such as a fine wire is mounted on the stalk of a high-power contact lens so as to yield a high-contrast stabilized image, it often reappears for quite long periods, especially if stabilization is not perfect. If, however, a normal unstabilized image is cast on the same retina (as for example by bringing up the finger into the focal plane of the contact lens), the 'stabilized' object disappears completely, in a manner reminiscent of interocular rivalry. Since retinal or other adaptation would if anything be disturbed rather than otherwise by the addition of fresh stimuli, this effect requires a different explanation. It suggests a model of an *ecological* type, in which the complex dynamic balance of ongoing internal activity in the neural population is upset by the arrival of sensory stimuli, and stabilization of persistent stimuli causes adaptation not only in the physiological sense but also in the ecological sense. Metaphorically speaking, once the new arrivals have settled in, the interneural traffic tends to settle down to something like its previous state of ecological balance between competing 'subroutines' [3]. New but unstabilized stimuli then have a big advantage in the competition for 'matching' subroutines, quite apart from any physiological adaptation that may have occurred in the signal strength representing the stabilized stimuli.

Whether or not a theory on these lines will be found satisfactory, the point to note is that the presence of unstabilized contours can affect the visibility of stabilized contours in ways not at present accounted for by the theory of lateral inhibitory processes.

3. Perception of Position and Motion

It has long been known that the acuity for relative motion of two visual stimuli over the retina is much higher than for the motion of an isolated stimulus. The addition of a stationary visual landmark increases the perceived velocity of contours moving in its vicinity. In recent experiments at Keele in collaboration with Dr. W. J. RIETVELD (see reference [3a]) we have found that the averaged occipital potential (EP) evoked by the onset of motion of a line of light on a C.R.T. screen can be correspondingly increased by placing a stationary line near the starting point to serve as a landmark. Moreover, the EP in response to a visual velocity of 4°/sec was found to be of the same magnitude with a stationary landmark as that in response to a velocity of 2°/sec with a landmark moving in the opposite direction at 2°/sec. In other words, the size of the EP here reflected the *relative* velocity between diverging contours, not the velocity relative to the retinal receptors. This and other evidence suggests that we need a model of visual information-processing in which a group of features moving over the retina as a whole would be identifiably 'unitary' and create less disturbance (in some specific sense) than the same number of features with motions of the same order of magnitude in different directions.

As a catalyst to fresh thinking we might look for example at the principle of the radar system used by police to estimate vehicle speed. Here a stationary or moving source emits waves which are reflected from moving objects with a frequency shift (due to Doppler effect) proportional to their velocity relative to the source. A group of objects all moving with the same speed relative to the source will return a coherent wave at a single frequency. A group moving with different velocities will return waves at different frequencies which will beat together to form a complex signal.

In this example, then, we have
a) sensitivity only to relative velocity of source and reflector;

b) a specially simple and 'unitary' signal if a number of reflecting objects move as a group at the same speed;

c) a more complex and readily detectable signal if different reflecting objects move at different speeds.

Without pressing the analogy in detail, it may be worth-while to explore (on another occasion!) the theoretical properties of a quasicontinuous visual network in which the elements excited by an optical contour on the retina could act as field discontinuities, serving to reflect or reradiate secondary echoes of the waves of ongoing neural activity that come their way. There would be no need to postulate sinusoidal waves at a single frequency (as in radar). Almost any pattern of signals would serve in principle provided that it could be cross correlated with the source. There could in general be more than one source; indeed if we return to the notion that the neural network is normally in an active state of dynamic equilibrium, it is unnecessary to postulate a special localized source at all. Given a wave-like propagation of background activity with a reasonably stationary statistical profile, relative motion between reflectors of it could be detected and measured by a variety of processes envisageable in neural terms. The resulting system would have the three desirable properties listed above for radar. That the auditory system can analyse complex sequences of signals and detect reflected components in this way is well-known [4]. It may not be too far-fetched to suggest that the visual system might have similar capacities.

4. 'Frame Adhesion' and the Auto-Kinetic Effect

Further evidence in this direction comes from studies with stimuli abnormally deficient in landmarks. A field of 'dynamic visual noise' [5, 6], for example, has no enduring structure, and is perceived as a collection of particles in random Brownian movement[1]. When a reference frame is provided, for example by a ring of wire placed over the noise field, the movement seen is not much affected (except that the 'particles' near the ring tend to be seen as moving perpendicular to it). But if the ring is moved, the whole field of 'particles' within it unmistakably seems to adhere to it. To put it otherwise, the perceived motion of the frame is strikingly transferred to the 'particles' within it. On the other hand, if one supplies a stationary reference point within the ring, say by placing a finger on the screen displaying the visual noise, this strongly tends to 'anchor' the field of 'particles', so that although still seen in violent Brownian motion, they no longer seem to move as a whole with the frame, but rather 'adhere' to the finger.

This effect may perhaps be regarded as pointing the same moral as the well-known Auto-kinetic effect — the continual and erratic drift seen in the perceived position of a point of light in an otherwise dark room. This is known not to depend on eye-movements, and indicates that in the absence of other clues our visual system is extremely bad at determining the absolute retinal coordinates of stimulation. Both these phenomena, in other words, are what would be expected if the visual network were sensitive primarily to the relative coordinates of stimulus contours rather than their absolute retinal location.

---

[1] A convenient source of visual noise is a detuned television receiver.

5. The Omega Effect

One further and specially puzzling sample of a 'proximity effect' was discovered when using dynamic visual noise to explore the effects on the visual system of systems of parallel contours, and named the 'Omega Effect'. This is a slow rotation seen in a visual noise field constrained within an annular region [7, 8]. Remarkably insensitive to the repetition rate of the noise source, the brightness and focus of the field and the like, the rotation period lies typically between 1 and 4 seconds. Almost the only parameter to have a strong effect on it is the diameter of the annulus, with which the angular velocity is negatively correlated, but not so as to make the linear velocity constant.

This phenomenon is still without even a plausible speculative explanation. (We have speculations, but doubt their plausibility!) It is mentioned only to show how multifarious are the effects which boundaries and landmarks in the visual field can have on what is perceived in their vicinity.

6. Conclusion

At the different stages through which visual signals pass to their final integration with central organizing activity, it is highly likely that different modes of representing information are used. There is plenty of room for models using 'feature filters' whose receptive fields are fixed[2] in the anatomical coordinate frame, and indeed for point-to-point mosaic-type mapping, as well as for the field processes we have been considering.

Gestalt psychologists such as KÖHLER, of course, have long advocated 'field models', and their evidence included a number of other 'figural effects' not mentioned here [9]. In KÖHLER's theory, however, the fields postulated were electrical, and crucial experiments, particularly by LASHLEY, failed to substantiate his ideas [10].

What I am suggesting [11] is that at one or more stages in the visual system we may need to consider a field model in which the waves are not electromagnetic but statistical (as in wave mechanics), and electrical forces are replaced by interactions of probability distributions. I very much hope that Dr. COWAN's mathematics may eventually give us the tools with which to handle such models, at least in special cases.

On the other hand it is difficult, and I think implausible, to envisage a general theory which could account for all of the foregoing 'proximity effects' in a single-stage model. My hope is only that a sufficient acquaintance with these phenomena may help shake us free from presuppositions which may remain unquestioned without their aid, and which may be inhibiting realistic model-making at the present time.

---

[2] Increasing evidence accumulates that receptive fields are not as stable, in unanaesthetised animals, as at first thought; but the phenomena discussed here raise no objection to their being fixed.

References

1. MACKAY, D. M.: A mind's eye view of the brain. In: Cybernetics of the nervous system (WIENER, N., and J. P. SCHADE, Eds.). Progr. Brain Res. 17, 321—332 (1965).
2. — Monocular "rivalry" between stabilized and unstabilized retinal images. Nature (Lond.) 185, 834 (1960).
3. — Towards an information-flow model of human behaviour. Brit. J. Psychol. 47, 30—43 (1956).

3a. MacKay, D. M. and Rietveld, W. J.: Electroercephalogram potentials evoked by accelerated visual motion. Nature (Lond.) **217**, 677—678 (1968).
 4. Wilson, J. P.: Psychoacoustics of obstacle detection using ambient or self-generated noise. Les systèmes sonars animaux (Symposium, Frascati, September 1966). Ed. by R. G. Busnel, Jouy-en-Josas, France **1**, 89—114 (1967), and other papers in that symposium.
 5. MacKay, D. M.: Moving visual images produced by regular stationary patterns. Nature (Lond.) **180**, 849—850 (1957).
 6. — Visual noise as a tool of research. J. gen. Psychol. **72**, 181—197 (1965).
 7. — The visual effects of non-redundant stimulation. Nature (Lond.) **192**, 739—740 (1961).
 8. Chamberlain, L. W.: An investigation of the omega effect. Ph. D. Thesis, University of Keele 1965.
 9. Köhler, W., and H. Wallach: Figural after-effects, an investigation of visual processes. Proc. Amer. Phil. Soc. **88**, 269—357 (1944).
10. Lashley, K. S.: In search of the engram. In: Physiological mechanisms in animal behaviour (S.E.B. Symposium No. 4), C.U.P., 454—482 (1950).
11. MacKay, D. M.: Modelling of large-scale nervous activity. In: Models and analogues in biology (S.E.B. Symposium No. 14), C.U.P., 192—198 (1960).

Logic and Closed Loops for a Computer Junket to Mars

W. S. McCulloch

Research Laboratory of Electronics M.I.T., Cambridge, Mass.

At present, three of us, Jose da Fonseca, Roberto Moreno Diaz and I, are assisting Louis Sutro of the Instrumentation Laboratory of M.I.T.; in his planning of a device to land on Mars to look for signs of life, say moving things or those bigger on top than on the bottom, like a tree or man. Because it must retrorocket in a thin atmosphere, it must crawl or roll out of the region it has blasted. Our primary work is with its vision, but it must have several other types of input for safe locomotion. It will have pressure and touch receptors on a hand to poke, and strain gauges on its wheels or springs and, of course, accelerometers to know which way is up and how it is moving. Without these it could not form, in its computer, a model of its surroundings to guide its motions. There is no possibility for it to send back to earth a full series of pictures detailed and fast enough for us to guide it. The channel back to earth is noisy and, with the little power promised, the rate of transmission is about what an amateur Radio Operator sends by hand. Worse yet! The time required for a single signal back to earth is of the order of 10 min. Hence we must build into it enough sense to observe a moving bug or worm and tell us what it saw or to study the landscape and describe it to us in a few well-chosen words.

It must be given programmed activities that are incompatible; such as go, turn, stop, retreat, look (for it cannot look except at rest). These routines can be built into it, not learned. The decision as to what to do, requires a different structure. To make a model of the world is an inductive process. To run a chain of command through its routines is a deductive process, like that in a surgical operation. To guess what its internal state and its surroundings demand of it, so that it does not make the wrong committment, is an abductive process — the apagoge of Aristotle. It is most like the differential diagnosis in which many doctors have examined one patient, each from his own angle but also more generally, and then consult among themselves until they come to a sensible agreement. This abductive process is carried out in all vertebrates by the core of its reticular system. The anatomy of that core is now well known thanks to J. Droogleever-Fortuyn, W. Nauta, and the Scheibels. It is composed of rather primitive cells whose dendrites, or fronts, fan out toward the periphery. These dendrites are long, thin, and sparsely branched. Their axons leave the cell opposite to the fan and divide into two branches, one running toward the head and the other toward the tail. They usually have a collateral branch that returns toward its cell's own dendrites, which is thought to be inhibitory to its cell and to its neighbors. These axons connect the cells of the core and send branches to all sensory and all motor systems. The number of these cells is variously estimated, but is usually thought to be less than the number of afferent peripheral neurons and greater than the number of motor neurons, say a couple of millions in man. Each cell samples all kinds of sensory inputs in a patchy fashion. It is this system that W. KILMER and I have been modeling for some years on a digital computer programmed earlier by R. WARREN and now by J. BLUM so that we know what the program is doing and can keep adjusting it. Appendix I will give you a good picture. The program does all we asked of it except that we had not then sufficient delays to make it perceive the relation of a warning signal followed by a signal to which it must repond. This is under way, but delay lines are huge and heavy. We would keep them to a minimum. Our first attempt to solve these difficulties was by looking into reverberation in nets of neurons. Appendix II was the first attempt, and Appendix III gives ROBERTO MORENO DIAZ's finding of the conditions for stability.

Since we are dealing with a string of modules talking to each other, it is possible that shift registers may serve our purposes. JOSE DA FONSECA has, therefore, looked into this, for the compression is logarithmic 2^N successive digits in N neurons serving as delays. Appendix VI gives our introductory note on this score and a good bibliography. The theory stems from prime polynomials over Galois fields. Logically it is manageable in the lower predicate calculus, which is consistent and complete. The theory of linear shift registers is itself complete, with and without inputs. MASSEY has the algorism for the construction of the minimum linear shift register to embody any finite chain. JOSE has recently shown how to handle the nonlinear shift registers by linearizing them at the cost of increasing their descriptive matrices from $N \times N$ to $2^N \times 2^N$ under the worst circumstances. Often these can be shorter than nonlinear shift registers for sequences of the length of 2^N. This approach is such that it can handle many problems of closed loops of formal neurons. This work will soon be made available by JOSE.

Simply because this conference is interested in models of visual systems, I include Appendix V, another note by ROBERTO on contrast detectors, but it is less important than his work on the calculus of relations of which Appendix IV is the beginning. That we have been able to get started we owe to L. GILSTRAP who elaborated a tensor calculus for handling information through ranks of neurons. He and we found it adequate for diadic relations and then we invented a "Mint", or three-dimensional matrix for Triadic relations. After that we were able to understand C. S. PEIRCE who had invented both. We want this logic to handle the triadic problems of the "words" of our Robot describing its "world" called Mars and our computer's model of that world. Such sentences as By____, the____, intends____. This is a much more difficult problem than you might imagine. Predicables, like hot and cold, have oppositions: Propositions have Negations: Classes have complements: Relations have ??? Certainly no one thing. We know how PEIRCE got stuck. We know how WHITEHEAD and RUSSELL and, after them, WIENER, by attempting to reduce them to classes, were snared. We have made, a beginning. We hope to continue and to be sure we do not fall into the trap of extension when we would build a logic to include intension.

Appendix

I. Summary of Research Progress: Theory of the Reticular Formation*

W. S. McCulloch and W. L. Kilmer

Research on the functional organization of the reticular core of vertebrate control nervous systems has reached a significant landmark. Our problem is as described in

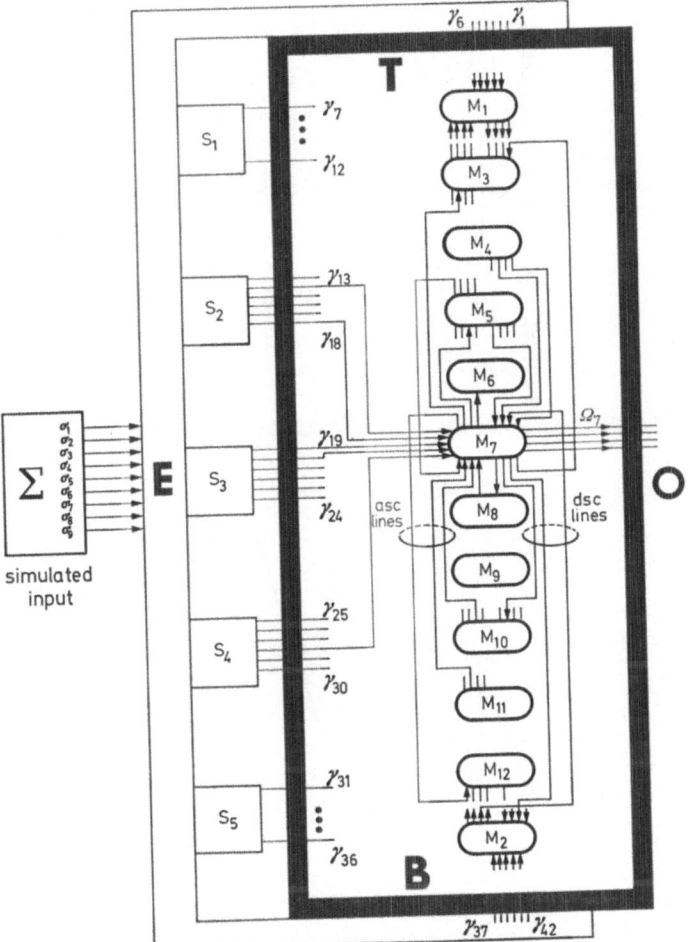

Fig. 1. Simulation model (*S*-retic)

Quarterly Progress Report No. 76 of the Research Laboratory of Electronics, (page 313), but our progress has been achieved with a somewhat different model than the one mentioned there.

The new model is enclosed within heavy lines in Fig. 1, with everything outside only for generating an appropriately structured environment for computer simulation.

* This work was supported by the National Institutes of Health (Grant NB-04985-04), the U.S. Air Force (Aerospace Medical Division) under Contract AF33(615)-3885, and by a grant from The Teagle Foundation, Inc.

5*

The γ_{ij} in Fig. 1 are all 3-variable symmetric switching functions of the binary σ_i. The typical module interconnection scheme is suggested by the M_7 hookup. Each module in Fig. 1 is a hybrid probability computer, with schematic as shown in Fig. 2.

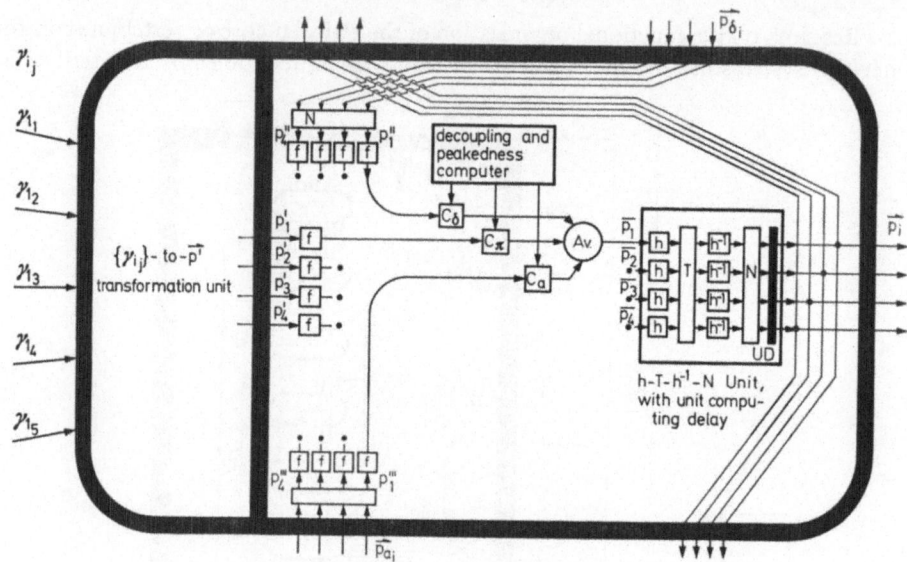

Fig. 2. A typical M_i of Fig. 1

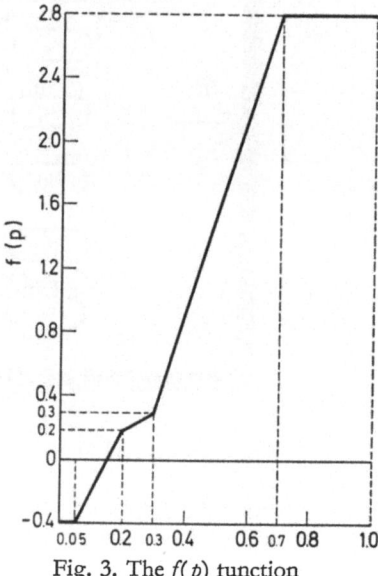

Fig. 3. The $f(p)$ function

It receives 4-component probability vectors $P_{\delta i}$ from above and $P_{\alpha i}$ from below, as well as generating a corresponding $P_{\pi i}$ from its $N_{i\alpha}$ part. The jth component in each case is the probability as computed by the module of origin that the over-all reticular formation model's present γ_{ij} input-signal configuration is properly a mode j one.

The P_{α_j}, P_{δ_j}, and P_{π_j} vectors are passed componentwise through an f function as shown in Fig. 3, and weighted in the subsequent 'Av' units according to formulas of the type

$$P = \frac{C_\pi P_\pi + C_\alpha P_\alpha + C_\delta P_\delta}{C_\pi + C_\alpha + C_\delta},$$

where $C_\pi = C_{\pi_1} C_{\pi_1} Q$, with all factors variable and determined according to two module decoupling principles and a potential command principle which demands that information constitute authority. The h, T, h^{-1}, N, and UD blocks in Fig. 2 are to

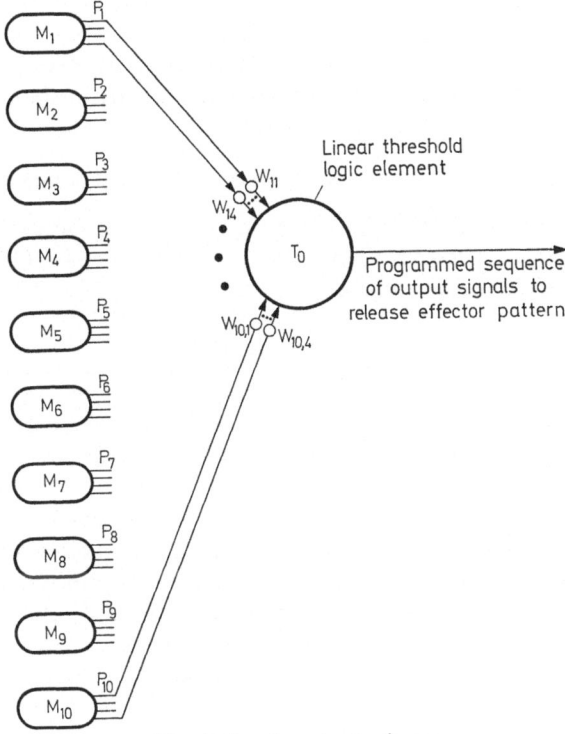

Fig. 4. S-retic output scheme

insure that every P_i is an appropriately normalized and delayed probability vector. Fig. 4 shows our Fig. 1 model's output modal detection scheme.

The model has been successfully simulated on the Honeywell Computer at Instrumentation Laboratory, M.I.T., in collaboration with J. BLUM, W. L. KILMER, E. CRAIGHILL, and D. PETERSON. The model converged to the correct output model indication in each of approximately 50 test cases, and always in from 5 to 25 time steps. This is just what we had hoped for.

We are now concentrating on the functional design of a considerably enriched model that can handle conditioning and extinction in a satisfactory time-domain sense. The design will again be programmed for simulation on the Instrumentation Laboratory computer.

References

1. McCulloch, W. L. Kilmer, J. Blum, and E. Craighill: Toward a theory of the reticular formation. A paper presented at the IEEE/cybernetics session, IEEE International Convention. New York 1966.
2. — — — — A cybernetic theory of the reticular formation. A paper presented at the Bionics Symposium. Dayton, Ohio 1966.

II. Realizability of a Neural Network Capable of all Possible Modes of Oscillation *

R. Moreno-Díaz

1. Introduction

Dr. McCulloch has called our attention to the need for investigating the modes of oscillation of neural nets with feedback and under constant input. The question "How many possible modes of oscillation are there for N neurons?" has already been answered by C. Schnabel. There are $\sum\limits_{k=2}^{k=2^N} (K-1)! \binom{2^N}{k}$ possible modes of oscillation. The next question is, "Are all of these modes realizable with a fixed anatomy?" The answer is affirmative, provided there is a minimum number of input lines to the network. The proof is presented here.

2. $\mathscr{L}$-Networks

Consider N formal neurons with interactions of afferents (those described by McCulloch in "Agathe Tyche" [2]) forming a onelayer network with M binary inputs, and in which each neuron binary output feeds back to the same neuron and to all the others. The number of inputs to each neuron is, then, $M + N$. At any time t the output (or state) — 0 or 1 — of any neuron is determined by the value of its inputs at time $t-1$. Therefore, the state of any neuron at time t is determined by the states of all of the neurons and the inputs to the network, both at time $t-1$. At any time t, the state of the network is defined as the array of N zeros and ones that indicate the state of each neuron at this time. Thus, we can say that the state of the network at time t is determined by the state of the network and the input configuration, both at time $t-1$.

For a network of N neurons, there are 2^N possible states. We can imagine some particular networks in which some of these 2^N states are never reached. We are interested in those networks in which any of the 2^N states may be reached from any initial state by at least 1 input sequence. Such networks are referred to here as $\mathscr{L}$-networks. Thus, an $\mathscr{L}$-network is a network of N neurons forming one layer in which the output of each neurons is connected to itself and all of the others, and any of the 2^N states may be reached from any initial state by some input sequence.

Consider the set of all possible states $S = (S_1, S_2, \ldots, S_{2^N})$ and the set of all possible configurations of the inputs $S = (W_1, W_2, \ldots, W_{2^M})$ of an $\mathscr{L}$-network with M inputs. From these sets, we form all possible doubles

$$(S_i, W_k),$$

* This report was prepared at the Instrumentation Laboratory under the auspices of DSR Project 55-257, sponsored by the Bioscience Division of National Aeronautics and Space Administration, Contract NSR 22-009-138.

where $W_k \in W$ and $S_i \in S$. We have $2^M \cdot 2^N = 2^{M+N}$ doubles. We now generate 2^{M+N} successors of the form

$$(S_i, W_k) \to S_j$$

by arbitrarily assigning to each double (S_i, W_k) an element $S_j \in S$ and only one, and using any $S_j \in S$ at least once. The set of 2^{M+N} successors generated in this manner is referred to as a "set of successors, $v(N, M)$." We generate all possible sets $v(N, M)$, and form from them a new ensemble $\mathscr{V}$. Thus, $\mathscr{V}$ is the ensemble of all possible sets of successors $v(N, M)$.

Returning to any one $\mathscr{L}$-network, if S_i is the state at any time $t - 1$, W_k is the input configuration at time $t - 1$, and S_j is the state at time t, we can form a set, v, of 2^{M+N} successors of the form

$$[S_i(t \to 1), W_k(t \to 1)] - S_j(t),$$

which describes completely the behavior of the net. Obviously $v \in \mathscr{V}$. We will prove that the inverse is also true, i.e., given any arbitrary v, there is an $\mathscr{L}$-network that is described by v.

Lemma 1. Given an arbitrary set of successors $v(N, M) \in \mathscr{V}$, it is always possible to design an $\mathscr{L}$-network of N neurons and M inputs that verifies $v(N, M)$.

Proof. The proof consists in generating, from $v(N, M)$, N Venn diagrams of $N + M$ inputs each. The network can be designed from the N Venn diagrams (see BLUM [3]).

We first note that each double (S_i, W_k) of each successor $(S_i, W_k) \to S_j$ of $v,(N, M)$ determines one area in a Venn diagram of $N + M$ inputs.

Let us assume that we have drawn the Venn diagram for the first neuron. Then, we put a jot in those areas of the Venn represented by all (S_i, W_k) for which the S_j indicate that the state of that neuron is 1 (fires). We repeat the same for all of the N neurons. Thus, for each combination (S_i, W_k), the corresponding S_j is determined.

3. Modes of Oscillation

Consider a system of N formal neurons and M inputs. If we define the state of the system at time t as the array of N zeros and ones that indicate the state of each neuron at time t, there are 2^N possible states. A mode of oscillation of the system is defined as any sequence of states that is repeated under a constant input and involves more than one member state. A k-dimensional mode of oscillation is a mode that passes through k different states.

The number N_o of possible modes of oscillation of N neurons is (see SCHNABEL, [1])

$$N_o = \sum_{k=2}^{k=2^N} (k-1)! \binom{2^N}{k}.$$

Lemma 2. All N_o possible modes of oscillation of N neurons can be described by a set of successors $v(N, M)$ such that

$$M \geq \log_2 \sum_{k=2}^{k=2^N} \frac{1}{\left(\frac{2^N}{k}\right)_B} (K-1)! \binom{2^N}{k},$$

where $\left(\dfrac{2^N}{k}\right)_B$ indicates the maximum whole number that is less than or equal to $2^N/k$.

Proof. Any k-dimensional mode of oscillation can be divided in k-steps. Each step can be expressed by a successor.

$$(S_i, W_k) \to S_j,$$

where S_i and S_j are the states of the step, and W_k is the constant input word that produces the mode. If we require that two modes with at least one state in common cannot be specified by the same input configuration, we can insure that for each double (S_i, W_k) there is one and only one S_j.

Thus the number of k-dimensional modes of oscillation that may result from any one input configuration is the largest integer that is less than or equal to $2^N/k$. We denote this integer by $\left(\dfrac{2^N}{k}\right)_B$. The number of input configurations necessary to specify all k-dimensional modes, is

$$\frac{(k-1)!\binom{2^N}{k}}{\left(\dfrac{2^N}{k}\right)_B}$$

(number of k-dimensional modes divided by the number of k-dimensional modes specified by each input configuration). The minimum total number of input configurations then is

$$\sum_{k=2}^{k=2^N} \frac{(k-1)!}{\left(\dfrac{2^N}{k}\right)_B} \cdot \binom{2^N}{k}$$

and therefore the number of input lines, M, has to be such that

$$2^M \geq \sum_{k=2}^{k=2^N} \frac{(k-1)!}{\left(\dfrac{2^N}{k}\right)_B} \binom{2^N}{k}$$

or

$$M \geq \log_2 \sum_{k=2}^{k=2^N} \frac{(k-1)!}{\left(\dfrac{2^N}{k}\right)_B} \binom{2^N}{k}.$$

Since $\sum_{k=2}^{k=2^N} k!\binom{2^N}{k}$ doubles have been used in describing all modes of oscillation, we can arbitrarily assign one and only one S_j to each of the remaining doubles; that is, to $2^{M+N} - \sum_{k=2}^{k=2^N} k!\binom{2^N}{k}$ doubles. This could be, for example, the state $S_{000\ldots00}$ to all of the doubles left.

Theorem. Given N neurons and M input lines such that

$$M \geq \log_2 \sum_{k=2}^{k=2^N} \frac{(k-1)!}{\left(\dfrac{2^N}{k}\right)_B} \cdot \binom{2^N}{k},$$

it is always possible to design an $\mathscr{L}$-network that verifies all possible modes of oscillation.

Proof. All possible modes of oscillation of N neurons can be expressed by a set $v(N, M)$ of successors such that

$$M \geq \log_2 \sum_{k=2}^{k=2^N} \frac{(k-1)!}{\left(\frac{2^N}{k}\right)_E} \binom{2^N}{k} \quad \text{(Lemma 2)} \, .$$

According to Lemma 1, it is always possible to design an $\mathscr{L}$-network that verifies any $v(N, M)$, in particular, that which describes all possible modes of oscillation.

The minimum number of jots, $\mathscr{N}$, per Venn diagram for such an $\mathscr{L}$-network is the same for all of the neurons of the network. This number can be computed as follows. The number of modes of oscillation that pass through any one state is

$$\sum_{k=2}^{k=2^N} (k-1)! \binom{2^N-1}{k-1} \, .$$

This number gives the number of doubles that correspond to the same S_j in all successors $(S_i, W_k) \to S_j$. In describing the first neuron, for example, we put jots in the Venn areas for which S_j indicates that the neuron fires. There are 2^{N-1} of these states S_j. Therefore, the number of jots, $\mathscr{N}$, for the Venn of that neuron is at least

$$\mathscr{N} = 2^{N-1} \cdot \sum_{k=2}^{k=2^N} (k-1)! \binom{2^N-1}{k-1} \, ,$$

and $\mathscr{N}$ is the same for all neurons.

References

1. SCHNABEL, C. P. T.: Number of modes of oscillation of a net of N neurons. Quarterly progress report No. 80, p. 253. Research Laboratory of Electronics, M.I., Jan. 15, 1966.
2. McCULLOCH, W. S.: Embodiments of mind, pp. 203—215. Cambridge, Mass.: The M.I.T. Press 1965.
3. BLUM, M.: Properties of a neuron with many inputs. Principles of self-organization, pp. 95—119 (VON FOERSTER, H., and R. ZOPF, Eds.). Oxford, London, New York and Paris: Pergamon Press 1962.

III. Stability of Networks with Loops * **

R. MORENO-DIAZ

1. State Transition Matrix of a Neural Network

Let $\mathscr{N}$ represent a network of N formal neurons with interacting afferents [1], i.e., neurons that are capable of computing any Boolian function of their inputs, which contain M external inputs, and are organized by means of internal loops. We denote by $x_1(t), x_2(t) \ldots x_M(t)$ the external inputs at time t, whereas $y_1(t), y_2(t) \ldots y_N(t)$ denotes the outputs at time t, which are also regarded as the state $(S\,t)$ of the network at that time. We may therefore write,

$$\vec{S}(t) = [y_1(t), y_2(t), \ldots y_N(t)] \, . \tag{1}$$

* This work was supported by the National Institutes of Health (Grant 5 RO1 NB-04985-04), the U.S. Air Force (Aerospace Medical Division) under Contract AF33(615)-3885, and by grants from The Teagle Foundation, Inc. and Bell Telephone Laboratories, Inc.

** This report was prepared at the Instrumentation Laboratory under the auspices of DSR Project 55-257, sponsored by the Bioscience Division of National Aeronautics and Space Administration through Contract NSR 22-009-138.

The number of network states is 2^N, which we denote by $\vec{S}_i(i = 1, 2, \ldots 2^N)$. We denote by $\vec{X}(t)$ the input configuration $x_1(t), x_2(t), \ldots x_M(t)$ at time t, of which there exist 2^M different input configurations, $\vec{X}_m(m = 1, 2, \ldots 2^M)$.

We define the network $\mathcal{N}$ by a set of N Boolian functions of the form:

$$y_1(t) = f_1[x_1(t-1), \ldots x_M(t-1); y_1(t-1), \ldots y_N(t-1)]$$
$$y_2(t) = f_2[x_1(t-1), \ldots x_M(t-1); y_1(t-1), \ldots y_N(t-1)] \qquad (2)$$
$$\vdots$$
$$y_N(t) = f_N[x_1(t-1), \ldots x_M(t-1); y_1(t-1), \ldots y_N(t-1)].$$

Equations 2 may be written as

$$y_1(t) = f_1[\vec{X}(t-1); \vec{S}(t-1)]$$
$$y_2(t) = f_2[\vec{X}(t-1); \vec{S}(t-1)] \qquad (3)$$
$$\vdots$$
$$y_N(t) = f_N[\vec{X}(t-1); \vec{S}(t-1)].$$

For a particular configuration, $\vec{X}_m$, of the inputs, Eqs. 3 are Boolian functions of $y_1, y_2, \ldots y_N$, i.e.,

$$y_1(t) = f_1[\vec{X}_m; \vec{S}(t-1)]$$
$$y_2(t) = f_2[\vec{X}_m; \vec{S}(t-1)] \qquad (4)$$
$$\vdots$$
$$y_N(t) = f_N[\vec{X}_m; \vec{S}(t-1)].$$

For each value of $\vec{S}(t-1) = \vec{S}_i$, we obtain a new state $(y_1(t), y_2(t), \ldots y_N(t)) = \vec{S}_j$. For each input $\vec{X} = \vec{X}_m$, we wish to consider the state transition matrix $\mathcal{M}(\vec{X}_m)$, i.e.

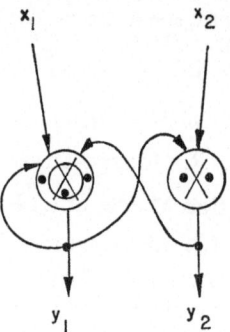

Fig. 5. Neuronal net with Venn diagram for function of 4 arguments

the Boolian matrix of 2^N rows and columns in which the $\mathcal{M}(\vec{X}_m)_{ij}$ term is 1 if the network goes from the state $\vec{S}_i$ to the state $\vec{S}_j$ under the input $\vec{X}_m$, and 0 otherwise. Therefore, these matrices $\mathcal{M}(\vec{X}_m)$ have one and only one 1 in each row. If $(\alpha, \beta, \ldots \nu)$ are the components of $\vec{S}_j$, i.e., they constitute the string of zeros and ones that define $\vec{S}_j$, $\mathcal{M}(\vec{X})_{ij}$ may be written

$$\mathcal{M}(\vec{X})_{ij} = f_1^\alpha(\vec{X}; \vec{S}_i) \cdot f_2^\beta(\vec{X}; \vec{S}_i) \cdot \ldots \cdot f_N^\nu(\vec{X}; \vec{S}_i) \qquad (5)$$

following the convention in which

$$f_n^0(\vec{X}; \vec{S_i}) = \overline{f_n(\vec{X}; \vec{S_i})} \quad \text{(negation)} \tag{6}$$
$$f_n^1(\vec{X}; \vec{S_i}) = f_n(\vec{X}; \vec{S_i}).$$

Example 1. Consider the network of Fig. 5, for which the functions f_1 and f_2 are given by

$$f_1 = x_1\bar{y}_1\bar{y}_2 + \bar{x}_1 y_1\bar{y}_2 + \bar{x}_1\bar{y}_1 y_2$$
$$f_2 = x_2\bar{y}_1 + \bar{x}_2 y_1.$$

The state transition matrix, $\mathcal{M}(\vec{X})$, is

$\vec{S}_j$ $\vec{S}_i$	00	01	10	11
00	$\bar{x}_1\bar{x}_2$	$\bar{x}_1 x_2$	$x_1\bar{x}_2$	$x_1 x_2$
01	$x_1\bar{x}_2$	$x_1 x_2$	$\bar{x}_1\bar{x}_2$	$\bar{x}_1 x_2$
10	$x_1 x_2$	$x_1\bar{x}_2$	$\bar{x}_1 x_2$	$\bar{x}_1\bar{x}_2$
11	x_2	$\bar{x}_2$	0	0

For example, the input $\vec{X}_m = (0,0)$, gives $\mathcal{M}$ $(0,0)$,

$$\mathcal{M}\ (0,0) = \begin{pmatrix} 1 & 0 & 0 & 0 \\ 0 & 0 & 1 & 0 \\ 0 & 0 & 0 & 1 \\ 0 & 1 & 0 & 0 \end{pmatrix}$$

which means that, under the input (0,0), the transitions of states are

$$(0,0) \rightarrow (0,0)$$
$$(0,1) \rightarrow (1,0)$$
$$(1,0) \rightarrow (0,1)$$
$$(1,1) \rightarrow (0,1)$$

2. Stability and Oscillations

Definition 1. A network $\mathcal{N}$ is stable under a constant input, $\vec{X}_m$, if, under that input, the network, after changing, or not to a new state, will remain in said state regardless of its initial state. Otherwise, the network is said to be unstable under $\vec{X}_m$.

Definition 2. A network is completely unstable under $\vec{X}_m$ if it is unstable for any given initial state.

Definition 3. If a network is unstable under $\vec{X}_m$, it oscillates in one or more modes depending upon the state of the network when $\vec{X}_m$ was applied. The order of a mode of oscillation [2] is the number of states that are involved in the oscillation.

The conditions of stability for $\mathcal{N}$-networks may be derived from their transition state matrices, $\mathcal{M}(\vec{X}_m)$, by using the following algorithm (which is a consequence of the meaning of $\mathcal{M}(\vec{X}_m)$; the proof of it is rather self-evident and has been left as an exercise for the reader):

a) If all terms in the diagonal of $\mathcal{M}(\vec{X}_m)$ are zero, the network is completely unstable, where the converse also holds true. Therefore, the necessary and sufficient condition for complete instability is that the equation

$$\sum_i \mathcal{M}(\vec{X})_{ii} = 0 \tag{7}$$

has solutions. Under these solutions the network will be completely unstable.

Example 2. For the network of Example 1, the inputs which provoke complete instability are the solutions of

$$\bar{x}_1\bar{x}_2 + x_1 x_2 + \bar{x}_1 x_2 + 0 = \bar{x}_1 + x_2 = 0$$

which has the unique solution $x_1 = 1$, $x_2 = 0$, i.e., under the input (1,0) the network is completely unstable.

b) If any terms in the diagonal of $\mathcal{M}(\vec{X}_m)$ are 1, we delete the rows and columns which correspond to them, ending in a new matrix in which two alternatives are possible;

b_1. Some rows have only 0's.

b_2. All rows have 1's.

Under the latter case, the network is unstable when the initial state is any of those states which are present in the reduced matrix. In the former case we delete rows and columns corresponding to the states whose rows are all zeros. A new matrix is obtained that follows either alternatives b_1 or b_2. If it follows b_1, we continue the process of reduction until we end in a minor that follows b_2. If, by iteratively applying b_1, we end in only one state, the network is stable.

Example 3. The matrix $\mathcal{M}(0,0)$ for the network of Fig. 5 is

$$\mathcal{M}(0,0) = \begin{pmatrix} 1 & 0 & 0 & 0 \\ 0 & 0 & 1 & 0 \\ 0 & 0 & 0 & 1 \\ 0 & 1 & 0 & 0 \end{pmatrix}$$

By deleting the first row and column, which have 1 in the diagonal, we obtain

$$\mathcal{M}'(0,0) = \begin{pmatrix} 0 & 1 & 0 \\ 0 & 0 & 1 \\ 1 & 0 & 0 \end{pmatrix}$$

which follows b_2. Therefore, under the input (0,0), the network is unstable if the initial state is either (0,1), (1,0), or (1,1).

For the same network, $\mathcal{M}(1,1)$ is

$$M(1,1) = \begin{pmatrix} 0 & 0 & 0 & 1 \\ 0 & 1 & 0 & 0 \\ 1 & 0 & 0 & 0 \\ 1 & 0 & 0 & 0 \end{pmatrix}$$

By deleting the second row and column, we conclude that the network is unstable under the input (1,1) if the initial state is either (0,0), (1,0), or (1,1). Similarly, the network is unstable for the input (0,1) if the initial state is either (0,0), (0,1), or (1,1).

Example 4. The network of Fig. 6 has no external inputs. The function of each neuron is, respectively,

$$f_1 = y_1 \bar{y}_3 + \bar{y}_1 y_3$$
$$f_2 = \bar{y}_1 \bar{y}_2$$
$$f_3 = y_2 \bar{y}_3 + \bar{y}_2 y_3$$

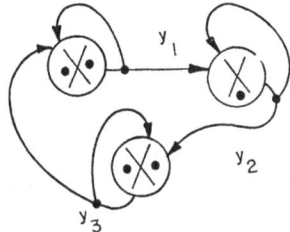

Fig. 6. Neuronal net with Venn diagram for functions of 2 arguments

The state transition matrix is (blanks are zeros)

(y_1, y_2, y_3)		(f_1, f_2, f_3)							
		1	2	3	4	5	6	7	8
1	000	1							
2	001								1
3	010		1						
4	011					1			
5	100					1			
6	101		1						
7	110							1	
8	111	1							

By inspection of the diagonal, we can delete rows and columns 1 and 5. Applying criterion b_1, we then delete 8 and 4. Reapplying criterion b_1, we delete 2; again, we delete 3 and 6, ending with a single state, the 7th. Therefore, the network is stable for any given initial state.

3. Stability for a Single Neuron

For the case of a single neuron computing any of the possible Boolian functions of its M inputs, the necessary and sufficient conditions for stability adopt a much simpler form. In this case, we have only one Boolian function that describes the neuron, which is of the form:

$$y(t) = f[X(t-1); y(t-1)] \tag{8}$$

The state transition matrix, $\mathcal{M}(\vec{X})$, is

$$\mathcal{M}(\vec{X}) = \begin{pmatrix} \overline{f(\vec{X}; 0)} & f(\vec{X}, 0) \\ \overline{f(\vec{X}; 1)} & f(\vec{X}; 1) \end{pmatrix} \tag{9}$$

Since there exist only two states, instability of any kind implies complete instability. Therefore, the necessary and sufficient conditions for stability are manifest in stipulating that the equation

$$\overline{f(\vec{X}; 0) + f(\vec{X}; 1)} = 0$$

has no solution, i.e., the solutions of Eq. 10 produce instability. If unstable, the neuron will be characterized by the simplest oscillation 010101... .

By negating Eq. 10, we obtain

$$f(\vec{X}; 0) \cdot \overline{f(\vec{X}; 1)} = 1. \tag{11}$$

Therefore, the solutions of

$$f(\vec{X}; 0) \cdot \overline{f(\vec{X}; 1)} = 0 \tag{12}$$

are inputs under which the neuron is stable, i.e., Eq. 12 gives the necessary and sufficient condition for stability.

Example 5. Consider the neuron of Fig. 7, which computes the function

$$f = x_1 x_2 \overline{x}_3 \overline{y} + (x_1 + x_2) y.$$

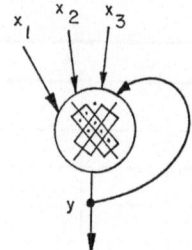

Fig. 7. Neuronal net with Venn diagram for functions of 3 and 2 arguments

Equation 12 now takes the form

$$x_1 x_2 \overline{x}_3 \cdot \overline{(x_1 + x_2)} = x_1 x_2 \overline{x}_3 \overline{x}_1 \overline{x}_2 = 0.$$

Therefore, the neuron is stable for any input.

References

1. McCulloch, W. S.: Agathe Tyche of nervous nets—the lucky reckoners. In: Embodiments of mind. Cambridge, Mass.: The M.I.T. Press 1965.
2. Moreno-Diaz, R.: Realizability of a neural net capable of all possible modes of oscillation. Quarterly progress report No. 82, pp. 280—285. Research Laboratory of Electronics, M.I.T., July 15, 1966.

IV. On a Calculus for Triadas

W. S. McCulloch and R. Moreno-Diaz

1. Introduction

De Morgan, obstructed by his terminology, thought the construction of a logic of relations impossible. A quarter of a century later, C. S. Peirce initiated it. Repeated attempts to understand him failed because in every paper he changed his terminology. It was not until we attempted to formulate family relations in Gilstrap's matricial calculus that he and we were able to understand PEIRCE, who had actually invented such a calculus and extended it to three-dimensional arrays which we call "mints". It is now clear what he had done and what stopped him. He also used a symbolism in molecular diagrams which is transparent. Finally, he interpreted these in terms of sentences containing n blanks to be filled by the names of things in the universe of discourse. Whether these be real or imaginary is immaterial to this calculus, which therefore can cope with intension, not merely extension, and hence is of value in psychophysiological contexts. Many theorems not involving negation can now be proved, but negation is not simple and we are struggling to discover its multifarious consequences. At the moment, we want to present the following useful results.

2. Triadas

A triada is a structure of any kind involving three elements or members of a given set at a time. For example, "a gives b to c" is a triada, G, involving the objects a, b, and c. PEIRCE suggested different ways to develop a calculus for triadas, i.e., "an art of drawing inferences." For cases in which triadas are of the nature of the previously mentioned example, i.e., of the nature of a sentence or phrase with three blanks that are to be filled by particular members of a given set, a calculus may be developed that is similar to the calculus of functional propositions of three arguments — or you have Boolian tensors of rank 3 — but that is richer in possibilities and consequences. One of the ways to develop such a calculus is to consider two kinds of variables or symbols, one for the elements of the set where the triadas apply (here lower-case letters are used), and the other for the triadas themselves (represented here by upper-case letters). A calculus involving only upper-case letters will be called a "proper calculus for triadas".

In the process of constructing the calculus, operations on or among triadas are defined which have a definite meaning. The object of the calculus is then to combine the operations and to obtain conclusions or theorems about the combined operations of triadas. We concern ourselves here only with closed operations, i.e., operations on or among triadas, which again generate triadas.

3. Definitions and Operations

A triada is a sentence or phrase with three blanks that are to be filled with specific names of objects, or members of a given set, in order for the sentence to have meaning. For example, if in the sentence "a gives b to c", we delete the names a, b, and c, we end with the triada "___ gives ___ to ___". We denote by i, j, and k the first, second, and third blanks, respectively. Furthermore, we represent the triada by G_{ijk}, i.e., G_{ijk} means "___ gives ___ to ___." If we want to express the fact that the particular member a gives the particular member b to the particular one c, we shall write G_{abc}. Therefore, the subscripts are regarded as variables, as are the blanks. Somewhere in the calculus we shall be able to delete subscripts without confusion, to obtain the calculus proper.

Two triadas are said to be equal if they have the same meaning, i.e., they originate equivalent sentences, when applied to any three objects in the same order. We represent the equality of two triadas by separating them with the sign $=$. In any expression in which triadas appear, any of them can be replaced by an equivalent one.

For example, the triadas "___ gives ___ to ___" and "___ is given to ___ by ___" are not equal because when applied to objects a, b, and c in this order the resulting sentences do not have the same meaning; however, the triadas "___ gives ___ to ___" and "___ is identical to the one who gives ___ to ___" are equal.

We now distinguish three kinds of closed operations. These are unary operations, involving one triada; binary, or nonrelative, involving two triadas; and triadic, or relative, involving three triadas.

a) Unary Operations. *Rotation* is the clockwise rotation of the order of the blanks in the triada one step. For example, let G_{ijk} be "___ gives ___ to ___". Its rotation, represented by $\widehat{G}_{ijk}$, is the triada "___ is given by ___ the gift ___". According to the definition of equality, we may write

$$\widehat{G}_{ijk} = G_{kij}$$

which indicates that if G applies to objects a, b, and c in this order, then $\widehat{G}$ applies to them in the order c, a, b.

Reflection, where the first and third blanks interchange positions, for example, the reflection of G_{ijk} is the triada "___ is given ___ by ___", that we represent by $\breve{G}_{ijk}$, that is, we may write

$$\breve{G}_{ijk} = G_{kji} .$$

By iteratively applying each unary operation to a triada, it is easy to see that

$$G_{ijk} = \breve{\breve{G}}_{ijk} \text{ and } G_{ijk} = \widehat{\widehat{\widehat{G}}}_{ijk} .$$

Since, in these expressions, subscripts are the same on both sides of the equality sign and they appear in the same order, we may delete them without confusion, to obtain

$$\breve{\breve{G}} = G \text{ and } \widehat{\widehat{\widehat{G}}} = G .$$

b) Binary Operations (or Nonrelative Operations). *Nonrelative Product*: The nonrelative product of two triadas is a triada obtained after joining the two original triadas with the logical connective "and", and making the subscripts in both triadas the same. For example, let G_{ijk} mean "___ gives ___ to ___" and let L_{ijk} mean "___ lies in between ___ and ___". The nonrelative product, represented by $G_{ijk} \cdot L_{ijk}$, is the triada "___ gives ___ to ___ and the first lies between the second and the third." It follows that $G_{ijk} \cdot L_{ijk} = L_{ijk} \cdot G_{ijk}$.

Nonrelative Sum: The nonrelative sum of two triadas is the triada obtained after joining the two original triadas with the logical connective "or" (inclusive or), and making the subscripts in both triadas the same. For example, the nonrelative sum of G_{ijk} and L_{ijk} is the triada "___ gives ___ to ___ or the first lies in between the second and the third". We represent it by $G_{ijk} + L_{ijk}$. It is clear that $G_{ijk} + L_{ijk} = L_{ijk} + G_{ijk}$.

c) Triadic Operations (or Relative Operations). Now we introduce the existential quantifier $\sum$ (read "there is some...") and the universal quantifier Π (read "all", or "everybody" or "everything"). Application of a quantifier to a triada gives a lower structure (a structure with a lower number of blanks). For example, $\sum_i G_{ijk}$ reads "there is some who gives ___ to ___", that is, a diadic structure. In order to obtain a closed operation, we could define an "open" or "external" product or sum to obtain a higher structure, and then reduce it to a triada, by applying one or the two quantifiers one or more times. For example, let "and" be the open operation between L_{ijk} and G_{emn} such that $L_{ijk} \cdot G_{emn}$ means "____ lies in between ____ and ____, and ____ gives ____ to ____", that is, a hexada. If we now "contract" by application of the Σ quantifier, we obtain the triada

$$\sum_{iem} L_{ijk} \cdot G_{emn} .$$

This reads "there is some individual who lies in between ____ and ____, and someone gives something to ____".

More interesting are the combinations of triadas with some elements, or blanks, in common, that is, having colligative terms. Such is the case of the so-called relative products and sum for binary, or diadic, relations. For triadas, let us write the product with one colligative term

$$L_{ijk} \cdot G_{kem}$$

that reads "____ lies in between ____ and ____ who gives ____ to ____", that is, a pentadic structure. If we now contract upon the repeated index, by means of the Σ quantifier, we obtain

$$\sum_{k} L_{ijk} \cdot G_{kem} ,$$

that is, the tetrada "____ lies in between ____ and someone who gives ____ to ____". If the operation between L_{ijk} and G_{kem} were a sum, we would obtain first the pentada

$$L_{ijk} + G_{kem}$$

that reads "____ lies in between ____ and ____ or this gives ____ to ____". By contracting now on the repeated index by means of the Π quantifier, we obtain

$$\prod_{k} L_{ijk} + G_{kem} ,$$

that is, "take any individual; then, either ____ lies in between ____ and this individual or this gives ____ to ____". This is similar to the relative sum of diadas.

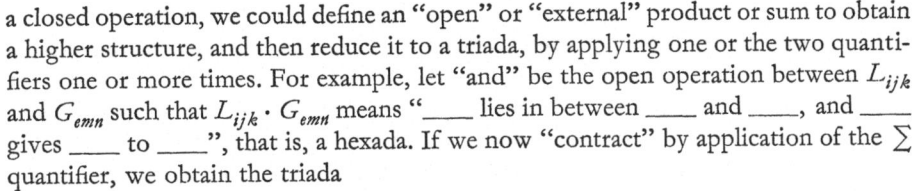

Fig. 8 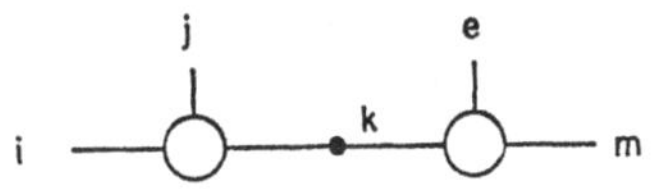   Fig. 9

Fig. 8. Atomic graphs of 2 triadic relations

Fig. 9. Molecular graph of resultant tetradic relation

The combination of triadas with colligative terms is amenable (PEIRCE) to clear graphical representation. For example, Fig. 8 represents the two triadas G_{ijk} and L_{kem}.

The two operations described above could be graphically represented by Fig. 9, in which the colligative term appears as a "common bound", and the number of blanks left is the number of "free bounds".

For convenience, we shall define closed relative products and sums among triadas in which the contraction or generalization by the quantifiers is realized upon repeated indexes, and in which each repeated index repeats only once. This permits the use of the above-mentioned type of graph as a means for visualizing the relative operations, and, at the same time, provides us with another tool to prove theorems. It turns out that many of the combinations of open operations which finally result in triadas are particular cases of closed products and sums defined with those rules. Briefly, the rules for forming relative operations of triadas, which permit the use of the above-mentioned graphs, may be stated as follows.

(i) Each repeated index repeats only once.

(ii) Quantifiers act on repeated indexes.

It follows from the graphs that at least three triadas are necessary to verify a closed operation. There are three different ways in which the triadas could be connected (see Fig. 10).

These lead to the relative products and sums that are defined below.

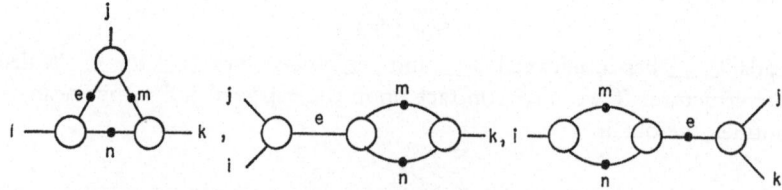

Fig. 10. Molecular graphs of Δ, $\succ$, $\prec$ relative products and sums of 3 triadas

Relative Products

Δ *Product* of three triadas A, B, and C is the triada

$$\sum_{nem} A_{nie} \cdot B_{ejm} \cdot C_{mkn}$$

which we represent by $\Delta\,(ABC)$.

$\succ$ *Product* of the triadas A, B, and C is the triada

$$\sum_{emn} A_{ije} \cdot B_{emn} \cdot C_{nmk}$$

which we represent by $\prec\,(ABC)$.

$\prec$ *Product* of the triadas A, B, and C is the triada

$$\sum_{emn} A_{iem} \cdot B_{men} \cdot C_{njk}$$

which we represent by $\prec\,(ABC)$.

For example, let G be the triada "____ gives ____ to ____"; let L be "____ lies in between ____ and ____"; and let T be "____ thinks ____ is ____". Then, $\Delta\,(GLT)$ reads "someone gives ____ to somebody who lies in between ____ and some other who thinks ____ is the first", or "there are three individuals such that the first gives ____ to the second, this lies in between —— and the third, and this thinks ____ is the first".

Relative Sums

$\varDelta$ *Sum* of three triadas A, B, and C is the triada

$$\prod_{nem} A_{nie} + B_{ejm} + B_{mkn}$$

which we represent by $\underset{+}{\Delta}\,(ABC)$.

➤ *Sum* of three triadas A, B, and C is the triada

$$\prod_{nem} A_{ije} + B_{emn} + C_{nmk}$$

which we represent by $\underset{+}{➤} (ABC)$.

➤ *Sum* of three triadas A, B, and C is the triada

$$\prod_{emn} A_{iem} + B_{men} + C_{njk}$$

which we represent by $\underset{+}{➤} (ABC)$.

For example, $\underset{+}{\triangle} (GLT)$ reads "take any three individuals; then, either the first gives ____ to the second, or the second lies in between ____ and the third, or the third thinks ____ is the first".

Resume of Closed Operations for Triadas

Unary $\begin{cases} \text{Rotation, } \widehat{A} \\ \text{Reflection, } \breve{A} \end{cases}$

Binary $\begin{cases} \text{Nonrelative Product } A \cdot B \\ \text{Nonrelative Sum } A + B \end{cases}$

Triadic $\begin{cases} \text{Relative Products} \begin{cases} \triangle(ABC) \\ ➤(ABC) \\ ➤(ABC) \end{cases} \\ \\ \text{Relative Sums} \begin{cases} \underset{+}{\triangle}(ABC) \\ \underset{+}{➤}(ABC) \\ \underset{+}{➤}(ABC) \end{cases} \end{cases}$

4. Immediate Theorems

By combining the closed operations among triadas, we can prove the set of equalities, or theorems, that follow.

First, let P_{ijk} be the triada that results from the nonrelative product of A_{ijk} and B_{ijk}. That is,

$$P_{ijk} = A_{ijk} \cdot B_{ijk} .$$

Rotation of P_{ijk} gives

$$\widehat{P}_{ijk} = P_{kij} = A_{kij} \cdot B_{kij} = \widehat{A}_{ijk} \cdot \widehat{B}_{ijk} ,$$

that is,

$$\widehat{P}_{ijk} = \widehat{A}_{ijk} \cdot \widehat{B}_{ijk} .$$

Since subscripts now appear in the same order, we may delete them to obtain

$$\widehat{A \cdot B} = \widehat{A} \cdot \widehat{B} . \tag{1}$$

Similarly, we can prove that

$$\widehat{A + B} = \widehat{A} + \widehat{B} . \tag{2}$$

By the same method, we can prove that

$$\overbrace{A \cdot B} = \breve{A} \cdot \breve{B} \tag{3}$$

$$\overbrace{A + B} = \breve{A} + \breve{B} . \tag{4}$$

6*

Let $\mathcal{Q}_{ijk}$ be the triada that results from the operation $\Delta\,(ABC)$, that is,

$$\mathcal{Q}_{ijk} = \sum_{emn} A_{nim} \cdot B_{mje} \cdot C_{ekn}\,.$$

Rotation of $\mathcal{Q}_{ijk}$ gives

$$\widehat{\mathcal{Q}}_{ijk} = \mathcal{Q}_{kij}\,.$$

From the definition of Δ product, we have

$$\mathcal{Q}_{kij} = \sum_{emn} A_{nkm} \cdot B_{mie} \cdot C_{ejn}\,.$$

Since the "and" operation is commutative, we have

$$\mathcal{Q}_{kij} = \sum_{emn} B_{mie} \cdot C_{ejn} \cdot A_{nkm}\,.$$

That is,

$$\widehat{\mathcal{Q}}_{ijk} = \sum_{emn} B_{mie} \cdot C_{ejn} \cdot A_{nkm}\,.$$

The subscripts that are not affected by the quantifier appear in the same order in both sides of the last equation. Therefore, we may write

$$\widehat{Q} = \Delta\,(BCA)\,.$$

That is,

$$\widehat{\Delta\,(ABC)} = \Delta\,(BCA)\,. \tag{5}$$

The reflection of $\mathcal{Q}_{ijk}$ gives

$$\widecheck{\mathcal{Q}}_{ijk} = \mathcal{Q}_{kji}\,.$$

From the definition of Δ product, we have

$$\mathcal{Q}_{kji} = \sum_{emn} A_{nkm} \cdot B_{mje} \cdot C_{ein}\,.$$

That is,

$$\mathcal{Q}_{kji} = \sum_{emn} C_{ein} \cdot B_{mje} \cdot A_{nkm}\,.$$

From the definition of reflection,

$$\widecheck{\mathcal{Q}}_{ijk} = \mathcal{Q}_{kji} = \sum_{emn} \widecheck{C}_{nie} \cdot \widecheck{B}_{ejm} \cdot \widecheck{A}_{mkn}\,.$$

By deleting subscripts, we obtain

$$\widecheck{Q} = \Delta\,(\widecheck{C}\widecheck{B}\widecheck{A})\,.$$

That is,

$$\widecheck{\Delta\,(ABC)} = \Delta\,(\widecheck{C}\widecheck{B}\widecheck{A})\,. \tag{6}$$

By similar procedures, it is possible to show that

$$\succ\!\widecheck{(ABC)} = \prec (\widecheck{C}\widecheck{B}\widecheck{A}) \tag{7}$$

$$\prec\!\widecheck{(ABC)} = \succ (\widecheck{C}\widecheck{B}\widecheck{A})\,. \tag{8}$$

Similarly, we can prove that

$$\underset{+}{\Delta}\,\widecheck{(ABC)} = \underset{+}{\Delta}\,(BCA) \tag{9}$$

$$\underset{+}{\Delta}\,\widecheck{(ABC)} = \underset{+}{\Delta}\,(\widecheck{C}\widecheck{B}\widecheck{A}) \tag{10}$$

$$\underset{+}{\succ} (ABC) = \underset{+}{\prec} (\breve{C}\breve{B}\breve{A}) \tag{11}$$

$$\underset{+}{\prec} \overbrace{(ABC)} = \underset{+}{\succ} (\breve{C}\breve{B}\breve{A}). \tag{12}$$

5. Constant Triadas

We define five particular triadas that we shall use in the calculus.

a. *Universal triada*, I_{ijk}, or simply I, is the triada "____, ____ and ____ are individuals". It has the following properties: Let A be any triada; then $A + I = I$ and $A \cdot I = A$. It is clear that $\breve{I} = I$ and $\widehat{I} = I$.

b. *Null triada*, θ, or θ_{ijk}, is the triada "neither ____ nor ____ nor ____ are individuals". Let A be any triada; then $A + \theta = A$ and $A \cdot \theta = \theta$. Also, $\breve{\theta} = \theta$ and $\widehat{\theta} = \theta$.

c. *Left and Right Identities*, denoted by I_λ and I_ϱ, respectively, are the following: I_λ is the triada "____ is an individual and ____ is identical to ____"; I_ϱ is the triada "____ is identical to ____, and ____ is an individual". It follows that

$$\breve{I_\lambda} = I_\varrho; \; \breve{I_\varrho} = \breve{I_\lambda} \text{ and } I_\lambda = I_\varrho. \tag{13}$$

Let A be any triada; then

$$\underset{\cdot}{\Delta} (I_\lambda A I_\varrho) = A. \tag{14}$$

For example, let A be "____ gives ____ to ____". $\underset{\cdot}{\Delta}(I_\lambda A I_\varrho)$ reads "there are three individuals such that, the first is an individual and ____ is identical to the second, this gives ____ to the third, the third is identical to ____, and the first is an individual". That is the same as "____ gives ____ to ____".

d. *Central Identity*, I_ϵ, is, by definition, $I_\epsilon = \widehat{I_\varrho}$. It follows that

$$\widehat{I_\epsilon} = I_\lambda \text{ and } \breve{I_\epsilon} = I_\epsilon. \tag{15}$$

Theorem. Let R be any triada. Then

$$R = \underset{\cdot}{\Delta}(R I_\varrho I_\lambda). \tag{16}$$

Proof. According to Eq. (14), $R = \underset{\cdot}{\Delta}(I_\lambda R I_\varrho)$. By rotating both members, we obtain

$$\widehat{R} = \underset{\cdot}{\Delta}(\overbrace{I_\lambda R I_\varrho}).$$

And, by applying Eq. (5), $\underset{\cdot}{\Delta}(\overbrace{I_\lambda R I_\varrho}) = \underset{\cdot}{\Delta}(R I_\varrho I_\lambda)$.

Theorem. Let A, B, and C be any three triadas. Then

$$\underset{\cdot}{\Delta}[\underset{\cdot}{\Delta}(\widehat{B}\breve{A}I_\epsilon) I_\lambda \widehat{C}] = \prec(ABC). \tag{17}$$

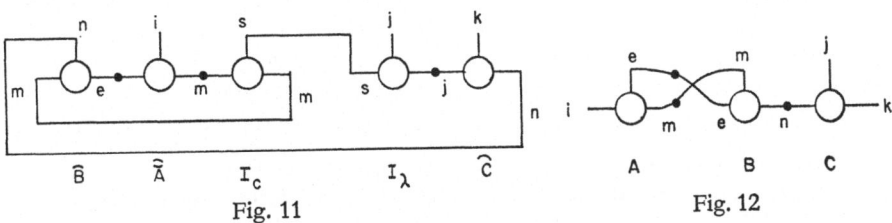

Fig. 11   Fig. 12

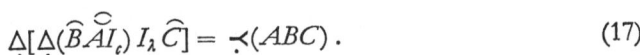

Fig. 11. Graph of $\underset{\cdot}{\Delta} [\underset{\cdot}{\Delta} (\widehat{B} \breve{A} I_\epsilon) I_\lambda \widehat{C}]$

Fig. 12. Graph of $\succ A B C$

This theorem could be proved by operating on subscripts, in a form simular to the proofs of Eqs. (5) and (6). It can also be proved by means of a graph. The proof by means of a graph is illustrated in the following diagrams.

The graph for $\Delta[\Delta(\overset{\frown}{B}\overset{\circ}{\overset{\frown}{AI_e}})I_\lambda \overset{\frown}{C}]$ is shown in Fig. 11.

The graph for $\succ (ABC)$ is shown in Fig. 12.

Because of the nature of the identities I_e and I, both graphs are the same. The introduction of the subscript s in the first does not affect this, since it is equivalent to saying that "someone is an individual".

Theorem. Let A, B, and C be any three triadas. Then

$$\Delta[\overset{\frown}{AI_e}\ \Delta(I_e\ \overset{\smile}{C}\overset{\frown}{B})] = \succ (ABC).\tag{18}$$

Proof. Let R, S, and T be any three triadas.
According to Eq. (17), we have

$$\prec(RST) = \Delta[\Delta(\overset{\frown}{SRI_e})\ I_\lambda\ \overset{\frown}{T}].$$

By reflecting both sides, and iteratively applying Eqs. (8) and (6), we obtain

$$\overset{\frown}{\prec(RST)} = \succ (\overset{\smile}{T}\overset{\smile}{S}\overset{\smile}{R}) = \Delta[\overset{\smile}{T}\overset{\smile}{I_\lambda}\ \Delta(\overset{\smile}{I_e}\overset{\smile}{\overset{\circ}{R}}\overset{\smile}{S})].$$

But $\overset{\smile}{I_\lambda} = I_e$ and $\overset{\smile}{I_e} = I_e$. Therefore

$$\succ (\overset{\smile}{T}\overset{\smile}{S}\overset{\smile}{R}) = \Delta[\overset{\smile}{T}I_e\ \Delta(I_e\overset{\smile}{\overset{\circ}{R}}\overset{\smile}{S})].$$

Let $A = \overset{\smile}{T}$, $B = \overset{\smile}{S}$, and $C = \overset{\smile}{R}$. Then

$$\overset{\frown}{T} = \overset{\frown}{A},\ \overset{\smile}{S} = \overset{\frown}{B},\ \text{and}\ \overset{\smile}{\overset{\circ}{R}} = \overset{\smile}{C}.$$

By substitution, we finally prove the theorem.

From theorems (16), (17), and (18), it follows that rotation ($\frown$) and the triadic products $\succ$ and $\prec$ are reducible to Δ products.

V. Contrast Detectors * **

R. Moreno-Díaz

Lateral subtractive inhibition may occur at the retinal bipolar level, thereby enabling a contrast-detection process in which each "contrast bipolar" cell could detect any spatial change of the intensity of light incident in its receptive field. In such a situation, the locus of the contrast bipolar cells that fire at any time gives the contour of any sharply contrasted image on the retina at this time. A contrast-detector ganglion cell receiving signals from an area that contains many contrast bipolar cells thereby senses a significant part of that contour as limited by the object size-ganglion field relationship. Its rate of firing is different for different shapes and sizes of the image

* This work was supported by the National Institutes of Health (Grant 5 RO1 NB-04985-04), and in part by the U.S. Air Force (Aerospace Medical Division) under Contract AF33(615)-3885.

** This work was done partly at the Instrumentation Laboratory under the auspices of DSR Project 55-257, sponsored by the Bioscience Division of National Aeronautics and Space Administration through Contract NSR 22-009-138.

and for different velocities of a moving image. It is, therefore, desirable to obtain simple expressions relating ganglion tone to the aforementioned parameters that are consistent with, and supported by, neurophysiological evidence.

In particular, we shall be concerned with the dependence of ganglion tone upon the length of the contrast, or edge, of the image and upon its velocity. By applying a process used to model a specific visual ganglion cell [1], we can obtain one expression for such a dependence. The process to which we refer is the lateral (nonlinear) inhibition at the level of the ganglion cell dendrites. All that we require is, first, that there be a single horizontal dendritic layer for the contrast ganglion cell, and second, that signals arriving there from bipolar cells interact by lateral nonlinear inhibition. Either divisive inhibition or exponential inhibition would be adequate for this task. We chose, for simplicity, to use exponential inhibition [2] in our formulations.

For the sake of simplicity, we assume: First, that the contrast bipolars are uniformly distributed throughout the retina and that their number is large enough to permit the assignment of "linear density" (λ), the number of contrast bipolar cells per unit retinal length, as a constant. Second, we assume that bipolar cells give rise to pulses (action potentials) of constant amplitude (p) and constant duration (τ), and that they contain refractory periods of sorts.

If the image of a sharply contrasted object is stationary with respect to the retina, and 1 is the length of the edge in the contrast ganglion cell receptive field, this cell receives pulses from n_o contrast bipolar cells, in which

$$n_o = 1\lambda . \tag{1}$$

If the image moves with respect to the retina, with velocity of absolute value u, the ganglion cell will receive pulses from n_e additional bipolar cells such that n_e is approximately given by

$$n_e = u \cdot \tau 1\lambda^2 . \tag{2}$$

The total number, n, of bipolar cells exciting the ganglion cell is given by

$$n = n_o + n_e = 1\lambda(1 + u\tau\lambda) . \tag{3}$$

If the lateral exponential inhibition occurs, the contribution of a single bipolar cell to the activity of the ganglion cell is given by

$$p \cdot e^{-kp(n-1)}, \tag{4}$$

where k is a constant that determines the strength of the inhibitory action. Under the assumption that contributions are additive, the total activity, A_c, of the ganglion cell is given by

$$A_c = \Sigma\, p\, e^{-kp(n-1)}, \tag{5}$$

where the summation is over all of the bipolar cells that are firing, that is, n. Then,

$$A_c = np\, e^{-kp(n-1)}. \tag{6}$$

By substituting Eq. (3) in Eq. (6) and renaming the constants, we obtain

$$A_c = K_1 1(1 + K_3 u)\, e^{-K_2 1(1+K_3 u)} , \tag{7}$$

where
$$K_1 = \lambda\, p\, e^{kp}$$
$$K_2 = k\, p\, \lambda$$
$$K_3 = \tau\, \lambda.$$

Let the frequency (tone), f, of the ganglion cell be linearly related to its activity; that is,

$$f = aA_c + b, f \geq 0,\tag{8}$$

where b, if positive, is the spontaneous firing frequency. A negative value of b may be interpreted as threshold.

Let us define z as

$$z \equiv 1(1 + K_3 u).\tag{9}$$

The maximum value of f occurs when $\dfrac{\partial f}{\partial z} = 0$, that is, for a value of z (represented by Z_{opt}), in which

$$Z_{opt} = \frac{1}{K_2}.\tag{10}$$

For a stationary object ($u = 0$) there is an optimum edge length in the retinal field which produces a maximum response. This is

$$1_{opt} = \frac{1}{K_2}.\tag{11}$$

For moving objects of constant edge length, 1_0, there is an optimum velocity, U_{opt}, which produces a maximum f and is given by

$$U_{opt} = \frac{1}{K_3}\left(\frac{1}{K_2 1_0} - 1\right).\tag{12}$$

In any case, the maximum frequency is given by

$$f_{max} = a\frac{K_1}{K_{2e}} + b.\tag{13}$$

Since only the absolute value of the velocity u appears in the expressions above, a negative value for U_{opt} has no meaning. Therefore, for a given edge length, 1_0, the maximum frequency can be obtained only if

$$K_2 1_0 \leq 1.\tag{14}$$

The case $K_2 1_0 = 1$ corresponds to the optimum stationary edge, that is, a maximum ganglion tone that is due to a stationary edge, as given by Eq. (11).

Properties that are qualitatively similar to the ones described here — and that have oriented our work — have been reported for the group 1 ganglion cells in the frog's retina [3, 4].

References

1. Moreno-Díaz, R.: Modeling the group 2, ganglion cell of the frog's retina. Quarterly progress report No. 81, pp. 227—236. Research Laboratory of Electronics, M.I.T. April 15, 1966.
2. Exponential inhibition may be formulated as follows: Let E and I be the excitatory and inhibitory signals. After inhibition, the resulting signal (activity) is $E \cdot e^{-KI}$, where K is a constant. See, for example: Shypperheyn, J. J.: Contrast detection in frog's retina. Acta physiol. pharmacol. neerl. 13, 231—277 (1965).
3. Lettvin, J. Y., H. R. Maturana, W. H. Pitts, and W. S. McCulloch: Two remarks on the visual system of the frog. In: Sensory communicatione, pp. 757—776 (W. A. Rosenblith, Ed.). Cambridge, Mass.: The M.I.T. Press, Cambridge, Mass., and New York and London: John Wiley and Sons, Inc. 1961.
4. Grusser-Cornehls, R., O. J. Grusser, and T. H. Bullock: Unit responses in the frog's tectum to moving and non-moving visual stimuli. Science 141, 820—822 (1963).

VI. Insight into Neuronal Closed Loops from Shift-Register Theory*

W. S. McCulloch, and J. L. S. da Fonseca

In 1943, Pitts and McCulloch [1] produced three theorems showing that nets with circles could compute only those numbers that a Turing machine could compute with a finite tape. Recently, Minsky and Papert [2] have reported several theorems applicable to them, and our group has presented some in previous reports [3 to 6]. Since Wiener's pioneering treatment of nonlinear filters, little progress has been made, until last year when Caianiello published two items in Kybernetik [7, 8].

In the meantime, a theory of shift registers has grown up independently, depending on Galois Fields, initiated by Huffman's [9, 10] analysis of their use in coding, and a subsequent evolution of theorems of limited generality [11 to 24]. It has not been recognized that all such devices are within the scope of nerve net theory, although the converse is not generally true in the present state of the art. As their theory is relatively complete [25 to 29] (except for fully nonlinear shift registers with inputs), it is clear that shift-register theory can sometimes be extended from Boolian functions of 0 and 1 to any finite field of integers, and in some cases to the field of real numbers, [30 to 32] and perhaps even of complex numbers.

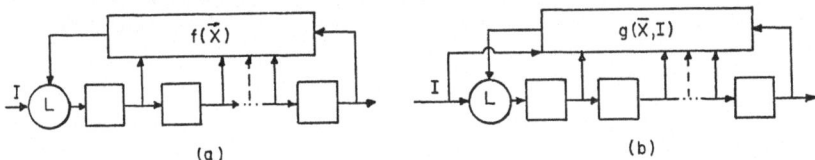

Fig. 13. Nonlinear feedback shift register for control (a) and command (b)

There is no apparent reason why these theories may not ultimately be extended to all closed-loop structures in finite automata of neuron nets of proper neuromimes. We still do not know how to extend this theory to the general problems of nonlinear anastomotic nets with inputs.

Even without that, the utility of these notions foreshadows a great extension of neuronal modelling in the design of circuits for command and control, as well as in the programming of commands for which shift registers are eminently suitable. We already have simple solutions for temporal sequences in nonlinear feedback shift registers.

For example, we have found conditions for driving the state of nonlinear feedback shift registers with input through any logical gate of types (a) and (b) (see Fig. 13). In this figure

I = Input

L = Logical gate

$\vec{X}$ = The vector that defines the state of the n delay elements of an nth-order shift register

$f(\vec{X})$ = Any Boolian function of the n components of $\vec{X}$,

$g(\vec{X}, I)$ = Any Boolian function of the components of $\vec{X}$ and I.

* This work was done partly at the Instrumentation Laboratory under the auspices of DSR project 55-257, sponsored by the Bioscience Division of the National Aeronautics and Space Administration through Contract NSR 22-009-138.

References

1. McCulloch, W. S., and W. H. Pitts: A logical calculus of the ideas immanent in nervous activity. Bull. Math. Biophys. **9**, 127—247 (1943).

2. Minsky, M. L., and S. A. Papert: Unrecognizable sets of numbers. Project MAC progress report III, pp. 18—20. Massachusetts institute of Technology, July 1965 to July 1966.

3. Blum, M.: Properties of a neuron with many inputs. In: Principles of self-organization, pp. 95—119 (von Foerster, H., and G. Zopf, Eds.). Oxford and New York: Pergamon Press 1961.

4. Schnabel, C. P. J.: Number of modes of oscillation of a net of N neurons. Quarterly progress report No. 80, p. 253. Research Laboratory of Electronics, M.I.T. Jan. 15, 1965.

5. Moreno-Diaz, R.: Realizability of a neural network capable of all possible modes of oscillation. Quarterly progress report No. 82, pp. 280—285. Research Laboratory of Electronics, M.I.T. July 15, 1966.

6. — Stability of networks with loops. Quarterly progress report No. 83, pp. 165—171. Research Laboratory of Electronics, M.I.T. Oct. 15, 1966.

7. Caianiello, E. R., and A. de Luca: Decision equation for binary systems. Application to neuronal behavior. Kybernetik **3**, 33—40 (1966).

8. — Decision equation and reverberation. Kybernetik **3**, 98—99 (1966).

9. Huffmann, D. A.: The synthesis of linear sequential coding networks. In: Information theory, pp. 77—95 (C. Cherry, Ed.). London: Butterworths 1955.

10. — A linear circuit viewpoint on error-correcting codes. IRE Trans. **IT-2**, 20—28 (1956).

11. Cohn, M.: Controllability in linear sequential networks. IRE Trans. **CT-9**, 74—78 (1962).

12. Elspas, B.: The theory of autonomous linear sequential networks. IRE Trans. **CT-6**, 45—60 (1959).

13. Fire, P.: Boolean operations on binary Markov chains. Report EDL-L 27. Sylvania Electronic Defense Laboratories 1964.

14. Friedland, B., and T. E. Stern: On periodicity of states in linear modular sequential circuits. IRE Trans. **IT-5**, 136—137 (1959).

15. — Linear modular sequential circuits. IRE Trans. **CT-6**, 61—68 (1959).

16. Golomb, W.: Sequences with Randomness properties. Final report on contract No. W 36-039 SC-54-36611. Baltimore, Md.: Glenn L. Martin Co. 1955.

17. Hartmanis, J.: Linear multivalued sequential coding networks, IRE Trans. **CT-6**, 69—74 (1959).

18. Massey, J.: Shift-register synthesis and BCH decoding. Pers. communication.

19. Mowle, F. J.: Enumeration and classification of stable feedback shift registers. Technical report No. EE-661. Department of Electrical Engineering. Notre Dame, Indiana: University of Notre Dame 1966.

20. Peterson, W. W.: Error-Correcting Codes. Cambridge, Mass.: The M.I.T. Press 1961.

21. Srinivasan, C. V.: State diagram of linear sequential machines. J. Franklin Inst. **273**, 383—418 (1962).

22. Stern, T. E., and B. Friedland: The linear modular sequential circuit generalized. IRE Trans. **CT-8**, 79—80 (1961).

23. Zierler, N.: Several binary-sequence generators. Technical report No. 95. Lincoln Laboratory, M.I.T. 1955.

24. — Linear recurring sequences. SIAM J. **7**, 31—48 (1959).

25. Golomb, S. W.: Non-linear shift register sequences. Memorandum No. 20-149. Jet Propulsion Laboratory. Pasadena, California: California Institute of Technology 1957.

26. —, L. R. Welch, and R. M. Goldstein: Cycles from non-linear shift registers. Jet Propulsion Laboratory. Pasadena, California: California Institute of Technology 1959.

27. Magleby, K. B.: The synthesis of nonlinear feedback shift registers. Technical report No. 6207-1. Stanford, California: Stanford Electronics Laboratories 1963.

28. Massey, J., and R. Liu: Equivalence of nonlinear shift registers. IEEE Trans. **IT-10**, 378—379 (1964).

29. Fukunaga, K.: A theory of nonlinear autonomous sequential nets using Z transforms. IEEE Trans. **EC-13**, 310—312 (1964).

30. KUBISTA, T., and J. MASSEY: Pseudo-linear generalized shiftregisters. Department of Electrical Engineering. Notre Dame, Indiana: University of Notre Dame 1966.
31. MASSEY, J., and R. LIU: Application of Lyapunov's direct method to the error-propagation effect in convolutional codes. IEEE Trans. IT-10, 248—250 (1964).
32. RADER, C. M., and B. GOLD: Digital filter design techniques in the frequency domain. Proc. IEEE 55, 149—170 (1967).

Neural Networks: Reverberations, Constants of Motion, General Behavior

E. R. Caianiello, A. de Luca, and L. M. Ricciardi

Laboratorio di Cibernetica del C.N.R., Arco Felice, Napoli, Italia

I. Basic Concepts and Equations

1. Suppose the brain is a machine made of variously structured and interconnected biological decision elements (the neurons), and attempt to approximate its behavior with some highly schematized model composed of artificial (hardware or purely mathematical) binary decisors (which are still called "neurons" for simplicity): this is, reduced to bare essentials, a "neural network", of which the theory is approached here from a novel angle, different from standard boolean algebra or probabilistic descriptions. Our tool is ordinary matrix algebra; our aim, the formulation and solution of some central theoretical problems (those mentioned in the title), the nature of which seems to discourage different approaches. We shall insist neither on details nor on generality, referring for lengthier discussions to the works cited in the references; we only note that most of our results hold also if the number of neurons is infinite, and in some cases even continuous: this should suffice to show the difference between standard automata theory and our methods.

A neural network differs from a computer in one essential aspect: both consist of decision elements of some sort, but a computer has its inputs, outputs, memories, arithmetic units, etc., well localized and separated from one another, whereas the network (the essential "thinking device" in any speculation on models or brains) has a *diffuse* structure, wherein all functions are necessarily spread among all parts in a uniform manner.

A mathematical description of how a network of decision elements might conceivably perform functions similar to those of a brain was given in an earlier work [1], and pushed since then in various directions [1—5]. The model of neural network used by us was derived from a drastic, though plausible, schematization of anatomical and physiological evidence, which was discussed in some detail in Ref. [1]. We forgo here any further reference to biology, and concentrate on the study of the main mathematical problems posed by this approach; these were already stated in Ref.[1] in qualitative terms and shown there to be the key to the understanding of the operation of a neural network as the analogue of a cortex.

Our model, be it conceived as a set of mathematical equations or an assembly of hardware implements, is based on three fundamental and *mutually independent* principles:

a) Its elements, which we call "neurons", perform binary decisions; their instantaneous behaviour is described by means of *Neuronic Equations* (N.E.), which we may also call *Decision Equations*.

b) The memory processes take place according to *Mnemonic Equations* (M.E.) (which we may also call *Evolution Equations*) expressing the changes of the coupling coefficients of the N.E. in time (the N.E. need not at all have the very special form hypothesized in Ref. [1] for a model which aims at some respondence to biological reality).

c) *The Adiabatic Learning Hypothesis* (A.L.H.), which serves to decouple the instantaneous behaviour of the network from its much slower learning processes. By virtue of the A.L.H. we can consider all coupling coefficients as constant for short durations of time.

The essential part of our work consists in taking such a description as the starting point for a mathematical formulation of the "problems" which must be associated with the neuronic equations in order that they make physical sense (for a discussion of this point see Ref. [3]).

2. In a neural network any neuron acts, or can act, at the same time as: a) *input*, b) *output*, c) *nodal element* in a mesh of connections, wherein memory lays; the connections can change according to the mnemonic equations and the A.L.H.

Consider the network with frozen connections; this we can do in virtue of the A.L.H. Then its state can be read from the outside (i.e. it becomes intelligible, or can be intelligibly put to work) in two ways: a) by recording at each instant (of a quantized sequence) which neuron is excited and which is not; or b) by recording at each instant the total amount of excitation (facilitatory as well as inhibitory) impinging upon each neuron from all others. Both methods can be useful, as it will be shown later; although they describe identical situations from the standpoint of the network, they may convey different types of information to the outside and afford different means of controlling the operation of the network.

After excitation, the network will exhibit an activity consisting of *transient* and *periodic modes (reverberations)*. We emphasize here that we purposely refrain from introducing probabilistic elements in the model; these we think should be reserved for future improvements, such as correcting failures or imperfections, as certainly occur in biological systems: the case we consider at present is the ideal one of a network free from any flaws. But then, the behaviour of a network would be unintelligible and unusable from the outside if the duration of the transients and the period of the reverberations were not known *a-priori*; this lack of information would bar completely the way to any concrete non-probabilistic use of the network, for one could not read satisfactorily its output without knowing exactly when and for how long to do it. In addition, reverberations are essential in many ways to our model, as is discussed in detail in Ref. [1]; they are instrumental, for instance, in effecting memory changes, and too long or too short reverberations would be useless for this purpose.

In problems of this nature, our concern must be with whole behavioral classes; the search for necessary *and* sufficient conditions is in general not possible, and not necessarily useful. Meaningful and useful are instead mostly conditions which are *either* necessary *or* sufficient. We shall therefore look mostly for general prescriptions which are sufficient to secure the wanted behaviours of the network.

Our discussion makes use essentially of the neuronic equations; it will be apparent in each instance what kind of variability may be allowed for adaptive changes in the couplings, as described by the mnemonic equations and the A.L.H., in order that they do not alter the global performance of the network (e.g., that it may only after excitation have state reverberations of period 7 or ≤ 7; or that at each time exactly 13 neurons be firing, etc.).

3. *Neuronic equations.* Let us introduce the Heaviside function:

$$1[x] \begin{cases} = 1, & x > 0 \\ = 0, & x \leq 0 \end{cases} \tag{1}$$

and the *signum* function

$$\text{sgn } x \equiv \sigma(x) = \begin{cases} +1, & x > 0 \\ 0, & x = 0 \\ -1, & x < 0; \end{cases} \tag{2}$$

if instead of (1) we consider the function:

$$\vartheta(x) = \begin{cases} 1[x], & x \neq 0 \\ \tfrac{1}{2}, & x = 0 \end{cases}$$

we have, clearly:

$$\vartheta(x) = \tfrac{1}{2} \left[1 + \sigma(x) \right] .$$

The use of the function $\vartheta(x)$, in terms of which several of the properties to be discussed in this work would still hold, might be of interest in the study of *ternary* decision elements; we wish however to restrict our attention to binary elements (neurons), so that we impose from now on the condition (quite trivially attainable with very little loss of generality in all cases of interest to us) that, whenever use if made of (2), the values of all the quantities involved be such that never the argument of a function (2) may assume the value 0. With this restriction we have thus

$$1[x] = \tfrac{1}{2} \left[1 + \sigma(x) \right] \quad (x \neq 0) . \tag{3}$$

The transformation (3) is a remarkable one from our point of view, since it obviously implies the possibility of exploiting the product law:

$$\sigma(xy) = \sigma(x) \, \sigma(y) ; \tag{4}$$

some non-trivial consequences of (4) were pointed out in Ref. [2].

The *neuronic equations* that describe a neural network consisting of N elements are:

$$u_h(t + \tau) = 1 \left[\sum_{k=1}^{N} \sum_{r=0}^{l(h)} a_{hk}^{(r)} u_k(t - r\tau) - s_h \right] \quad (h = 1, 2, \ldots, N) ; \tag{5}$$

we briefly recall from Refs. [1] and [2] the meaning of the symbols used in (5): $u_h(t)$ is a piece-wise constant function admitting only the values 0 and 1; τ is the common characteristic delay time of all neurons; the coefficients $a_{hk}^{(r)}$ describe the coupling (facilitatory for positive, inhibitory for negative values) of neuron k with h, which is effective $r\tau$ seconds after the firing of k into the channel $k \to h$; s_h is the threshold of the neuron h.

It is expedient [2] to quantize time into multiples of τ. We introduce the notation:

$$v_h(m\tau) = v_{h, m}$$

$$\vec{v}_m \equiv \begin{pmatrix} v_{1, m} \\ v_{2, m} \\ \vdots \\ v_{N, m} \end{pmatrix} ; \quad \vec{1} \equiv \begin{pmatrix} 1 \\ 1 \\ \vdots \\ 1 \end{pmatrix}$$

$$1[\vec{v}_m] \equiv \begin{pmatrix} 1(v_{1,\,m}) \\ 1(v_{2,\,m}) \\ \vdots \\ 1(v_{N,\,m}) \end{pmatrix} ; \qquad \sigma(\vec{v}_m) \equiv \begin{pmatrix} \sigma(v_{1,\,m}) \\ \sigma(v_{2,\,m}) \\ \vdots \\ \sigma(v_{N,\,m}) \end{pmatrix}$$

and recall that, setting

$$v_h(t) = \sum_{k=1}^{N} \sum_{r=0}^{l(h)} a_{hk}^{(r)} \, 1[v_k(t - r\tau)] - s_h$$

the N.E. (5) are transcribed into the equivalent form:

$$v_h(t + \tau) = \sum_{k=1}^{N} \sum_{r=0}^{l(h)} a_{hk}^{(r)} \, 1[v_k(t - r\tau)] - s_h . \qquad (6)$$

When vector notation is handier we write (6) as

$$\vec{v}_{m+1} = \sum_{r=0}^{L} A^{(r)} \, 1[\vec{v}_{m-r}] - \vec{s} \qquad (7)$$

(where r ranges up to the highest value L of the $l(h)$ contained in (5), with 0's replacing any supernumerary coefficients thus introduced); $A^{(r)}$ denotes the matrix

$$A^{(r)} \equiv \left\| a_{hk}^{(r} \right\| .$$

The most interesting case, at this stage of development, is certainly that with $L = 0$. Whatever the value of L in (7), however, the situation can always be brought into the same formalism by considering non-square matrices and higher-dimensional vector spaces; (7) may be written, thus:

$$\vec{v}_{m+1} = (A^{(0)} \, A^{(1)} \ldots A^{(L)}) \begin{pmatrix} 1[\vec{v}_m] \\ 1[\vec{v}_{m-1}] \\ \vdots \\ 1[\vec{v}_{m-L}] \end{pmatrix} - \vec{s} \qquad (8)$$

or

$$\vec{v}_{m+1} = \mathscr{A} \, 1[\vec{V}_m] - \vec{s} , \qquad (9)$$

where the rules for interpreting the notation used in (9) are read from the transcription (8) of (7). The considerations which follow apply, with only common-sense changes, to equations of the type (9) as well as to the situation with $L = 0$; this latter we denote simply with the notation

$$\vec{v}_{m+1} = A \, 1[\vec{v}_m] - \vec{s} ; \qquad (10)$$

we emphasize, in fact, that nowhere in our later discussions the condition that A be a square matrix, or the particular definitions of $\vec{v}_{m+1}$ and $\vec{V}_m$ in (9) are relevant. For the sake of simplicity we shall refer most often only to the case $L = 0$; the generalization to higher values of L will be obvious in all cases, the only warning being that the duration of transients shall have to be estimated accordingly; likewise, it is not necessary that $N < \infty$.

Eq. (10) can be written equivalently:

$$\vec{v}_{m+1} = B \, \sigma(\vec{v}_m) + \tfrac{1}{2} A \vec{1} - \vec{s} , \qquad \text{with } B = \tfrac{1}{2} A \qquad (11)$$

which becomes of particular interest when

$$A \vec{1} = 2 \vec{s} ,$$

a condition that characterizes *normal systems*, as they were called in Ref. [2], where they were shown to have some remarkable properties, due to (4) and to the homogeneity of their defining equations:

$$\vec{v}_{m+1} = B\,\sigma(\vec{v}_m)\,. \tag{12}$$

We recall that for normal systems the following problems were solved in Ref. [2]

a) Given a network of N neurons, to change the solution of the equations for reverberations of preassigned period (7) and (13) into a standard algebraic problem.

b) Given an arbitrary reverberation, to find coupling coefficients and threshold which guarantee that a network thus built will admit of that reverberation.

c) To determine conditions sufficient for a system (12) to admit of no solution at all.

II. Reverberations

1. The condition for a solution of Eq. (7) to describe a state reverberation of the network of period $R\tau$ is clearly

$$\vec{v}_{m+R} \equiv \vec{v}_m \tag{13}$$

for all m in a range of L consecutive values starting from an arbitrary m_0.

The problem of determining conditions which secure that a network, after excitation, can only reverberate with a pre-assigned period, or with a period not exceeding a pre-assigned value, was exhaustively considered in a previous work [5]. There we studied also the problem of adding controlling elements to the network which could force it into having a periodic, or any other wanted behavior. We recall here the main results thus obtained, which are of central interest in our treatment. Indeed the behavior of a network described by equations of the type (7), or more generally of any finite *state-state machine*, exhibits in general a *transient phase* of maximum length 2^n, and a periodic activity, or *state reverberation*, also with maximum length 2^n. For a network containing 100 neurons, the maximum length of the transient phase, is $2^{100} \sim 10^{30}$ which is an astronomic number. This would amount, for all practical purposes, to a total lack of knowledge, in any concrete use of a machine: we would not know for how long to read its output or states, nor whether some observed output may yield or not the relevant information that the machine can produce.

The main role is played in our theory by the *rank* K of the coupling matrix which appears in Eqs. (7), (8) or (12). To see this we consider first, for simplicity, the latter equation under the assumption that B be of rank $K = 1$. This example will prepare the ground for the general discussion which will follow, and has some non-trivial features which may be of interest *per se*.

If B is of rank 1, its elements have the form:

$$b_{hk} = a_h\,b_k\,; \tag{14}$$

(12) becomes:

$$v_{h,\,m+1} = a_h \sum_k b_k\,\sigma(v_{k,\,m})\,. \tag{15}$$

Setting:

$$q_0 = \sum_k b_k\,\sigma(v_{k,\,0})$$

$$q = \sum_k b_k\,\sigma(a_K)$$

we find easily, from (4) and (15):

$$v_{b,1} = a_b \, q_0$$
$$v_{b,m+1} = a_b \, q[\sigma(q)]^{m-1} \, \sigma(q_0), \qquad m \geq 1 \tag{16}$$

so that:

$$v_{b,m+1} = v_{b,m-1}, \qquad m \geq 1. \tag{17}$$

We see thus that, except possibly for one single initial transient state, this network can only exhibit: a) reverberations of period 1, if $q > 0$, or b) reverberations of period 2, if $q < 0$.

This case is highly instructive for its simplicity, which is due both to the normal form of the system and to the rank 1 of the matrix B.

2. It is appropriate at this point to make a brief digression on the effects of learning processes on such a network. Of these, we only suppose that they may not change the rank of the matrix B, i.e.: $a_{bk}(m) = a_b(m) \, b_k(m)$ always.

Setting now:

$$q_0 = \sum_k b_k(0) \, \sigma(v_{k,0})$$
$$q^{(i)} = \sum_k b_k(i) \, \sigma[a_k(i-1)]$$

we find that (16) is replaced by:

$$v_{b,1} = a_b(0) \, q_0$$
$$v_{b,m+1} = a_b(m) \, q^{(m)} \prod_{i=1}^{m-1} \sigma[q^{(i)}] \, \sigma[q_0] \tag{18}$$

During the learning period one cannot expect periodicity; when learning is completed (some device will stop it somehow when the wanted goal is reached), the observer will notice it immediately, from the fact that the network falls again into the behaviours a) or b) mentioned in 1. It is also apparent that this discussion holds true for normal systems of type (9) with any rectangular matrix A of rank 1.

3. In general, an arbitrary matrix Γ, with p rows and q columns, of rank K, can be brought by simple permutations to the form

$$\Gamma = \begin{pmatrix} A & A\Lambda \\ MA & MA\Lambda \end{pmatrix} \tag{19}$$

with $\det(A) \neq 0$, rank $(A) = K$, A, M and Λ being otherwise arbitrary matrices with the appropriate number of rows and columns for (19) to hold. The number of arbitrarily assignable elements in Γ is thus $K(p + q - K)$.

For a normal system (12) with $B = \Gamma$ of form (19) we find then, writing the matrices

$$Z = (\vec{v}_1 \, \vec{v}_2 \, \vec{v}_3 \ldots)$$
$$Y = [\sigma(\vec{v}_0) \, \sigma(\vec{v}_1) \, \sigma(\vec{v}_2) \ldots]$$

that

$$Z = \begin{pmatrix} A & A\Lambda \\ MA & MA\Lambda \end{pmatrix} Y \tag{20}$$

so that the rank of the matrix Z is $\leq K$.

This remark can be exploited for the construction of a general theory of reverberations and controls of a neural network, for which we refer to Ref. [5]; it is the main lemma for generalizing to arbitrary networks the discussion made before on the specific example with $K = 1$, i.e.

It is indicated in Ref. [5] how, by properly choosing M and Λ, and using well defined additional controlling elements, any wanted reverberating pattern can be obtained; in particular the neurons corresponding to the submatrix A of Γ can be made to play the role of controlling elements of the network. It is thus possible to design networks whose reverberations are *either independent of the initial stimulation*, or are, instead, *dependent upon it*. Both can be of great interest, according to the purpose for which the network is planned.

We shall say no more about these matters here, in order to avoid excessive technicalities, and begin instead to discuss neural networks from the point of view of an observer *who records the total amount of excitation which reaches each neuron*. This situation was also touched upon in Ref. [5], but we shall give here a more complete presentation of it, adding some statements and results which may be not without interest.

III. Constants of Motion and Collective Modes

1. Consider a network of type (7) with $L = 0$:

$$\vec{v}(t) = A \, 1[\vec{v}(t - \tau)] - \vec{s} . \qquad (21)$$

Let $\vec{\gamma}$ be an arbitrary N-component vector, and consider the scalar product:

$$W(t) = \vec{\gamma} \cdot \vec{v}(t) = \sum_{b=1}^{N} \gamma_b \, v_b(t) = \vec{\gamma} \cdot A \, 1[\vec{v}(t - \tau)] - \vec{\gamma} \cdot \vec{s} . \qquad (22)$$

If $\vec{\gamma}$ satisfies the equation (A^T is the transpose of A):

$$A^T \vec{\gamma} = 0 \qquad (23)$$

we obtain:

$$W = \vec{\gamma} \cdot \vec{v}(t) = - \vec{\gamma} \cdot \vec{s} . \qquad (24)$$

Suppose the elements γ_b denote the values of couplings which bring the total excitation $v_b(t)$ impinging upon neuron b at time t to an external summation element $\sum$ (which may be or not another neuron); then, provided Eq. (23) is satisfied, the sum total of the excitations reaching $\sum$ from the whole network is given by (24), and is constant throughout the operation of the network if $\vec{s}$ is a constant vector, or a function of time which follows the variations of $\vec{s}$ if $\vec{s}$ is itself a function of time $\vec{s}(t)$ (and acts therefore as a controlling device of a new type).

This method of reading the excitation falling upon the neurons, instead of their "yes-or-no" states, conveys therefore to the outside information of a quite different nature from that discussed thus far, as it was mentioned in the introduction; it is indeed to be emphasized that the constancy, for instance, of (24) does by no means carry in itself, *a priori* at least, any information on the actions of the neurons of the network.

We remark that an expression such as $W(t)$ represents the natural definition for a non-linear network such as (21) (the Heaviside or signum functions being here replaceable by any functions at will) of a *collective mode* (think of the normal modes of linear systems).

It can be easily seen (Ref [5]) that the number of these collective modes, or linear "constants of motion" is $N\text{-}K$, if A is of rank K; note also that interesting possibilities arise if $L > 0$ in (7): this we forgo discussing here.

2. We proceed now to show that it is also possible to obtain *quadratic* constants of motion. We refer again, for the sake of simplicity to the case of a normal system (12); writing both (12) and its transpose we find:

$$\vec{v}_{m+1} = B\,\sigma(\vec{v}_m) \qquad \vec{v}^T_{m+1} = \sigma(\vec{v}^T_m)\,B^T \tag{25}$$

so that, with M an arbitrary matrix:

$$\vec{v}^T_{m+1}\,M\vec{v}_{m+1} = \sigma(\vec{v}^T_m)\,B^T\,MB\,\sigma(\vec{v}_m)\,. \tag{26}$$

Choose now M so that

$$B^T\,MB = \Delta \equiv ||d_r \delta_{rs}|| \tag{27}$$

is diagonal; it follows that

$$\vec{v}^T(t)\,M\vec{v}(t) = Tr(\Delta) = \sum_{r=1}^{N} d_r \tag{28}$$

is a *constant of motion* of one network of a quite different sort from the linear ones discussed before.

If, for instance, $\Delta \equiv 1$ and B is an orthogonal matrix we find from (28):

$$\vec{v}^T(t)\,\vec{v}(t) = |\vec{v}(t)|^2 = N \tag{29}$$

so that the vector $\vec{v}_m = \vec{v}(m\tau)$ in N-space ("neuronic space") moves having its end point always on a hypersphere of radius $\sqrt{N}$.

As another simple example, suppose that B is of rank 1; then, whatever M, since $b_{hk} = a_h\,b_k$

$$\vec{v}^T_{m+1}\,M\vec{v}_{m+1} = (\vec{a}^T\,M\vec{a})\,[\vec{b}\cdot\sigma(\vec{v}_m)]^2\,; \tag{30}$$

we know from previous discussions that in this case $\sigma(\vec{v}_{m+1}) = \pm\,\sigma(\vec{v}_m)$, so that the expression (30) is a constant of motion, whose value depends only upon M and B, after the transient phase is over.

We end our discussion here. Its aim is mainly to show that a remarkable amount of deterministic information on the behavior of neural networks can be gathered with simple mathematical tools; any knowledge obtained in this way is a useful prerequisite for the application of statistical considerations. We think it quite reasonable that the latter might play a relevant role in studies on the optimization of adaptive behavior, i.e. learning as is described by mnemonic equations in our model; a deterministic framework, such as the one supplied by the present treatment or any other one may wish to use, seems however not dispensable with, if a model of brain functions must have a structure capable of performances apt to lead beyond the very crude stage of present devices. Our work shows, in particular, ways to introduce adaptive behavior without altering, after learning has taken place, the general deterministic structure of the system, such as the period of its reverberations.

References

1. CAIANIELLO, E. R.: Outline of a theory of thought processes and thinking machines. J. theor. Biol. 1, 204—235 (1961).
2. — Decision equations and reverberations. Kybernetik 3, 98—100 (1966); Non linear problems posed by decision equations. Summer School, Ravello 1965.
3. — Mathematical and physical problems in the study of brain models. Ojai Valley Symposium 1964.
4. —, and A. DE LUCA: Decision equation for binary systems. Application to neuronal behavior. Kybernetik 3, 33—40 (1966).
5. — —, and L. M. RICCIARDI: Reverberations and control of neural networks. Kybernetik 4, 10—18 (1967).

Probabilistic Description of Neurons *

A. DE LUCA and L. M. RICCIARDI

Laboratorio di Cibernetica del C.N.R., Arco Felice, Napoli, Italia

Abstract

In connection with the model of the neuron presented by CAIANIELLO (1961), an approach to the study of a formalized linear threshold element is outlined, and the firing probability is calculated in the most general case of continuous input random variables. It is then considered the case when the number of input lines becomes very large, in order to make use of asymptotic theorems. The probability for a neuron to have a given histogram of the intervals between successive spikes is then derived, making use of some results previously worked out by several authors (see FISZ, 1963 and references there cited), for the "theory of runs". An explicit expression for this probability is presented in the case when the neuron exhibits a refractory period after each spike. Finally, a finite summation time is introduced in the model, and in a specific case the firing probability is calculated, and the behaviour of two asymptotic cases is discussed.

1. Introduction

In the previous lecture reference was made to a model of the neuron and to some of the properties that a neural net exhibits provided suitable constraints are introduced (CAIANIELLO, DE LUCA and RICCIARDI, 1967). Here we will be concerned with a probabilistic description of the same neural model. Other authors have previously used the probabilistic approach, but in a different context.

In the second section we will deal primarily with an analysis of the conditions under which use can be made of the Central Limit Theorem (C.L.T.) for calculating the probability density function (d.f.) of the net excitation arriving at the decision element of the neuron. A more detailed description was presented in a previous paper (DE LUCA and RICCIARDI, 1967), and it is of interest also since some authors (BRAITENBERG, 1966; BRAITENBERG, GAMBARDELLA, GHIGO and VOTA, 1965) have also used the C.L.T. in connection with the analysis of spike trains from Purkinje cells in the frog's brain. The justification for their use of the C.L.T. is that the Purkinje cells receive a very large number of inputs from separated sources, which, in the case of invertebrates, is of the order of 10^5, and, even in the case of mammals, it remains quite high ($\sim 10^4$). However, as we will show in the following, to make use of the C.L.T. in the case of a neuron with a large number of input lines, some further conditions must be fulfilled: if this is not the case, the error one makes when approximating the d.f. of the net excitation by a Gaussian has in general an infinite upper limit.

* This work has been performed with the joint sponsorship of the U.S.A.F. and their European Office of Aerospace Research under contracts no. AF EOAR 66-37 and AF33 (615)2786.

In the general case of arbitrary (stationary) input d.f.'s, the probability for the neuron to fire (which is itself stationary) is calculated in a standard way; the determination of the probability for the neuron to exhibit a preassigned frequency of firing, in a fixed time interval, is then straightforward, and, obviously, depends on the parameters of the neuron (coupling coefficients and threshold) and on the d.f.'s of the random input variables. In the specific case when the C.L.T. can be applied, the frequency probability is only a function of the ratio $(S - \langle E \rangle)/\mu_n$, where the numerator is the difference between the threshold and the mean value of the excitation, and the denominator is the standard deviation of the excitation.

In all the above (except for the calculation of the frequency probability) time does not need be quantized. If, however, as in Sec. 3, we look at the time variable as a sequence of discrete instants (intervals between any pair need not be equal), we can make use of the previously determined firing probability, to calculate the probability for any given histogram of intervals between successive spikes. The more realistic case when the neuron has a constant dead time R is then considered in Sec. 4, and the interval histogram probability is calculated. The problem of evaluating the neuron's parameters by making best fit of the experimentally obtained histograms with the ones theoretically predicted is left open, although it does not offer any intriguing difficulty.

Finally, we give some simple examples to show how the problem of calculating the effect of the dead time can, apart of some tedious formal complications, easily be solved, and use of the C.L.T. is then made for a neuron with a large number of Poisson inputs in the case when a finite summation time is introduced in the model.

2. Firing Probability and Asymptotic Theorems

Following CAIANIELLO (1961) we shall consider, as mathematical model of neuron, a linear threshold element, with n input lines (labeled from 1 to n) and as many (constant) *coupling coefficients* a_k ($k = 1, 2, \ldots, n$). At any time each one of these input lines can be in one of two possible states, labeled 1 and 0, corresponding to the physiological situation of *activity* and *inactivity* respectively. The inputs are connected to an adder element, by means of the coupling coefficients a_k ($k = 1, 2, \ldots, n$) which transform the state $\varkappa_k$ of the k-th input line into $a_k \varkappa_k$ ($k = 1, 2, \ldots, n$), so that for a_k positive there is *excitation*, while for a_k negative there is *inhibition*.

At the output of the adder the *net excitation* $E(t)$ at the time t is thus

$$E(t) = \sum_{i=1}^{n} a_i \varkappa_i(t) \tag{1}$$

A binary decision element follows the adder. Denoting the constant threshold of the neuron by S, the neuron fires if and only if

$$E(t) > S.$$

By firing, we mean that the output line becomes active after a (constant) delay τ.

Denoting the state of the output by a two valued variable u whose values can only be 0 and 1, again corresponding to the inactivity and activity state of the line, we may then write:

$$u(t + \tau) = 1 \, [E(t) - S]$$

where $1[\varkappa]$ denotes the Heaviside unit step-function:

$$1[\varkappa] \begin{cases} = 1, & \varkappa > 0 \\ = 0, & \varkappa \leq 0 \end{cases}$$

We will not consider time as a continuous variable, but as a discrete sequence of equidistant intervals:

$$\tau, 2\tau, \ldots, m\tau, \ldots$$

where τ again denotes the neuron's delay. This time quantization is not a strong constraint, in this context, and its usefulness will be pointed out in the following.

In order to give a probabilistic description of the neuron, we will consider the input variables $\varkappa_i$ as two valued *random variables*, which can be represented by means of the following *finite schemes*:

$$\varkappa_i \equiv \begin{pmatrix} 1 & 0 \\ p_i & q_i \end{pmatrix} \qquad (i = 1, 2, \ldots, n) \tag{2}$$

where the first row of the matrix specifies the values of the random variables, and the second row the corresponding probabilities, which we shall assume *stationary* and normalized:

$$p_i + q_i = 1 \qquad (i = 1, 2, \ldots, n)$$

For later use, let us also introduce the random variables e_i $(i = 1, 2, \ldots, n)$ defined by the schemes

$$e_i \equiv \begin{pmatrix} a_i & 0 \\ p_i & q_i \end{pmatrix} \qquad (i = 1, 2, \ldots, n) \tag{2'}$$

whose mean (m.v.) $\langle e_i \rangle$ and standard deviation (s.d.) σ_i^2 are:

$$\langle e_i \rangle = p_i \, a_i \qquad \sigma_i^2 = p_i \, q_i \, a_i^2 \qquad (i = 1, 2, \ldots, n) \tag{3}$$

The net excitation E is then itself a random variable whose m.v. $\langle E \rangle$ is:

$$\langle E \rangle = \sum_{i=1}^{n} p_i \, a_i$$

and whose s.d. μ^2 (assuming the $\varkappa_i$'s are independent) is:

$$\mu^2 = \sum_{i=1}^{n} p_i \, q_i \, a_i^2 . \tag{4}$$

In the most general case when all the e_i's are continuous random variables[1], the neuron's firing probability P_f can be calculated in terms of their d.f. 's $\varphi_i(z_i)$ $(i = 1, 2, \ldots, n)$. In fact, by definition, it is

$$\varphi_i(z_i) \, dz_i \equiv Pr\{z_i \leq e_i \leq z_i + dz_i\}$$

so that the d.f. of the net excitation E is:

$$\Phi(z) = \int_{-\infty}^{+\infty} dz_1 \int_{-\infty}^{+\infty} dz_2 \ldots \int_{-\infty}^{+\infty} dz_{n-1} \prod_{i=1}^{n-1} \varphi_i(z_i) \, \varphi_n(z - \sum_{i=1}^{n-1} z_i) , \tag{5}$$

---

[1] The discrete case is contained in the continuous one, provided we assume:

$$\varphi_i(z_i) = p_i \, \delta(z_i - a_i) + q_i \, \delta(z_i) \; (i = 1, 2, \ldots n) .$$

which allows us to calculate the firing probability as:

$$P_f = \int_S^\infty \Phi(z)\, dz \equiv 1 - F(S) \tag{6}$$

where $F(x)$ denotes the distribution function (D.f.) of E, defined in the following way:

$$F(x) \equiv \int_{-\infty}^x dz\, \Phi(z) \equiv Pr\{-\infty < z \leq x\}$$

Special cases making explicit use of (5) and (6) are contained in a previous paper (DE LUCA and RICCIARDI, 1967).

All of the previous considerations hold, under the specified hypothesis, for a neuron with any finite number of input lines. We wish now to outline some conditions under which limit theorems can be applied, in particular, we will deal with the central limit theorem (C.L.T.).

Although an infinite number of input lines makes no physical sense, using the C.L.T. allows us to make useful approximations of the d.f. of the net excitation, and interesting properties of the firing probability will emerge in some cases.

Let us denote by X the sum of n zero mean-valued independent[2] random variables x_i of s.d. given by $\sigma_i^2 (i = 1, 2, \ldots, n)$, and be μ_n its s.d. It is:

$$\langle X \rangle = 0$$

$$\mu_n^2 = \sum_1^n \sigma_i^2 .$$

Now introduce the r.v. Y defined by:

$$Y \equiv \frac{\sum_1^n x_i}{\mu_n} \equiv \frac{X}{\mu_n} .$$

Then Y also has zero mean value, whereas its s.d. is 1. Denoting the D.f. of Y by $\psi_n(Y)$, the C.L.T. states that (under fairly general conditions which we will specify shortly):

$$\lim_{n \to \infty} \psi_n(Y) = G(Y) \equiv \frac{1}{\sqrt{2\pi}} \int_{-\infty}^Y dt\, e^{-\frac{t^2}{2}} , \tag{7}$$

i.e. the D.f. of Y asymptotically tends to the Gauss distribution function.

Although there is a good deal of literature on the C.L.T., we will restrict ourselves to outline only two theorems, which we will need in the following: the first one is due to LINDEBERG (CRAMER, 1963), and the second one to LIAPOUNOFF (1900).

Theorem I

Under the hypothesis:

$$\lim_{n \to \infty} \mu_n = +\infty$$

$$\lim_{n \to \infty} \frac{\sigma_n}{\mu_n} = 0$$

---

[2] As it is easily seen one can always satisfy this requirement, provided a suitable coupling of the dependent input lines is performed.

a necessary and sufficient condition for (7) *to hold is that:*

$$\lim_{n \to \infty} = \frac{1}{\mu_n^2} \sum_{k=1}^{n} \int_{|y| > \varepsilon \mu_n} y^2 \, df_k = 0 \tag{8}$$

for any arbitrarily fixed $\varepsilon > 0$, *where* f_i *'s*$(i = 1, 2, \ldots, n)$ *are the D.f. 's of the variables* $\varkappa_i$ *'s.*

Denoting now by $\alpha_{k,h}$ the absolute moment of order k of the variable $\varkappa_h$, and setting:

$$m_n^p \equiv \sum_{b=1}^{n} \alpha_{p,b}$$

one can easily demonstrate (see e.g. DE LUCA and RICCIARDI, 1967) the following

Theorem II

A sufficient condition for the C.L.T. to hold is that there exists a real number $\delta > 0$ *such that:*

$$\lim_{n \to \infty} \frac{m_n^{2+\delta}}{\mu_n^{2+\delta}} = 0 . \tag{9}$$

For the case of the neuron, we make a transformation of the variable e_i introduced in eq. (2') to

$$y_i = e_i - p_i \, a_i \quad (i = 1, 2, \ldots, n)$$

The mean value and standard deviation of e_i (eq. 3) then imply:

$$\langle y_i \rangle = 0 \qquad \sigma_i^2 = a_i^2 \, p_i \, q_i \qquad (i = 1, 2, \ldots, n)$$

Moreover, straightforward calculations yield:

$$\alpha_{3,i} = |a_i|^3 \, p_i \, q_i \, (p_i^2 + q_i^2) \le |a_i|^3 \, p_i \, q_i$$
$$\mu_n = [\sum_{i=1}^{n} a_i^2 \, p_i \, q_i]^{1/2} , \qquad\qquad (i = 1, 2, \ldots, n) \tag{9'}$$

so that we finally have:

$$\frac{m_n^3}{\mu_n^3} \le \frac{\sum\limits_{i=1}^{n} |a_i|^3 \, p_i q_i}{[\sum\limits_{1}^{n} p_i \, q_i \, a_i^2]^{3/2}} . \tag{10}$$

It is than easily seen that, under the realistic hypothesis:

$$0 < A \le |a_i| \le B \qquad (i = 1, 2, \ldots, n)$$

the right hand side of (10) is less or equal to:

$$\left(\frac{B}{A}\right)^3 [\sum_{i=1}^{n} p_i \, q_i]^{-1/2}$$

from which it follows that a sufficient condition for the validity of (9) (in this case is $\delta = 1$) is that the series

$$\sum_{i=1}^{\infty} p_i \, q_i$$

be divergent. If this is true, in the case of a finite but large n, the D.f. $F_n(E)$ of the net excitation E is approximatively given by:

$$F_n(E) \sim \frac{1}{\sqrt{2\pi}\, \mu_n} \int_{-\infty}^{E} dt\, e^{-\frac{(t-\langle E \rangle)^2}{2\mu_n^2}},$$

and therefore, using (6), the firing probability is

$$P_f \sim \frac{1}{\sqrt{2\pi}\, \mu_n} \int_{S}^{\infty} dE\, e^{-\frac{(t-\langle E \rangle)^2}{2\mu_n^2}}, \qquad (10')$$

or:

$$P_f \sim \frac{1}{\sqrt{2\pi}} \int_{\xi}^{\infty} e^{-\frac{t^2}{2}} dt = 1 - G(\xi)$$

where

$$\xi \equiv \frac{S - \langle E \rangle}{\mu_n}.$$

In other words, we find that P_f only depends on the value of ξ, and is not separately function of threshold S, the probabilities p_i and the coupling coefficients a_k. The probability $P(k, N, \xi)$ for the neuron to fire k times in the time interval $N\tau$ is then given by:

$$P(k, N, \xi) = \binom{N}{k} [G(\xi)]^{N-k} [1 - G(\xi)]^k$$

whose maximum, as function of ξ, is:

$$P(k, N, \eta) = \binom{N}{k} \left(1 - \frac{k}{N}\right)^{N-k} \left(\frac{k}{N}\right)^k,$$

where η is solution of the equation

$$\frac{1}{\sqrt{2\pi}} \int_{-\infty}^{\eta} dt\, e^{-t^2/2} = \frac{N-k}{N}.$$

Moreover, the following limit relation holds

$$\lim_{\xi \to \pm\infty} P(k, N, \xi) = 0$$

To conclude this section, let us remark that when use of the C.L.T. is made in the realistic case of a finite number of input lines, we need to know the order of magnitude of the error we make, in order to quantitatively justify the approximation. To this end, we can utilize a theorem essentially due to LIAPOUNOFF (1901) which says that, under very general hypothesis, the following inequality holds:

$$|\psi_n(Y) - G(Y)| < 3\lambda_{3,\,n} \frac{\ln n}{\sqrt{n}}$$

where $\lambda_{3,n}$ is given by

$$\lambda_{3,\,n} = \frac{\sqrt{n}\, m_n^3}{\mu_n^3}.$$

If we apply this theorem to our neural model, assuming that (as it may happen for Purkinje cells) the number n of input lines is of the order of 10^5, under the simplifying hypothesis:

$$\begin{cases} p_i = q_i = p \\ |a_i| = a \end{cases} \quad (i = 1, 2, \ldots, n)$$

remembering (9') we get:

$$|\psi_n(Y) - G(Y)| < 3\frac{\ln n}{\sqrt{n}} \sim 0 \cdot 11$$

i.e. the deviation of the distribution $\psi_n(Y)$ from the Gaussian is less than 11%.

3. Histograms

We consider now the problem of determining the probability for the neuron to exhibit a preassigned histogram of intervals between successive spikes in a time interval $N\tau$, by knowing the (stationary) firing probability P_f. To this end, following Fisz (1963) we consider the random variable

$$X \equiv \begin{pmatrix} 1 & 0 \\ p & 1-p \end{pmatrix}$$

and N repetitive trials (this corresponds to record the neuron's activity for a time $N\tau$). The result will be a sequence

$$\varkappa_1, \varkappa_2, \ldots, \varkappa_N \quad (\varkappa_i = 0, 1) \quad (i = 1, 2, \ldots, N)$$

where the suffixes represent the time.

We will say that the sequence

$$\varkappa_j, \varkappa_{j+1}, \ldots, \varkappa_{j+l} \quad \begin{pmatrix} l = 0, 1, 2, \ldots N-j \\ j = 1, 2, \ldots, N \end{pmatrix}$$

is a run of length $l+1$ if:

$$\varkappa_{j-1} \neq \varkappa_j = \varkappa_{j+1} = \ldots = \varkappa_{j+l} \neq \varkappa_{j+l+1} .$$

For $j = 1$ and $j = l+1$ the symbol $\neq$ is unnecessary.

Let us now introduce the following notation:

$\varkappa_{1,j}$ = number of runs of 1's of length j
$\varkappa_{0,j}$ = number of runs of 0's of length j
N_1 = total number of 1's
N_0 = total number of 0's
k_1 = total number of runs of 1's
k_0 = total number of runs of 0's

These definitions yield the following relations:

$$\begin{aligned} N_0 &= N - N_1 \\ \sum_j \varkappa_{0,j} &= N_0 \\ \sum_j \varkappa_{1,j} &= N_1 \\ k_1 &= \sum_j \varkappa_{1,j} \\ k_0 &= \sum_j \varkappa_{0,j} \end{aligned} \quad (11)$$

Also define by $P(\ldots \chi_{0,j} \ldots, N_1, N)$ the probability of finding in a time interval $N\tau$ a number N_1 of 1's, arranged in such a way that $\chi_{0,1}, \chi_{0,2} \cdots \chi_{0,N_0}$ runs of length $1, 2, \ldots, N_0$ respectively are found. In other words, this is the probability for the neuron to emit (in the time interval $N\tau$) $\chi_{0,1}$ pairs of consecutive spikes at distance τ, $\chi_{0,2}$ at distance 2τ, and χ_{0,N_0} at distance $N_0\tau$. By means of very simple arguments (for a detailed exposition see Fisz, quoted reference) we find the following expression for the probability P:

$$P(\ldots \chi_{0,j} \ldots; N_1, N) = \frac{k_0!}{\chi_{0,1}! \, \chi_{0,2}! \ldots \chi_{0,N_0}!} \binom{N_j+1}{k_0} P_f^{N-N_1} (1-P_f)^{N_1} \quad (12)$$

for any $\chi_{0,j}$, N_1, N which satisfy $(11)_1$ and $(11)_2$. From (12), by summing over all the $\chi_{0,r}$ except $\chi_{0,j}$ with the only constraint

$$\sum_r r \chi_{0,r} \leq N$$

one obtains the probability of having $\chi_{0,j}$ intervals of length $j\tau$, e.g. the probability that, no matter what the other intervals are, the histogram has height $\chi_{0,j}$ in the bin $j\tau$.

4. The Problem of the Dead Time

The model introduced in Sec. 2 represents a very drastic schematization of the anatomical and physiological evidence, though still retaining some of the typical features observed in the biological neurons. Now we want to consider two different instances where the model is slightly modified, in order to account for the existence of a refractory period effective after each firing and a finite summation time of the signals coming along the input lines.

1. Time Quantized and Existence of a Constant Dead Time

In this case the effect of the refractory period is to keep the neuron off for a time interval of duration $R\tau$ after each firing. Formula (12) for the probability of finding a preassigned histogram does not hold any more, and (see de LUCA and RICCIARDI, manuscript in preparation) has to be substituted with the following one:

$$P(\ldots \chi_{0,j+R} \ldots; N_1, N; R)$$
$$= \frac{k_0!}{\chi_{0,R+1}! \, \chi_{0,R+2}! \ldots \chi_{0,R+N-N_1(R+1)}!}$$
$$\times \binom{N_1+1}{k_0} P_f^{N-N_1(R+1)} (1-P_f)^{N_1},$$

where now:

$$k_0 = \sum_j \chi_{0,j+R}$$

2. No Time Quantization and Constant Dead Time

Problems can be set in quite general cases, but their solutions offer quite intringuing formal difficulties, as one can gather from a very simplified example which we are going to outline, and which is of interest also because it finds applications in the Cascade Theory for the so called Type I counters (BHARUCHA-REID, 1960). The problem is the evaluation of the probability $p_n(T, \sigma)$ of finding n spikes at the output of a neuron with threshold S and dead time σ, when its input is stimulated by Poisson distributed impulses. The existence of a threshold is not relevant at all for this particular problem[3]. The resulting output distribution is (RICCIARDI and ESPOSITO, 1966) the following:

$$p_n(T, \sigma) = 1[T-(n-1)\sigma] \left\{ 1 - e^{-\alpha[T-(n-1)\sigma]} \sum_{k=0}^{n-1} \frac{\alpha^k [T-(n-1)\sigma]^k}{k!} \right\} +$$

$$- 1[T-n\sigma] \left\{ 1 - e^{-\alpha(T-n\sigma)} \sum_{k=0}^{n} \frac{\alpha^k [T-n\sigma]^k}{k!} \right\}$$

where $1[x]$ denotes again the Heaviside unit step-function introduced in Sec. 2.

3. Finite summation time of the inputs

For simplicity let us assume $a_i = 1$ $(i = 1, 2, \ldots, n)$ and a random (Poisson) distribution of unitary impulses on each input line:

$$P_r^{(i)}(T) = \frac{(\alpha_i T)^r}{r!} e^{-\alpha T} \qquad (i = 1, 2, \ldots, n) \qquad (13)$$

and let us suppose that the adder sums all the signals reaching it in a time interval T. To the i-th input line $(i = 1, 2, \ldots, n)$ we associate the random variable

$$x^{(i)} \equiv \begin{pmatrix} 0 & 1 & 2 & \ldots \\ P_0^{(i)}(T) & P_1^{(i)}(T) & P_2^{(i)}(T) \ldots \end{pmatrix}$$

where $P_r^{(i)}(T)$ is given by (13). It is easily seen that:

$$\langle x^{(i)} \rangle = \sigma_i^2 = \alpha_i T.$$

Setting then

$$X \equiv \sum_{i=1}^{n} x^{(i)}$$

we have

$$\langle X \rangle = T \sum_{i=1}^{n} \alpha_i.$$

As done in Sec. 2, let us now introduce the new zero meanvalued random variables

$$y^{(i)} \equiv x^{(i)} - \alpha_i T$$

whose standard deviations are:

$$\sigma_i^2 = \alpha_i T$$

so that the variable

$$Y \equiv \sum_{i=1}^{n} y^{(i)}$$

has standard deviation

$$\mu_n^2 = T \sum_{i=1}^{n} \alpha_i.$$

Under the reasonable hypothesis

$$0 < \alpha_{min} \leq \alpha_i \leq \alpha_{max} \qquad (i = 1, 2, \ldots)$$

it is easily seen that:

$$\frac{m_n^3}{\mu_n^3} \leq \frac{1}{\sqrt{n}} \frac{\alpha_{max}(\alpha_{max}^2 T^2 + 3T \alpha_{max} + 1)}{T^{1/2} \alpha_{min}^{3/2}}.$$

[3] Its effect is only to cut off some input pulses, still the input distribution remaining POISSON.

It follows that the Liapounoff condition (9) is satisfied, so that the firing probability P_f for the neuron is given, according to (10'), by:

$$P_f \sim \frac{1}{\sqrt{2\pi}\, T\, \gamma_n} \int\limits_S^\infty dt\, e^{-\dfrac{(t - T\gamma_n)^2}{2\, T^2\, \gamma_n^2}} \tag{14}$$

having set:

$$\gamma_n \equiv \sum_{i=1}^n \alpha_i$$

By performing the following transformation

$$\frac{t - T\,\gamma_n}{T\,\gamma_n} = y$$

(14) becomes:

$$P_f \sim \frac{1}{\sqrt{2\pi}} \int\limits_{\frac{S}{T\gamma_n} - 1}^\infty e^{-y^2/2}\, dy\,. \tag{15}$$

From (15) we see that, keeping S constant and making n tend to infinity it is:

$$\lim_{n \to \infty} P_f(S) = \frac{1}{\sqrt{2\pi}} \int\limits_{-1}^\infty dy\, e^{-y^2/2} \sim 0.84\,.$$

If, instead, n is kept large enough but finite, making use of the identity:

$$e^{-y^2/2} = -\frac{1}{y^2} - \frac{d}{dy}\left(\frac{1}{y}\, e^{-y^2/2}\right) \tag{16}$$

we obtain for large values of S [i.e. misregarding the first term on the right hand side of (16)]:

$$P_f(S) \sim \frac{T\,\gamma_n}{\sqrt{2\pi}} \cdot \frac{e^{-\dfrac{S^2}{2\,T^2\,\gamma_n^2}}}{S}$$

which shows that for large values of S, the probability for a neuron to fire is a very rapidly decreasing function of its threshold.

References

BARUCHA-REID, A. T.: Elements of the theory of Markov processes and their applications New York: McGraw-Hill 1960.

BRAITENBERG, V.: J. theoret. Biol. 8, 419 (1965).

—, G. GAMBARDELLA, G. GHIGO, and U. VOTA: Kybernetik 2, 197 (1965).

CAIANIELLO, E. R.: J. theoret. Biol. 2, 204 (1961).

—, A. DE LUCA, and L. M. RICCIARDI: Kybernetik 4, 10 (1967).

CRAMER, H.: Random variables and probability distributions. Cambridge: Cambridge University Press 1963.

FISZ, M.: Probability theory and mathematical statistics. New York: John Wiley and Sons 1961.

LIAPOUNOFF, A.: Bull. Acad. Sci. St. Pétersbourg 13, 359 (1900).

— Mém. Acad. Sci. St. Pétersbourg 12, No. 5 (1901).

DE LUCA, A., and L. M. RICCIARDI: J. theoret. Biol. 14, 206 (1967).

RICCIARDI, L. M., and F. ESPOSITO: Kybernetik 3, 148 (1966).

Models of Certain Nonlinear Systems

J. D. APLEVICH

Committee on Mathematical Biology, University of Chicago

Abstract

A continuous model of linear binary threshold elements and some of its properties are discussed.

The purpose of this discussion is to demonstrate some of the similarities — and differences — between time-discrete and time-continuous models of linear threshold networks, examples of both of which are often used to represent neural nets.

A finite linear threshold net will be defined by the following:

1. I, a finite nonempty set of n elements, the collection of threshold gates.

2. E, a real n-vector with elements ε_i, $i \in I$, termed the threshold vector.

3. A, a real $n \times n$ matrix with elements α_{ij}, $i, j \in I$, termed the weight matrix.

Let $X(t)$ be a vector function of time t, with elements $x_i(t) \in \{a, b\}$ where a and b are real and distinct and $i \in I$. $X(t)$ is supposed to represent the state of the net at time t. The state at time $t + 1$ is given by

$$x_i(t+1) = \begin{cases} b & \text{if } \varepsilon_i + \sum_{j \in I} \alpha_{ij} x_j(t) \geq 0 \\ a & \text{otherwise} \end{cases} \tag{1}$$

The set $\{a, b\}$ is usually taken to be $\{0,1\}$ or $\{-1, 1\}$. It is easy to show that as long as a and b are distinct, for any two distinct numbers c, d, an equivalent linear threshold net exists with state vector elements in $\{c, d\}$.

The above definition is usually made or assumed when linear threshold nets are considered. If $\alpha_{ij} > 0$ or $\alpha_{ij} = -\infty$ for $(i, j) \in I \times I$ and $\varepsilon_i > 0$ for $i \in I$, then the net is known as a McCulloch-Pitts net [6, 12].

Threshold nets are used in studies of learning [1, 2] processes which usually involve adjustment of the parameters α_{ij}. Individual gates are known to have powerful logical properties [3, 4, 5].

It is important to note that a model defined on a discrete time-scale is a realistic description of a real network in only a limited number of cases:

(a) the trivial case where all functions of t are constant,

(b) the case in which a network is clocked, i.e. all variables are synchronized to a time-function in such a way that transients decay "sufficiently" in each time epoch,

(c) the case in which a dynamical system is described by a differential equation. The system

$$\frac{dX}{dt} = F(X) \tag{2}$$

may be represented by the time-discrete system

$$X(t+v) = X(t) + vF(t) + \frac{1}{2!}(v)^2 F'(t) + \cdots \qquad (3)$$

in a finite region provided the derivatives exist. In the first-order case the series is

$$X(t+v) = X(t) + vF(t) \qquad (4)$$

which has arbitrarily small error only for arbitrarily small v.

(d) the case of a free network for which it is known *a priori* that at certain points in time the system state is arbitrarily near that predicted by a discrete time equation.

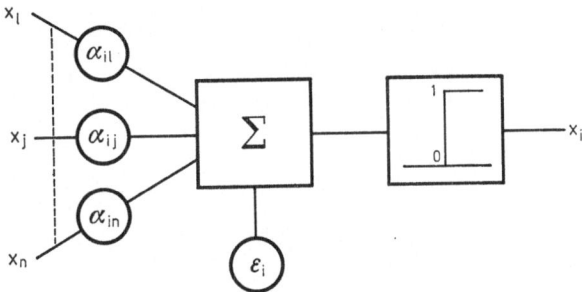

Fig. 1. A Network Element

Case (c) applies only to continuous functions: it does not apply, for example, to systems described by Eq. (1).

Fig. 1 represents an element which obeys Eq. (1). The dynamics of such elements involves a pure delay and perfect step response associated with each element. An attempt must be made to account for the actual response of physical

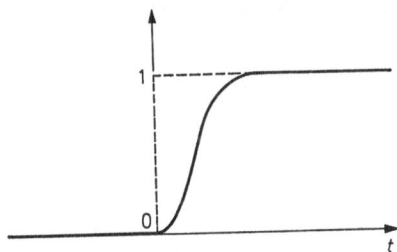

Fig. 2. Transient Response

gates, which may resemble Fig. 2. Of course other transient responses are possible, i.e. "ringing" behavior.

A model will be presented which has the response of Fig. 2, and which is a dynamical system, that is, its behavior is described by differential equations. Two further restrictions exist for models of real systems: the dynamics of real systems always involves dissipation and nonlinearity. The object is to find a simple model of a threshold gate which obeys the above two restrictions.

Consider Fig. 3, which is an operational diagram for the equation

$$\left(\tau_i \frac{d}{dt} + 1\right)\beta_i \psi(x_i) = \varepsilon_i + \sum_j \alpha_{ij} x_j, \qquad (5)$$

where $\tau_i, \beta_i > 0$, $i \in I$. The inverse function $\psi^{-1}(\beta_i y_i)$ is shown in Fig. 4, normalized so that it is asymptotic to the values 0 and 1. This function is assumed to be analytic and to have the property

$$\frac{d}{dq} \psi^{-1}(q) > 0 .\tag{6}$$

A suitable function is

$$\psi^{-1}(q) = \frac{1}{1 - e^{-q}}\tag{7}$$

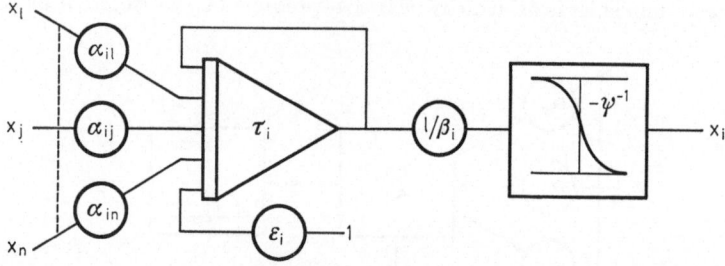

Fig. 3. Operational Diagram

with inverse

$$\psi(x_i) = \log \frac{x_i}{1 - x_i} .\tag{8}$$

For some small v we may write, because ψ is differentiable and $x_i(t)$ is continuous,

$$\frac{d}{dt} \psi[x_i(t)] = \frac{\psi[x_i(t+v)] - \psi[x_i(t)]}{v} .\tag{9}$$

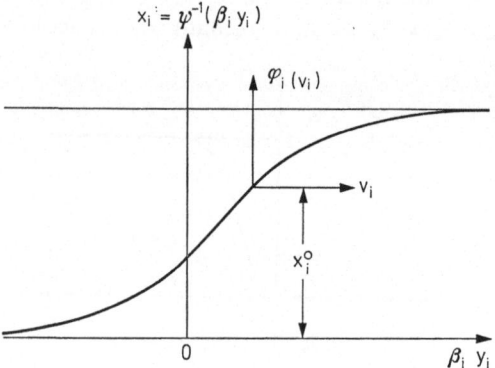

Fig. 4. Nonlinear Function

Hence

$$\psi[x_i(t+v)] \simeq \left(v \frac{d}{dt} + 1\right) \psi[x_i(t)] .\tag{10}$$

From (5) and (10),

$$x_i(t+v) \simeq \psi^{-1}\left[\left(1 - \frac{v}{\tau_i}\right) \psi(x_i(t)) + \frac{v}{\beta_i \tau_i}\left(\varepsilon_i + \sum_j \alpha_{ij} x_j(t)\right)\right]\tag{11}$$

which is a difference equation and always has arbitrarily small error in the trivial case that v is arbitrarily small. Now as the parameter β_i approaches 0, the equation becomes

$$x_i(t+v) = U\{\varepsilon_i + \sum_j \alpha_{ij} x_j(t)\}\tag{12}$$

where $U\{.\}$ is the step function, that is, the system obeys Eq. (1). This situation is nontrivial since approximation (11) does not necessarily hold in the limit as $\beta_i \to 0$.

Consider a network of gates. If there exist numbers t_{0i}, $i \in I$ and a sequence $\nu_1, \nu_2, \ldots$ with $\nu_0 = 0$ and all $\nu_{r+1} > \nu_r$ such that

$$| x_i(t_{0i} + \nu_{r+1}) - U\{\varepsilon_i + \sum_j \alpha_{ij} x_j(t_{0i} + \nu_r)\} | < \mu \tag{13}$$

for all $i \in I$ and a specified constant $\mu > 0$, then the system may be termed time-discrete.

Nets satisfying cases (b) or (d) have long been assumed to represent forms of neural behavior [6, 8]. They also are the basis of the design of sequential logic [10] circuits, in which case the parameters ε_i are no longer constant, but are replaced by the sequences of values ε_{ir} of linear functionals of the "external" inputs. Another limiting case [7] arises as follows: Assume that the parameters β_i approach 0, but that the product $\beta_i \tau_i$ remains constant. Then Eq. (5) becomes

$$\beta_i \tau_i \frac{d}{dt} \psi[x_i(t)] = \varepsilon_i + \sum_j \alpha_{ij} x_j(t) \tag{14}$$

which, under certain constraints on the parameters α_{ij}, can be shown [7, 11] to exhibit conservative oscillatory behavior.

Networks of elements described by Eq. (5) are autonomous dynamical systems conforming to case (c). Algebraic or combinatorial methods must be used for analysis and design of cases (b) and (d); here some analytical techniques will be indicated, and the results with apply in limiting cases to Eqs. (12) and (14).

Eq. (5) will be put in a normal form. Let $x_i = x_i^0$ be the solution of the equation

$$\varepsilon_i + \sum_{j \in I} \alpha_{ij} x_j - \beta_i \psi(x_i) = 0 . \tag{15}$$

Then it is possible to write

$$\left(\tau_i \frac{d}{dt} + 1 \right) \beta_i [\psi(x_i) - \psi(x_i^0)] = \sum_{j \in I} \alpha_{ij}(x_j - x_j^0) , \tag{16}$$

and letting

$$\beta_i [\psi(x_i) - \psi(x_i^0)] = v_i , \tag{17}$$

$$x_i - x_i^0 = \psi^{-1}(\beta_i y_i) - x_i^0 = \varphi_i(v_i) , \tag{18}$$

the equation becomes

$$\left(\tau_i \frac{d}{dt} + 1 \right) v_i = \sum_j \alpha_{ij} \varphi_j(v_j) . \tag{19}$$

The network equation is

$$V = - T^{-1} V + T^{-1} A\Phi(V) \tag{20}$$

where $T = \text{diag} [\tau_i]$, $V = [v_i]$, and $\Phi = [\varphi_i(v_i)]$. The functions $\varphi_i(v_i)$ satisfy the condition (see Fig. 4).

$$0 \le v_i \varphi_i \le k v_i^2 \tag{21}$$

for some finite k, as long as all $\beta_i > 0$. The point $V = 0$ is a singularity of (20) which is therefore in a normal form. By integrating this equation, the following is obtained:

$$V(t) = e^{-t T^{-1}} V(0) + T^{-1} \int_0^t e^{-T^{-1}(t-\tau)} A\Phi(\tau) \, d\tau . \tag{22}$$

This system is in the Lur'e form and results concerning its stability are well known [9, 13]. Indeed, Eq. (20) may be generalized as follows: Let the system be separable into linear time-invariant dynamical subsystems and nonlinear memoryless elements which obey restriction (21). Let the system be described by the equation

$$V(t) = Z(t) + \int_0^t G_\delta(t - \tau)\, \Phi(\tau)\, d\tau \qquad (23)$$

where $G_\delta(t)$ is the $n \times n$ impulse response matrix of the linear portion $G = [g_{ij}]$ of the system, and $Z(t) = [z_i(t)]$ is a linear function of the "zero-input" response of G. It is assumed that the following conditions are satisfied for $i, j \in I$:

(i) for all initial states, z_i is bounded, $z_i(t) \to 0$ as $t \to \infty$, and $z_i, \dot z_i \in L_2(0, \infty)$;
(ii) $g_{ij} \in L_1(0, \infty)$.

If $G(s)$, the Laplace transform of $G(t)$, is rational with all poles in the left half-plane, i.e. the system is dissipative, then the above conditions are satisfied. In such a case it is possible to apply the extended Popov [13, 14] criterion for finding Lyapunov functions of the system.

A second, simpler method of analysing such a network is to consider linearizations of it at the singular points. Eq. (20) is a particular form of (2). The procedure is as follows: The Jacobian matrix $\left[\dfrac{\partial F}{\partial X}\right]$ is evaluated at a singular point X^0, and the linear equation

$$\frac{d}{dt}(X - X^0) = \left[\frac{\partial F}{\partial X}\right]_{X^0}(X - X^0) \qquad (24)$$

is investigated (by solving for latent roots, by the Hurwitz technique, or by solving the Lyapunov equation). The system behavior is then known in a small neighborhood of the singularites X^0. It can be shown [11] that the particularly simple form of the nonlinearities $\varphi_j(v_j)$ in (19) allows conclusions to be reached about system global behavior by considering the linearized system.

Acknowlegdements. Much of the work presented here was done in the Communications and Electronics Section at Imperial College, London, with the financial assistance of the Athlone Fellowships and the National Research Council of Canada. It is a pleasure to acknowledge discussions with Mr. P. Johannesma in the preparation of this work.

References

1. Rosenblatt, F.: Principles of Neurodynamics. Washington, D.C.: Spartan 1962.
2. Widrow, B., and M. E. Hoff: Adaptive Switching Circuits, 1960 Wescon Convention Record (IV), Aug. 1960, p. 96—104.
3. Muroga, S., I. Toda, and S. Takasu: Theory of Majority Decision Elements, J. Franklin Inst. **271**, 376—418 (1961).
4. McNaughton, R.: Unate Truth Functions. I.R.E. Trans. Elect. Comp. (EC-10), **1961**, 1—6.
5. Winder, R. O.: Enumeration of Seven-Argument Threshold Functions. I.E.E.E. Trans. Elect. Comp. (EC-14). **1965**, 315—325.
6. McCulloch, W. S., and W. Pitts: A logical Calculus of the Ideas Immanent in Nervous Activity. Bull. Math. Biophys. (5), Sept. **1943**, 115—133.
7. Cowan, J. D.: Neuronal Oscillators, Revised Version of a lecture given at the Norbert Wiener Memorial Meeting on the Idea of Control, Genoa, Italy, October 1965.

8. CAIANIELLO, E. R., A. DE LUCA, and L. M. RICCIARDI: Reverberations and Control of Neural Networks, Kybernetik **4**, 10—18 (1967).
9. MINORSKI, N.: Nonlinear Oscillations. Van Nostrand 1962. London.
10. HUFFMAN, D. A.: The Synthesis of Sequential Switching Circuits. J. Franklin Inst. **257**, 3 and 4.
11. APLEVICH, J. D.: Stability of Networks of Nonlinear Elements with Logical Properties. Ph. D. Thesis, University of London 1968.
12. KROHN, K., and J. RHODES: Nets of Threshold Elements, Inf. and Cont. **8**, 579—588 (1965).
13. DEWEY, A. G.: Frequency Domain Stability Criteria for Non-linear Multi-variable Systems. Intern. J. Control **5**, 1, 77—84 (1967).
14. POPOV, V. M.: Automat. Telemech., Moscow **22**, 961 (1961).
— Automation and Remote Control **22**, 857 (1962).

Diffusion Models for the Stochastic Activity of Neurons *

P. I. M. Johannesma

Laboratory of Medical Physics, University of Nijmegen, The Netherlands**

Abstract

The activity of a neuron, subjected to an input of many small excitatory and inhibitory pulses, is considered. Diffusion equations for transition probabilities and first passage times are derived.

Exact expressions result for the moments of the distribution of intervals between action potentials. The determination of the distribution from the moments is discussed.

The theory is applied to a model with proportional decay of the postsynaptic potential and to the equivalent circuit of the membrane.

Ways of treating refractory properties are described.

Introduction

It is well known that the interpretation of neurophysiological measurements of the intervals between action potentials of single neurons requires in many cases a probabilistic approach. Already a fair amount of work has been done to model the stochastic behaviour of neurons, most of it by computer simulation. For a survey see MOORE, PERKEL and SEGUNDO (1966), STEIN (1967).

Only in two cases have there been analytical results:

1. Time constant of summation of the postsynaptic potential $\tau = \infty$, that is: no decay of the P.S.P.,

2. Excitatory and inhibitory incoming pulses have a Poisson distributed life time instead of a proportional decay (TEN HOOPEN, 1966).

In this paper we derive analytical formulas for the moments of the interval distribution. Because of the very general and powerful nature of the approach using diffusion equations, the derivation turns out to be applicable to a group of neural models, including the equivalent circuit for the dentritic membrane, with an input consisting of a Poisson sequence of excitatory and inhibitory pulses and/or additive or multiplicative noise.

If we can assign numerical values to the required physiological parameters of the neuron, the moments of the interval distribution can be computed numerically by the evaluation of a manifold integral and compared with the results of experiments.

* This work was supported by a NATO Science Fellowship through the Netherlands Organisation for the Advancement of Pure Research (Z.W.O.).

** The main part of this work was performed when the author was on leave at: Department of Electrical Engineering, Imperial College of Science and Technology, London, S.W.7.

Statement of the Model

Though an accurate mathematical representation of the neuron would have to be based on the Hodgin-Huxley equations and should take into account the non-uniform distributed character of the system (RALL, 1964), this approach is much too difficult.

We shall start from a simpler, widely used model which reflects rather satisfactorily many of the properties of the behaviour of a neuron. A logical diagram of this model is given in Fig. 1.

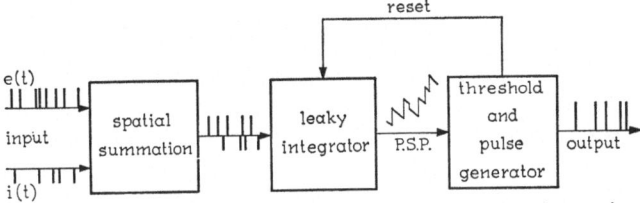

Fig. 1. Logical diagram of the model. $e(t)$ = probabilistic excitatory input signal, $i(t)$ = probabilistic inhibitory input signal, s = time of occurrence of latest output pulse, x = value of the post synaptic potential immediately, after generation of an action potential, τ = time constant of summation, $Y(t)$ = post synaptic potential at time t

$$Y(t) = \frac{1}{\tau} \int_s^t du\, e^{-\frac{t-u}{\tau}} [e(u) + i(u)] + xe^{-\frac{t-s}{\tau}}$$

The functional behaviour of this model is expressed in the following *assumptions*:

1. The state of the neuron is characterized by one parameter only: $Y(t)$, the post-synaptic potential (P.S.P.).

2. Incoming pulses are uncorrelated, of two modalities, each with its own frequency and its own effect

modality	frequency	effect
excitation	n_e	$e > 0$
inhibition	n_i	$i < 0$

the arrival of an excitatory pulse causes a change in the P.S.P.: $Y \to Y + e$,
the arrival of an inhibitory pulse causes a change in the P.S.P.: $Y \to Y + i$,

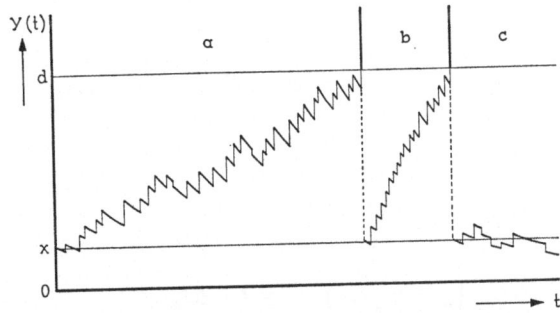

Fig. 2a—c. Examples of the time course of the post synaptic potential. (a) Excitation and inhibition, (b) high excitation, no inhibition, (c) nearly equal intensity of excitation and inhibition

3. As long as the postsynaptic potential $Y(t)$ is smaller than the threshold potential d, $Y(t)$ has a decay proportional to $Y(t)$: $dY = - Ydt$ ($\tau =$ time constant of summation).

4. If $Y(t)$ reaches the threshold value d, an output pulse is generated and the P.S.P. reset to the starting value x.

5. The threshold potential is independent of time or occurrence of output pulses (refractory properties will be incorporated later).

A pictorial representation of these assumptions, in the presence of several sources of excitation and inhibition, is given in Fig. 2.

The Equation for the Distribution of $Y(t)$

If we do not yet take the threshold into account, then Fig. 3 gives a picture of the transitions involved.

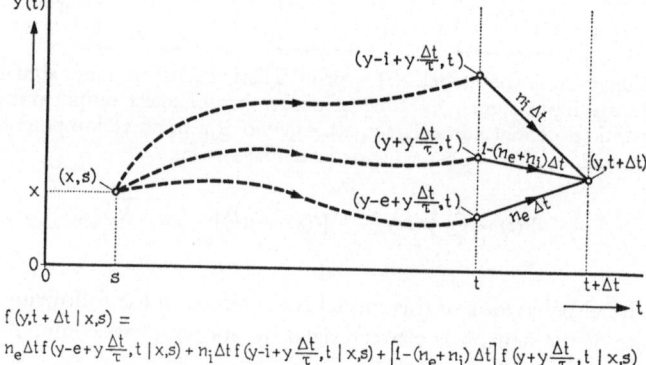

$$f(y, t+\Delta t \mid x,s) =$$
$$n_e \Delta t\, f(y-e+y\tfrac{\Delta t}{\tau}, t \mid x,s) + n_i \Delta t\, f(y-i+y\tfrac{\Delta t}{\tau}, t \mid x,s) + \left[1-(n_e+n_i)\,\Delta t\right] f\left(y+y\tfrac{\Delta t}{\tau}, t \mid x,s\right)$$

Fig. 3. The transition probability

For Δt very small with respect to the mean interval between arriving pulses the probability of more than one pulse in the time interval $(t, t + \Delta t)$ is negligible and we have:

probability of excitatory pulse in $(t, t + \Delta t) = n_e\, \Delta t$

probability of inhibitory pulse in $(t, t + \Delta t) = n_i\, \Delta t$

probability of no pulse in $(t, t + \Delta t) = 1 - (n_e + n_i)\, \Delta t$

amount of decay in $(t, t + \Delta t) = - y\dfrac{\Delta t}{\tau}$

where y is the value of $Y(t)$.

The possible transitions, which start at t and have y as an endpoint at time $t + \Delta t$ are

$$\left(y - e + y\frac{\Delta t}{\tau}, t\right) \rightarrow (y, t + \Delta t)$$

$$\left(y - i + y\frac{\Delta t}{\tau}, t\right) \rightarrow (y, t + \Delta t)$$

$$\left(y + y\frac{\Delta t}{\tau}, t\right) \rightarrow (y, t + \Delta t)$$

We define now a fundamental quantity for the description of a stochastic process: *the transition probability*.

$$f(y, t \,|\, x, s) = P(Y(t) = y \,|\, Y(s) = x)$$

= probability that P.S.P. has value y at time t, given that the value was x at time s,

= transition probability $(x, s) \rightarrow (y, t)$.

With the help of Fig. 3 we can directly write down the following relation for the transition probability

$$f(y, t + \Delta t \,|\, x, s) = n_e \Delta t f\!\left(y - e + y\,\frac{\Delta t}{\tau}, t \,|\, x, s\right)$$

$$+ n_i \Delta t f\!\left(y - i + y\,\frac{\Delta t}{\tau}, t \,|\, x, s\right) \tag{1}$$

$$+ \left[1 - (n_e + n_i)\,\Delta t\right] f\!\left(y + y\,\frac{\Delta t}{\tau}, t \,|\, x, s\right).$$

The assumptions 1 to 5 made previously as well as the form of Eq. (1), indicate that the stochastic process under consideration is Markovian. The mathematical representation of the Markovian property is the Smoluchowski integral relation

$$f(y, t + \Delta t \,|\, x, s) = \int_{-\infty}^{\infty} d z\, f(y, t + \Delta t \,|\, z, t)\, f(z, t \,|\, x, s). \tag{2}$$

It is possible to derive from Eq. (2) the series form of the Smoluchowski equation

$$\frac{\partial}{\partial t} f(y, t \,|\, x, s) = \sum_{n=1}^{\infty} \frac{(-1)^n}{n!} \left(\frac{\partial}{\partial y}\right)^n [A_n(y, t)\, f(y, t \,|\, x, s)] \tag{3}$$

where

$$A_n(y, t) = \lim_{\Delta t \to 0} \frac{1}{\Delta t} \int_{-\infty}^{\infty} d z\, z^n f(y + z, t + \Delta t \,|\, y, t)$$

(MIDDLETON, 1960, p. 448—450; STRATONOVICH, 1963, ch. 4.).

The incremental moments A_n characterise the stochastic process completely. If $A_n(y, t) = A_n(y)$, the process is stationary and the transition probability depends only on time differences: $f(y, t \,|\, x, s) = f(y, t - s, x)$, in which case we write $f(y, t, x)$ instead of $f(y, t - s, x)$.

For the process modelling the stochastic activity of a neuron the Smoluchowski relation has the form of Eq. (1) and the incremental moments are

$$A_1(y, t) = A_1(y) = -y/\tau + n_e e + n_i i$$
$$A_n(y, t) = A_n(y) = n_e e^n + n_i\, i^n.$$

Substitution in Eq. (3) results in

$$\frac{\partial}{\partial t} f(y, t, x) = \frac{\partial}{\partial y}\left[\frac{y}{\tau} f(y, t, x)\right] + \sum_{n=1}^{\infty} \frac{(-1)^n}{n!} [n_e e^n + n_i\, i^n] \left(\frac{\partial}{\partial y}\right)^n f(y, t, x)$$

which is equivalent to the equation

$$\frac{\partial}{\partial t} f(y, t, x) = \frac{\partial}{\partial y}\left[\frac{y}{\tau} f(y, t, x)\right] + n_e\,[f(y - e, t, x) - f(y, t, x)]$$

$$+ n_i[f(y - i, t, x) - f(y, t, x)]. \tag{3 S}$$

By integration over y this equation can be shown to be equivalent with the relation derived by Stein (1965, p. 182, Eq. 13); under the boundary conditions resulting from the threshold property a solution is unknown.

The model of ten Hoopen (1966) with exponentially distributed life time and equal size of the excitatory and inhibitory quanta ($e = j = -i$), results in

$$A_n^{(H)}(y, t) = -\frac{y}{\tau}(-j)^{n-1} + n_e e^n + n_i i^n$$

which shows that $A_1(y)$ is identical in both cases and the relative differences for the incremental moments are small if n_e and/or $n_i \gg \tau^{-1}$ and $j \ll d$.

However, the most important is the second moment, where the descriptions of Stein and Ten Hoopen show the relative difference

$$\frac{A_2^{(H)} - A_2^{(S)}}{A_2^{(S)}} = \left[\frac{(n_e + n_i)j\tau}{y}\right]^{-1} \equiv \left[\frac{m\tau}{y}\right]^{-1} \leq \left[\frac{m\tau}{d}\right]^{-1}.$$

Numerical results indicate that $\frac{m\tau}{d}$ may be of the order of 1.

The equation for the transition probability is in the approach of Ten Hoopen

$$\frac{\partial}{\partial t}f(y, t, x) = \frac{1}{j\tau}[(y+j)f(y+j, t, x) - yf(y, t, x)]$$

$$+ n_e[f(y-j, t, x) - f(y, t, x)] + n_i[f(y+j, t, x) - f(y, t, x)] \quad (3\text{ H})$$

which can also be derived directly from first principles.

For a treatment of this equation with the appropriate boundary conditions see Ten Hoopen (1966). Numerical evaluation of the solution derived by Ten Hoopen seems to be feasible if d is only a few units of j, that is a small number of excitatory pulses are sufficient to elicit an output pulse.

However, we shall proceed in another way by assuming that e and i are small with respect to the quantities we are interested in. In this case these quantities are the difference between threshold and equilibrium potential ($d - 0 = d$) and the difference between threshold and reset potential ($d - x$).

We add now a sixth *assumption*:

6. The pulse amplitudes e and i are small with respect to d and $d - x$.

Under this assumption, which is made throughout this paper, we may neglect in Eq. (3) all terms with $n \geq 3$. The resulting equation for the transition probability is then:

$$\frac{\partial}{\partial t}f(y, t \mid x, s) = \left[-\frac{\partial}{\partial y}(m - y/\tau) + \frac{1}{2}\left(\frac{\partial}{\partial y}\right)^2 s^2\right]f(y, t \mid x, s) \quad (4)$$

where

$m = n_e e + n_i i =$ average value or D.C.-component of input,

$s^2 = n_e e^2 + n_i i^2 =$ variance or A.C.-component of input.

In order that Eq. (4) defines the solution unequivocally we need one initial and two boundary conditions:

— since $Y(s) = x$, the initial condition is: $f(y, s \mid x, s) = \delta(y - x)$;

— since the potential cannot change an infinite amount in a finite time, the boundary conditions without threshold are: $f(\pm \infty, t \mid x, s) = 0$.

To get an indication of the error introduced by neglecting the terms higher than the second in Eq. (3), we assume again equal size of excitatory and inhibitory pulse: ($e = j = -i$). The incremental moments are then

$$A_n = [n_e + (-1)^n n_i] j^n, \quad n \geq 2 .$$

Using the abbreviation

$$C_n = \frac{1}{n!} \frac{A_n}{d^n}$$

the relative error of the diffusion approximation with respect to the behaviour near the threshold d is mainly dependent on

$$\frac{C_3}{C_2} = \frac{1}{3} \frac{n_e - n_i}{n_e + n_i} \frac{j}{d}$$

$$\frac{C_3}{C_2} \lesssim 0.03 \text{ for } j \leq 0.1 \, d \text{ if } n_i = 0$$

$$\frac{C_3}{C_2} \lesssim 0.01 \text{ for } j \leq 0.1 \, d \text{ if } n_i = \tfrac{1}{2} n_e$$

and

$$\frac{C_4}{C_2} = \frac{1}{12} \left(\frac{j}{d}\right)^2$$

$$\frac{C_4}{C_2} \lesssim 0.001 \text{ for } j \leq 0.1 \, d .$$

So we expect that the continuous description of Eq. (4) gives a reasonable approximation, if the change in the P.S.P. caused by one excitatory or inhibitory pulse is smaller than 10% of the distance between equilibrium and threshold potential.

(Compare: GERSTEIN and MANDELBROT, 1964; STEVENS, 1964; GLUSS, 1964.)

The Diffusion-Equations

We write down Eq. (4) in a slightly different and more general form

$$\frac{\partial}{\partial t} f(y, t \mid x, s) = \left[-\frac{\partial}{\partial y} a(y, t) + \tfrac{1}{2} \left(\frac{\partial}{\partial y}\right)^2 b(y, t) \right] f(y, t \mid x, s) \tag{5a}$$

$$f(y, s \mid x, s) = \partial(y - x), \qquad f(\pm \infty, t \mid x, s) = 0 .$$

This equation, the *forward equation*, describes the divergence of probability from the "start-point" (x, s) to all "points" (y, t).

We could be equally well interested in the convergence of probability from all "points" (x, s) to one "end-point" (y, t).

For this we need an equation describing the past, with a related final, instead of initial, condition. In the theory of stochastic processes it is well known that, under the conditions which allow derivation of the forward Eq. (5a), it is always possible to derive the corresponding *backward equation* (see for instance PHRABU, 1965)

$$-\frac{\partial}{\partial s} f(y, t \mid x, s) = \left[a(x, s) \frac{\partial}{\partial x} + \tfrac{1}{2} b(x, s) \left(\frac{\partial}{\partial x}\right)^2 \right] f(y, t \mid x, s) \tag{5b}$$

$$f(y, t \mid x, t) = \delta(x - y), \qquad f(y, t \mid \pm \infty, s) = 0 .$$

The expressions between square brackets in the equations (5) occur many times in the rest of this paper, therefore we introduce the notations

$$P = P\left(\frac{\partial}{\partial y}, y, t\right) = -\frac{\partial}{\partial y} a(y, t) + \frac{1}{2}\left(\frac{\partial}{\partial y}\right)^2 b(y, t)$$

$$Q = Q\left(x, \frac{\partial}{\partial x}, s\right) = a(x, s)\frac{\partial}{\partial x} + \frac{1}{2} b(x, s)\left(\frac{\partial}{\partial x}\right)^2$$

where P and Q are linear operators.

Eq. (5a) supplies information with regard to the distribution of the postsynaptic potential.

Eq. (5b) will prove to be the basic relation for the treatment of first passage time problems.

Conditions for derivation or applicability of the diffusion equations:

a) the underlying stochastic process is *Markovian*

$$f(y, t \mid x, s) = \int_{-\infty}^{\infty} dz\, f(y, t \mid z, u) f(z, u \mid x, s), \quad s < u < t;$$

the probability of a transition is only dependent on the value of the variables at that time, and possibly, time itself.

b) the underlying stochastic process is *continuous*

$$\lim_{\Delta t \to 0} \frac{1}{\Delta t} \int_{|z| > \varepsilon} dz\, f(y + z, t + \Delta t \mid y, t) = 0 \qquad \text{for all } \varepsilon > 0;$$

the probability of finite transitions in the interval $(t, t + \Delta t)$ approaches zero for $\Delta t \to 0$.

We can summarize a and b in the condition: the change of the stochastic variable $Y(t)$ is, apart from deterministic fully known influences, dependent on (infinitely) many independent occurring events, each having only an (infinitely) small effect during an (infinitely) small time.

Processes which fulfil this condition are called diffusion processes and are characterised by

drift
$$a(y, t) = \lim_{\Delta t \to 0} \frac{1}{\Delta t} \int_{-\infty}^{\infty} dz\, z f(y + z, t + \Delta t \mid y, t)$$

and

dispersion
$$b(y, t) = \lim_{\Delta t \to 0} \frac{1}{\Delta t} \int_{-\infty}^{\infty} dz\, z^2 f(y + z, t + \Delta t \mid y, t).$$

In the time homogeneous case $a(y, t) = a(y)$ independent of time, $b(y, t) = b(y)$ independent of time and $f(y, t \mid x, s)$ is not dependent any more on t and s separately but only on the time difference $(t - s)$.

Using now as before t instead of $t - s$ we define:

$f(y, t, x)$ = probability density of the transition from x to y in time interval t.

Eq. (5) then takes the form

$$\frac{\partial}{\partial t} f(y, t, x) = P\left(\frac{\partial}{\partial y}, y\right) f(y, t, x) \qquad (6a)$$

$$\frac{\partial}{\partial t} f(y, t, x) = Q\left(x, \frac{\partial}{\partial x}\right) f(y, t, x). \qquad (6b)$$

See appendix A for diffusion models of non-Markovian physical processes and appendix B for some remarks on the diffusion equations.

The First Passage Time[1]

We incorporate now assumption 2 of the model: the threshold. At the moment that the postsynaptic potential $Y(t)$ reaches the threshold value d, an output pulse is generated (see Fig. 2). Since the main purpose of this paper is the derivation of the distribution of the intervals between the output pulses, we are interested in the amount of time which is required for the P.S.P. to reach the threshold for the first time after a start at x: this is called the first passage time from x to d.

Since the underlying process is probabilistic, the first passage time is also a probabilistic quantity which can be described through the related probability density. Using the Brownian motion language (see appendix B), we define:

$g(t) = g(d, t \mid x, s)$
   = probability that particle reaches d for the first time at t if it started from x at s,
   = $P[Y(t) = d, Y(u) < d$ for all $s < u < t \mid Y(s) = x]$.

The introduction of an *absorbing barrier* at d has the consequence that an arrival of the particle at d is a first arrival.

The absorbing barrier is mathematically expressible through the imposition of a zero boundary condition at d, instead of the condition at $+\infty$, in Eq. (5).

The conservation of probability requires that the sum of the amount of probability that the particle is somewhere between $-\infty$ and d and the amount of probability that the particle is absorbed in the barrier is constant

$$\int_s^t du\, g(d, u \mid x, s) + \int_{-\infty}^d dy\, f(y, t \mid x, s) = 1$$

or

$$g(d, t \mid x, s) = -\frac{\partial}{\partial t} \int_{-\infty}^d dy\, f(y, t \mid x, s) . \tag{7}$$

Here $f(y, t \mid x, s)$ is the solution of Eq. (5a) or Eq. (5b) with the boundary condition $f(d, t \mid x, s) = 0$.

To get a more general description and avoid at the same time possible convergence problems, we introduce also a reflecting barrier at $r < x$. This gives some more complicated boundary condition in r, which expresses the fact that there is no flow of probability at r. If this reflecting barrier does not occur in our neural model, we may insert the value $-\infty$ for r in the resulting expression.

In the time homogeneous case only $(t - s)$ is relevant and we can take, instead of Eq. (7):
$g(d, t, x)$ = probability of first arrival at d after time interval t, starting from x,

$$= -\frac{\partial}{\partial t} \int_r^d dy\, f(y, t, x) . \tag{8}$$

---

[1] Much of the theory of this section and the next one can be found in Cox and MILLER (1965).

Since d is an arbitrary, but fixed parameter, we write $g(t, x)$ instead of $g(d, t, x)$. Because we can interchange the order of some operations

$$-\frac{\partial}{\partial t}\int_r^d dy\,\frac{\partial}{\partial t}f(y, t, x)=\frac{\partial}{\partial t}\left[-\frac{\partial}{\partial t}\int_r^d dy\,f(y, t, x)\right]=\frac{\partial}{\partial t}g(t, x)$$

$$-\frac{\partial}{\partial t}\int_r^d dy\,Q\left(x,\frac{\partial}{\partial x}\right)f(y, t, x)=Q\left(x,\frac{\partial}{\partial x}\right)\left[-\frac{\partial}{\partial t}\int_r^d dy\,f(y, t, x)\right]=Q\left(x,\frac{\partial}{\partial x}\right)g(t, x)$$

Eq. (6b) supplies an identical equation for the first passage time probability density $g(t, x)$ in the time homogeneous case

$$\frac{\partial}{\partial t}g(t, x)=Q\left(x,\frac{\partial}{\partial x}\right)g(t, x),\qquad r<x<d \tag{9}$$

however, with different initial and boundary conditions:

the particle can only make an infinitesimal jump in an infinitesimal time: $g(0, x) = 0$ for $r < x < d$;

a start at d causes immediate absorption: $g(t, d) = \delta(t)$; reflecting barrier:

$$\frac{\partial}{\partial x}g(t, x)/_{x=r} = 0 .$$

Eq. (9) is again a second order partial differential equation, with rather unpleasant boundary conditions.

To our knowledge, there exists only in the most simple case a closed expression for the solution. This case, which is known as the Wiener-Einstein model of diffusion does occur if drift a and dispersion b are independent of the state of the neuron:

$$a(x) = m, \quad b(x) = s^2.$$

Then for $r = -\infty,\ m > 0$

$$g(t, x) = \frac{d-x}{mt}\,2\pi\,(s^2t)^{-1/2}\exp\left[-\frac{1}{2}\left(\frac{d-x-mt}{s\sqrt{t}}\right)^2\right]$$

is the probability density of first passage times. The mean interval is

$$\mu = \frac{d-x}{m}$$

and the variance of intervals

$$\sigma^2 = \frac{1}{2}\frac{d-x}{m}\cdot\left(\frac{s}{m}\right)^2.$$

(see Gerstein and Mandelbrot, 1964.)

In the general case the solution can be represented as an infinite sum of orthogonal functions, with combinations of moments or cumulants as coefficients.

On the basis of Eq. (9) it will prove to be possible to derive a mathematical expression for any moment (cumulant) of the first passage time probability density in terms of the previous moment (cumulants), which enables numerical computation of successive moments (cumulants) and gives a quantitative understanding of the influence of the different parameters. In order to get these results we have to transform Eq. (9).

Laplace transformation of the first passage time equation

We take the following steps:
— multiply both sides of Eq. (9) with e^{-pt},
— integrate t from 0 to ∞,
— interchange the order of operations at the right-hand side,
— define $\hat{g}(p, x) = \int_0^\infty dt\, e^{-pt} g(t, x)$,
— derive through partial integration and use of the initial condition $g(o, x) = 0$

$$\int_0^\infty dt\, e^{-pt} \frac{\partial}{\partial t} g(t, x) = p\hat{g}(p, x), \qquad r < x < d,$$

— transform the boundary conditions:

$$\hat{g}(p, d) = \int_0^\infty dt\, e^{-pt} g(t, d) = \int_0^\infty dt\, e^{-pt} \delta(t) = 1$$

$$\frac{\partial}{\partial x} \hat{g}(p, x)|_{x=r} = \frac{\partial}{\partial x} \int_0^\infty dt\, e^{-pt} g(t, x)|_{x=r} = \int_0^\infty dt\, e^{-pt} \frac{\partial}{\partial x} g(t, x)|_{x=r} = 0.$$

The result is then

$$p\hat{g}(p, x) = Q\left(x, \frac{\partial}{\partial x}\right) \hat{g}(p, x) \tag{10}$$

$$\hat{g}(p, d) = 1, \qquad \frac{\partial}{\partial x} \hat{g}(p, x)|_{x=r} = 0.$$

Eq. (10) is a second order ordinary differential equation, with varying coefficients. Though in the case of the proportional decay, when $a(x) = m - x/\tau$, $b(x) = s^2$ it is possible to formulate the solution of Eq. (10) in terms of Weber functions, this result is so complicated that it seems of no use. So we proceed again to transform Eq. (10).

The Moments

Since $g(t, x) = 0$ for $t < 0$, $\hat{g}(p, x)$ is the moment generating function of $g(t, x)$. This implies that we can expand $\hat{g}(p, x)$ in a power series in p, with the moments as coefficients

$$\hat{g}(p, x) = \sum_{n=0}^\infty M_n(x) \frac{(-p)^n}{n!} \tag{11}$$

and $M_n(x)$ is the nth derivative of the moment generating function in $p = 0$

$$M_n(x) = \langle t^n \rangle = \int_0^\infty dt\, t^n g(t, x) = \left(-\frac{\partial}{\partial p}\right)^n \hat{g}(p, x)|_{p=0}. \tag{12}$$

Now we proceed as follows:
— substitution of Eq. (11) in Eq. (10),
— change of some indices,
— interchange of order of operations,

and get

$$- \sum_{n=0}^{\infty} n M_{n-1}(x) \frac{(-p)^n}{n!} = \sum_{n=0}^{\infty} Q\left(x, \frac{\partial}{\partial x}\right) M_n(x) \frac{(-p)^n}{n!}.$$

Since this equation is valid for all values of p, the coefficients of equal powers of p must be equal, which generates the infinite set of equations

$$Q\left(x, \frac{\partial}{\partial x}\right) M_n(x) = - n M_{n-1}(x), \qquad n \geq 0, r < x < d. \tag{13}$$

Solving the nth equation for M_n we may assume M_{n-1} already to be solved. Now recalling

$$Q\left(x, \frac{\partial}{\partial x}\right) = a(x) \frac{\partial}{\partial x} + \tfrac{1}{2} b(x) \left(\frac{\partial}{\partial x}\right)^2,$$

we see at the left hand side of Eq. (13), only the first and second derivative of M_n, not M_n itself. This enables us to separate each second order Eq. (13) into two first order equations

$$m_n(x) = \frac{d}{dx} M_n(x) \tag{14a}$$

$$\left[a(x) + \tfrac{1}{2} b(x) \frac{d}{dx}\right] m_n(x) = - n M_{n-1}(x) \tag{14b}$$

with the matching boundary conditions

$$M_0(d) = 1, \qquad M_n(d) = 0 \text{ for } n \geq 1 \tag{14a}$$

$$m_n(r) = 0 \text{ for } n \geq 0. \tag{14b}$$

The solution of Eq. (14) is straightforward and results, using now finally the boundary conditions, in

$$M_0(x) = 1$$

$$\frac{M_n(x)}{n!} = \int_x^d dy \exp\left[- C(y)\right] \int_r^y dz \frac{\exp[C(z)]}{\tfrac{1}{2} b(z)} \cdot \frac{M_{n-1}(z)}{(n-1)!} \tag{15}$$

where

$$C(y) = \int^y dz \frac{a(z)}{\tfrac{1}{2} b(z)}.$$

So we now have an analytical expression which enables us to compute (numerically) the various moments of the interval distribution. There are no restrictions on the form of the functions $a(z)$ and $b(z) > 0$.

A simpler derivation of Eq. (13) from Eq. (9) is given in appendix C.

The Cumulants

Instead of the moments we can take the cumulants: the coefficients in a power-series expansion in $p = 0$ of $\ln \hat{g}(p, x)$

$$\ln \hat{g}(p, x) = \sum_{n=1}^{\infty} K_n(x) \frac{(-p)^n}{n!} \tag{16}$$

with

$$K_n(x) = \left(- \frac{\partial}{\partial p}\right)^n \ln \hat{g}(p, x)|_{p=0}. \tag{17}$$

Now we take the following steps:
— substitution of

$$\exp\left[\sum_{n=1}^{\infty} K_n(x) \frac{(-p)^n}{n!}\right] \text{ for } \hat{g}(p, x) \text{ in Eq. (10)},$$

— multiply all terms with $[\hat{g}(p, x)]^{-1}$,
— use the relation

$$\left[\sum_{n=1}^{\infty} a_n y^n\right]^2 = \sum_{n=1}^{\infty} y^n \sum_{m=1}^{n-1} a_m a_{n-m},$$

— sort out coefficients of equal powers of p and take the equation for each coefficient, then we get finally the set of equations

$$k_n(x) = \frac{d}{dx} K_n(x) \tag{18a}$$

$$\left[a(x) + \tfrac{1}{2} b(x) \frac{d}{dx}\right] k_n(x) = -\delta(n, 1) - \sum_{m=1}^{n-1} \frac{n!}{m!(n-m)!} k_m(x) k_{n-m}(x) \tag{18b}$$

and the solution

$$\frac{K_n(x)}{n!} = \int_x^d dy \exp[-C(y)] \int_r^y dz \frac{\exp[C(z)]}{\tfrac{1}{2} b(z)}\left[\delta(n, 1) + \sum_{m=1}^{n-1} \frac{k_m(z)}{m!} \frac{k_{n-m}(z)}{(n-m)!}\right]. \tag{19}$$

Remark: The right-hand sides of Eq. (19) and Eq. (15) are identical for $n = 1$, as should be expected since $M_1 = \mu = K_1$.

Since the cumulants, also called semi-invariants, do not seem very well-known, we list some of their properties.
— The following relations can be directly derived:

$K_1 = M_1 = \mu = $ mean;

$K_2 = M_2 - M_1 = \sigma^2 = $ variance;

$K_3 = M_3 - 3M_1 M_2 + 2M_1^3 = $ third central moment;

$\qquad K_3/\sigma^3 = \gamma_1 = $ skewness;

$K_4 = M_4 - 3M_2^2 - 4M_1 M_3 + 12M_1^2 M_2 - 6M_1^4;$

$\qquad K_4/\sigma^4 = \gamma_2 = $ excess;

— analytical expressions for the cumulants of a large number of distributions are known (ABRAMOWITZ and STEGUN, 1965);
— cumulants are additive for independent processes;
— play a fundamental role in the description of the filtered Poisson process (shot noise);
— they are in a simple algebraical way related to the coefficients of expansions of the probability density in orthogonal polynomials;
— unbiased estimators for estimating the value of cumulants from experimental results are known (tabulated up to $n = 8$ in KENDALL and STUART, 1963);
— the importance of K_n for the description of a physical process decreases in general with increasing n;
— though the sample length required for the estimation, with preassigned reliability and precision, of K_n increases steeply with n, the lower cumulants can be found from relatively short samples.

Because of these properties and since it proved to be possible to derive an exact expression for K_n, we suggest that the cumulants may in a number of cases (unimodal distributions) be well suited for making quantitative connections between theory and experiment.

The First Passage Time Distribution

It would be possible to conclude here the general theoretical part: the relations (15) and (19), which are the most important equations of this paper, can be applied directly on a specific model and quantitative results derived. However, we should like to know how expressions for the probability density of the intervals can be inferred from a knowledge of moments or cumulants. Firstly we have to investigate if the distribution exists for a given sequence of moments.

FELLER [II, VII, **6**, 229—230 (1966)] states that the moments M_n uniquely determine the distribution if

$$\sum_{n=0}^{\infty} M_n \frac{(-p)^n}{n!}$$

converges in an interval $0 \leq p < p_0$.

Since $\exp [\pm C(y)]$ and $b(y)$ are positive for all $r \leq y \leq d$ and $M_1(x) \leq M_1(r)$ for all $r \leq x \leq d$ it is not difficult using Eq. (15), to prove by induction

$$M_n(x)/n! \leq [M_1(r)]^n .$$

The choice of

$$p_0 = [M_1(r)]^{-1}$$

leads then to the conclusion that the interval distribution is uniquely defined if the mean interval is finite, when the post synaptic potential is reset to the lowest possible value: $M_1(r) < \infty$. This will be the case under quite general conditions, including proportional decay of the P.S.P.

The second question is related to the mathematical form of the distribution function. One way to approach this problem is to represent the distribution function by an expansion in orthogonal functions and relate the coefficients with cumulants or moments. The best known expansion for probability density functions is the one in terms of the normal density and its derivatives (Hermite functions). The next section gives this approach and the reasons why this does not seem very promising. Thereafter we demonstrate an expansion based on the gamma density (Laguerre functions).

Both representations give, in theory, a complete description of the probability density function, and in practice approximating expressions which have correct moments up to any desired order. Drawbacks of these methods are that they may result in negative values for the probability density and the goodness of fit does not necessarily increase with the number of terms in the expansion. Another way is to assume the density to be unimodal and take only the first four moments into account. Then it is possible to apply a method devised by PEARSON which is sketched in a later section.

Expansion of the first passage time density in Hermite functions

The density distribution and the characteristic function form a Fourier-related pair

$$\check{g}(\omega) = \int_{-\infty}^{\infty} dt \, e^{i\omega t} g(t) , \qquad (20a)$$

$$g(t) = \frac{1}{2\pi} \int\limits_{-\infty}^{\infty} d\omega\, e^{-i\omega t}\, \check{g}(\omega). \tag{20b}$$

the characteristic function is given by

$$\check{g}(\omega) = \exp\left[\sum_{n=1}^{\infty} K_n \frac{(i\omega)^n}{n!}\right], \tag{21}$$

compare Eq. (16).

We take Eq. (21) and substitute this in Eq. (20b)

$$g(t) = \frac{1}{2\pi} \int\limits_{-\infty}^{\infty} d\omega\, \exp[-i\omega t]\, \exp\left[\sum_{n=1}^{\infty} K_n \frac{(i\omega)^n}{n!}\right]$$

$$= \frac{1}{2\pi} \int\limits_{-\infty}^{\infty} d\omega\, \exp[-i(t-K_1)\omega - \tfrac{1}{2} K_2\omega^2]\, \exp\left[\sum_{n=3}^{\infty} K_n \frac{(i\omega)^n}{n!}\right] \tag{22}$$

Now we define the *quasi-moments* B_n through the relation:

$$\exp\left[\sum_{n=3}^{\infty} K_n \frac{(i\omega)^n}{n!}\right] = \sum_{n=0}^{\infty} B_n \frac{(i\omega)^n}{n!} \tag{23}$$

which gives

$$B_0 = 1 \qquad\qquad B_1 = 0 \qquad\qquad\qquad B_2 = 0$$
$$B_3 = K_3 \qquad\qquad B_4 = K_4 \qquad\qquad\qquad B_5 = K_5$$
$$B_6 = K_6 + 10K_3^2 \qquad B_7 = K_7 + 35K_4K_3 \qquad B_8 = K_8 + 56K_5K_3 + 35K_4^2$$
$$B_n = B_n(K_n, K_{n-1}, \ldots, K_3)$$

Substitution of Eq. (22) in Eq. (23) gives

$$g(t) = \sum_{n=0}^{\infty} \frac{1}{n!} B_n \frac{1}{2\pi} \int\limits_{-\infty}^{\infty} d\omega (i\omega)^n \exp[-i(t-\mu)\omega - \tfrac{1}{2}\sigma^2\omega^2]$$

$$= \sum_{n=0}^{\infty} \frac{B_n}{n!} \left(-\frac{\partial}{\partial t}\right)^n \int\limits_{-\infty}^{\infty} d\omega \frac{1}{2\pi} \exp[-i(t-\mu)\omega - \tfrac{1}{2}\sigma^2\omega^2],$$

but under the integral sign is now precisely the characteristic function of a Gaussian distribution with mean μ and variance σ^2.

So for

$$\varphi\left(\frac{t-\mu}{\sigma}\right) = \frac{1}{\sigma\sqrt{2\pi}} \exp\left[-\tfrac{1}{2}\left(\frac{t-\mu}{\sigma}\right)^2\right]$$

we have

$$g(t) = \sum_{n=0}^{\infty} \frac{B_n}{n!} \left(-\frac{\partial}{\partial t}\right)^n \varphi\left(\frac{t-\mu}{\sigma}\right)$$

$$= \sum_{n=0}^{\infty} \frac{B_n}{n!} \frac{1}{\sigma^n} \varphi_n\left(\frac{t-\mu}{\sigma}\right) \tag{24}$$

with

$$\varphi_n(x) = n\text{th Hermite function}$$

$$= \left(-\frac{\partial}{\partial x}\right)^n \varphi(x)$$

$$= n! \sum_{m=0}^{[n/2]} \frac{(-1)^m\, x^{n-2m}}{2^m\, m!(n-2m)!} \cdot \varphi(x). \tag{25}$$

Conclusion: $\dfrac{B_n}{n!}\dfrac{1}{\sigma^n}$ is the coefficient of the *n*th term of an orthogonal expansion of $g(t)$, or, less exactly, the total quantity we see of $g(t)$ looking through the *n*th Hermite window, centered in μ, width σ. The expansion (24) is known as the Gram-Charlier A series or as the Edgeworth expansion (KENDALL and STUART, 1963).

Theoretically the problem of the interval distribution of output pulses is now solved, since all terms at the right hand side of Eq. (24) are known. However, if we would like to use this procedure for practical purposes, there are two important questions: a) does the series (24) converge? uniformly in x?, b) if the series (24) does converge, how fast?

There are strong indications that the answers to both questions are rather disappointing.

A theorem of CRAMER gives as sufficient, and nearly necessary, conditions for the convergence of the right hand side of Eq. (24):

$g(t)$ of bounded variation and $\displaystyle\int_{-\infty}^{\infty} dt\,|g(t)|\,\exp[t^2/4]$ exists.

At least many of the measured interval distributions have a tail which is not far from exponential, which implies that the integral diverges.

But if the series does not converge the meaning of the orthogonal expansion is questionable and we cannot expect that a finite number of terms (which is all we can take in practice) of the expansion (24) will give a reasonable approximation.

We can understand this more directly from the facts: $g(t) = 0$ for $t < 0$, highly skewed, mode $\neq$ mean, but the normal density $\varphi(t)$ is positive for all t and symmetrical. So the normal density and its derivatives do not seem the appropriate expressions for describing a first passage time density.

The generalized Laguerre functions

For an orthogonal expansion of a function defined on $(0, \infty)$, strongly asymmetrical and with a nearly exponential tail, an expansion in generalized Laguerre functions should be much better.

Definition

$$L_n^{(a)}(x) = \sum_{k=0}^{n} \frac{(-1)^k}{k!}\binom{n+a}{n-k} x^k, \qquad 0 < x < \infty,\; -1 < a \tag{26}$$

the orthogonality relation is

$$\int_0^{\infty} dx\, L_n^{(a)}(x)\, x^a\, e^{-x}\, L_m^{(a)}(x) = \frac{\Gamma(a+n+1)}{\Gamma(n+1)}\,\delta(n, m).$$

So we have as expansion for $g(t)$

$$g(t) = t^a\, e^{-t} \sum_{n=0}^{\infty} d_n\, L_n^{(a)}(t) \tag{27}$$

with the coefficients

$$d_n = \frac{\Gamma(n+1)}{\Gamma(a+n+1)} \int_0^{\infty} dt\, L_n^{(a)}(t)\, g(t)$$

$$= \sum_{k=0}^{n} (-1)^k \frac{\Gamma(n+1)}{\Gamma(n-k+1)\,\Gamma(a+k+1)\,\Gamma(k+1)}\, M_k \tag{28}$$

where

$$M_k = \int\limits_0^\infty dt\ t^k\ g(t) = \langle t^k \rangle$$

is the kth moment of the interval distribution.

The first term of this expansion is the gamma density with parameter $(a+1)$

$$\gamma_{a+1}(t) = \frac{1}{\Gamma(a+1)}\ t^a\ e^{-t}.$$

Pearson distributions

For distributions which have a single mode and smooth contact at the extremities

$$f = 0 \rightarrow \frac{df}{dx} = 0,$$

PEARSON devised a family of distributions, defined by

$$\frac{df(x)}{dx} = \frac{x-a}{b_0 + b_1 x_2 + b_2 x^2} f(x), \qquad a = \text{mode}. \tag{29}$$

A number of well-known distributions belong to this family: Normal, beta, gamma distribution.

The parameters a, b_0, b_1 and b_2 are in a rather simple way related to the first four cumulants.

The type of distributions depends on the value of

$$\varkappa = \frac{\gamma_1^2(\gamma_2 + 6)^2}{4(3\gamma_1^2 - 12 - 4\gamma_2)(3\gamma_1^2 - 2\gamma_2)}.$$

If

$$\varkappa = \infty \longleftrightarrow 2\gamma_2 = 3\gamma_1^2 \longleftrightarrow b_2 = 0$$

then the distribution is a Pearson type III, which is a generalized gamma distribution

$$\gamma_p\left(\frac{x-\alpha}{\beta}\right) = \frac{1}{\beta\Gamma(p)}\left(\frac{x-\alpha}{\beta}\right)^{p-1}\exp\left[-\frac{x-\alpha}{\beta}\right] \tag{30}$$

$$\alpha \le \varkappa < \infty, \qquad -\infty < \alpha < \infty \quad, \quad 0 < p < \infty, \qquad 0 < \beta < \infty$$

where π

$$\alpha = \mu - 2\sigma/\gamma_1, \quad \beta = \tfrac{1}{2}\sigma\gamma_1, \quad p = (2/\gamma_1)^2$$

and the cumulants are

$$K_1 = \alpha + \beta p, \quad K_n = \beta^n p\ \Gamma(n) \text{ for } n \ge 2.$$

(KENDALL and STUART, 1963.)

More investigations will be needed, both theoretically and with regards to experimental results, before it is possible to decide if these methods are useful. We suggest however, that a description of unimodal interval histograms may start from the generalized gamma distribution producing correct mean, variance and skewness. Additional refinements may then be produced by adding terms of the associated Laguerre expansion.

Application to the Diffusion Model with Proportional Decay

This paper started with a specific model for the stochastic activity of a neuron. The results based on the diffusion equation turned out to be quite general.

9*

Now we return to the original model with proportional decay. Not considering refractory properties it is evident that, if the assumptions 1—6 hold, we need only to know: drift $a(z) = m - z/\tau$ and dispersion $b(z) = s^2$.

To gain some insight in the relation between output and input variables Eq. (15) is made more explicit.

The substitution of

$$C(y) = \int^y dz \, \frac{a(z)}{\frac{1}{2} b(z)} = \int^y dz \, \frac{m - z/\tau}{\frac{1}{2} s^2} = -\left(\frac{y - m\tau}{s\sqrt{\tau}}\right)^2$$

in Eq. (15) results in

$$\frac{M_n(x)}{n!} = \frac{2}{s^2} \int_x^d dy \, \exp\left[\left(\frac{y - m\tau}{s\sqrt{\tau}}\right)^2\right] \int_r^y dz \, \exp\left[-\left(\frac{z - m\tau}{s\sqrt{\tau}}\right)^2\right] \frac{M_{n-1}(z)}{(n-1)!}.$$

A change in variables leads to the simpler form:

$$\frac{M_n(X)}{n!} = 2\tau \int_D^X dy \, e^{-y^2} \int_y^R dz \, e^{z^2} \frac{M_{n-1}(z)}{(n-1)!} \tag{31}$$

where

$$X = \frac{m\tau - x}{s\sqrt{\tau}}, \qquad D = \frac{m\tau - d}{s\sqrt{\tau}}, \qquad R = \frac{m\tau - r}{s\sqrt{\tau}}.$$

Eq. (31) allows the conclusion: in the case of proportional decay are the moments of the interval distribution not dependent on all six parameters m, s, τ, x, d, and r, but only on the three dimensionless parameters X, D, and R and the time constant τ.

A further simplification results if we express time in units of the time constant τ and define the, dimensionless, quantity

$$\mu_n = \frac{1}{n!} \frac{M_n}{\tau^n}.$$

Since the model does not contain a reflecting barrier, which would have otherwise only a small effect, $r = -\infty$.

Now Eq. (31) gives

$$\mu_n(X, D) = 2 \int_D^X dy \, e^{y^2} \int_y^\infty dz \, e^{-z^2} \mu_{n-1}(z, D). \tag{32}$$

In particular the equation for the mean interval

$$\mu_1(X, D) = 2 \int_D^X dy \, e^{y^2} \int_y^\infty dz \, e^{-z^2}. \tag{33a}$$

There are various ways to approximate or transform Eq. (33a), of which one seems well fit for numerical computation

$$\mu_1(X, D) = \int_0^\infty du \, e^{-u^2} \frac{e^{-2Du} - e^{-2Xu}}{u}. \tag{33b}$$

A representation as a series is also possible

$$\mu_1(X, D) = \sum_{n=1}^\infty (-2)^{n-1} \frac{\Gamma(n/2)}{\Gamma(n+1)} (X^n - D^n). \tag{33c}$$

From Eq. (32) follows: if time is expressed in units of the time constant τ, then all moments of the interval distribution, and thus also the distribution itself, are only dependent on two combinations of system and input parameters

$$X = \frac{m\tau - x}{s\sqrt{\tau}} \quad , \quad D = \frac{m\tau - d}{s\sqrt{\tau}} .$$

In the limit $s \to 0$, that is the input signal approaches a constant current, it can be derived directly

$$\mu_1(X, D) = \ln \frac{X}{D} = \ln \frac{m\tau - x}{m\tau - d} , \qquad m\tau > d . \tag{34}$$

We are engaged in a numerical evaluation of Eq. (32), which should result in a better understanding of the interrelations between the moments of the interval histogram and the dependency of these moments on the input variables m and s^2.

Application of the Diffusion Model on the Equivalent Circuit of the Membrane

This section is mainly intended as a demonstration of the wide range of possible applications of the diffusion approach and as a first step toward a more accurate

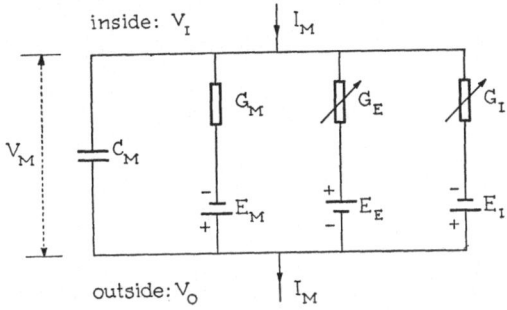

Fig. 4. The equivalent circuit of the membrane

description of the stochastic behaviour of the post synaptic potential and the generation of action potentials.

The model of the membrane is taken here in the form given by RALL(1964). As long as no action potential occurs a small uniform patch of membrane is represented by the circuit of Fig. 4.

The equivalent equation reads

$$I_M = C_M \frac{dV_M}{dt} + G_M(V_M - E_M) + G_E(V_M - E_E) + G_I(V_M - E_I)$$

or

$$\tau \frac{dV}{dt} = -V + I_M R_M + (E_e - V)e + (E_i - V)i , \tag{35}$$

where

$$\tau = C_M/G_M = R_M C_M = \text{membrane time constant},$$
$$V = V_M - E_M , \qquad V_M = V_I - V_0 ,$$
$$E_e = E_E - E_M , \qquad E_i = E_I - E_M ,$$
$$e = G_E/G_M , \qquad i = G_I/G_M .$$

We assume I_M to be constant and the input signal to consist of unpredictable changes in the relative excitatory and inhibitory conductances G_E/G_M and G_I/G_M only means and variances are known

$$m_e = \langle e \rangle \qquad s_e^2 = \langle e^2 \rangle - \langle e \rangle^2$$

$$m_i = \langle i \rangle \qquad s_i^2 = \langle i^2 \rangle - \langle i \rangle^2 .$$

Eq. (35) can be written as

$$\tau \frac{dV}{dt} = [I_M R_M + m_e E_e + m_i E_i] - [m_e + m_i + 1]\, V$$

$$+ s_e(E_e - V) \frac{e - m_e}{s_e} + s_i(E_i - V) \frac{i - m_i}{s_i}$$

or in the simpler looking form

$$\frac{dV}{dt} = m - \beta V + s_e(V)\, n_e(t) + s_i(V)\, n_i(t) \tag{36}$$

with

$$m = \tau^{-1}[I_M R_M + m_e E_e + m_i E_i], \qquad \beta = \tau^{-1}[m_e + m_i + 1],$$
$$s_e(V) = s_e[E_e - V], \qquad\qquad s_i(V) = s_i[E_i - V],$$
$$n_e(t) = \frac{e(t) - m_e}{s_e}, \qquad\qquad n_i(t) = \frac{i(t) - m_i}{s_i}.$$

Under certain conditions it might be justified to approximate $n_e(t)$ and $n_i(t)$ in Eq. (36) through Gaussian white noise with zero mean and unit variance (see appendix A). This leads then to the stochastic differential equation

$$\frac{dV}{dt} = m - \beta V + s(V)\, n(t) \tag{37}$$

with

$n(t) = $ Gaussian white noise ;

$s(V) = s_e(V) + c s_i(V), \; -1 \le c \le 1$, if $n_e(t)$ and $n_i(t)$ are completely correlated;
$s^2(V) = s_e^2(V) + s_i^2(V)$, \qquad if $n_e(t)$ and $n_i(t)$ are totally independent.

Since the autocorrelation function for white noise is a delta-function, it follows from appendix A, that Eq. (37) leads to

drift $\qquad\qquad a(V) = m - \beta V + \tfrac{1}{4} \dfrac{d}{dV} [s(V)]^2 ,$

dispersion $\qquad\quad b(V) = [s(V)]^2 .$

In the case where $n_e(t)$ and $n_i(t)$ are independent

$$a(V) = [\tau^{-1}(I_M R_M + m_e E_e + m_i E_i) + \tfrac{1}{2}(s_e^2 E_e + s_i^2 E_i)]$$
$$- [\tau^{-1}(m_e + m_i + 1) - \tfrac{1}{2}(s_e^2 + s_i^2)]V$$
$$= a_1 - a_2 V , \tag{38a}$$

$$\tfrac{1}{2} b(V) = [s_e^2 E_e^2 + s_i^2 E_i^2] - 2[s_e^2 E_e + s_i^2 E_i]\, V + [s_e^2 + s_i^2]\, V^2$$
$$= a_3 - 2a_4 V + a_5 V^2 . \tag{38b}$$

The behaviour of the post synaptic potential is then described by the diffusion Eqs. (5a, b) with drift and dispersion given by Eqs. (38a, b) and appropriate boundary conditions at the reflecting barrier $V = E_I - E_M$ and at an absorbing barrier $V = V_T - E_M$.

Application of Eq. (15) gives for the nth moment of the first passage time distribution:

$$M_n(V) = n \int_V^{VT-EM} dy \exp[-C(y)] \int_{EI-EM}^y dz \frac{\exp[C(z)]}{\frac{1}{2} b(z)} M_{n-1}(z) \qquad (39)$$

with

$$C(y) = \int^y dz \frac{a(z)}{\frac{1}{2} b(z)} = \int^y dz \frac{a_1 - a_2 z}{a_3 - 2a_4 z + a_5 z^2}$$

$$= -\frac{a_2}{a_5} \ln(a_3 - 2a_4 y + a_5 y^2) + \frac{a_1 a_5 - a_2 a_4}{a_5 \sqrt{a_3 a_5 - a_4^2}} \operatorname{arctg}\left[\frac{-a_4 + a_5 y}{\sqrt{a_3 a_5 - a_4^2}}\right]. \qquad (39a)$$

The description of this section takes more properties of the membrane into account then the proportional decay model of the preceding paragraph; as a consequence it contains also more parameters.

It appears that this more precise description will only make sense quantitively, if the values of all parameters and variables can be measured and proper regard is paid to the geometrical properties of the neuron.

The Refractory Period

The formulation of a simplifying description of the refractory effects, resulting from the Hodgkin-Huxley equations combined with the geometrical properties of the membrane, is not obvious.

The usual approach is to consider the threshold as a time dependent quantity:

$$d(t) = d + d_R(t - s).$$

Here s is the time at which the latest output pulse started and $d_R(u)$ is a function which decreases from infinity at $u = 0$ to zero at $u = \infty$. This model is, at least in the present context, not analytically tractable. We present now two descriptions of the refractory period. Description (a) resembles the traditional one and seems also unsuited for mathematical treatment. Description (b), though conceptually completely different, will in practice not give large quantitative deviations from the results of (a); approach (b) will appear to be amenable to mathematical analysis.

Let s be as defined before and $i(u)$ a function such that $i(u) > 0$ for all $u > 0$ and

$$\int_0^\infty du\, i(u) = \infty,$$

(a) For $t > s$ all distances are magnified with a factor $[i(t - s)]^{-1}$,

then

$$d(t) = \frac{d}{i(t - s)}.$$

Though the same holds for

$$x(t) = \frac{x}{i(t - s)}$$

and

$$r(t) = \frac{r}{i(t - s)},$$

this has no consequences if $x = 0$ and $r = -\infty$, and only a small effect for $x \ll d$ and $r < 0$. Some reflection leads to the conclusion that this space transformation is equivalent with a multiplication of drift $a(x)$ with $i(t-s)$ and dispersion $b(x)$ with $[i(t-s)]^2$, while leaving space unchanged.

(b) For $t>s$ all processes are slowed down with a factor $i(t-s)$. This is equivalent with a multiplication of $a(x)$ as well as $b(x)$ with $i(t-s)$, while not transforming time.

Though (a) might be preferable on physiological grounds, we choose (b) for the reasons already mentioned. The difference between the two descriptions bears only on the dispersion and is quantitatively small.

One more *assumption* has then to be added to the six already describing the neural model:

7. If the latest output pulse started at s,

then for $t>s$:
$$a(x, t) = i(t-s)\, a(x),$$
$$b(x, t) = i(t-s)\, b(x),$$

with $i(u)$ as defined.

The way to treat the refractory effect is then to define a transformed time

$$I(t-s) = \int_0^{t-s} du\, i(u) ,$$

in terms of which the Eqs. (5a, b) can be made homogeneous and the resulting equations analogous to those already derived for the non-refractory case. We omit the mathematical proofs and present only two final theorems.

If: drift $a(y)$ and dispersion $b(y)$ result in
interval probability density: $g(t)$,
and cumulative distribution: $G(t)$;

then: drift $i(t)\, a(y)$ and dispersion $i(t)\, b(y)$ result in
interval probability density: $g_R(t) = i(t)\, g[I(t)]$,
and cumulative distribution: $G_R(t) = G[I(t)]$. $\qquad$ (40)

If: drift $a(y)$ and dispersion $b(y)$ result in the moments of the interval probability density $g(t)$:

$$M_n = \int_0^\infty dt\, t^n g(t) ,$$

$t(I)$ is the inverse function of $I(t)$ and

$$[t(I)]^n = \sum_m a_{nm} I_m ,$$

drift $i(t)\, a(y)$ and dispersion $i(t)\, b(y)$ result in moments of the interval probability density $g_R(t)$:

$$M_{Rn} = \int_0^\infty dt\, t^n\, g_R(t) ;$$

then:

$$M_{Rn} = \sum_m a_{nm} M_m . \qquad (41)$$

It will be evident that non-monotonic forms of $i(u)$ may lead to multimodal distributions.

Discussion and Summary

The main purpose of this paper is an investigation of the scope, limitations and analytical results of diffusion models for the time course of the post synaptic potentials of formalized neurons and the resulting intervals between output pulses.

In mathematical respects, there is not much new here, most of it can be found in the quoted references and other books on stochastic processes. On the other hand, the results of probability theory and the theory of stochastic processes presented here have, to our knowledge not yet been systematically explored with respect to the distributions of neural firing intervals.

The important limitation of the diffusion approach is related to the input signal: the full complexities of the time configurations of the input sequence are not taken into account, but it is considered as (white, Gaussian) noise of which the average value and the power (or the sum of excitation and inhibition and the proportion of excitation and inhibition) are the effective, informationally significant quantities. This amounts to assuming that the input consists of many independent contributions of short duration, each of these changing the P.S.P. by only a small amount: 10% or less of the distance between equilibrium and threshold value. For an alternative approach see SEGUNDO, PERKEL and MOORE (1966).

It is evident that this assumption has important consequences for the possibilities of application to real neurons.

On the basis of this hypothesis two partial differential equations are derived for the transition probabilities of the P.S.P. (5a, b). The formulation of these equations is such a general one, that it allows the effect of incoming excitation and inhibition on the P.S.P. to be dependent in an arbitrary way on the existing value of this P.S.P.

The interval distribution for the generation of action potentials appears to be logically equivalent to the first passage time distribution, which fact is then expressed in Eq. (9) based on the backward diffusion equation for a stationary input (6b).

Since the derived partial differential equation for the first passage time distribution is in general not solvable, we take Laplace transforms, which results in the equally unsolvable ordinary differential Eq. (10). However, a series expansion of its Laplace-transform (or its logarithm) leads finally to a set of solvable equations for the moments (or cumulants): Eqs. (14a, b) and Eqs. (18a, b).

The solution of these equations forms the central result of this paper: a formula for the nth moment (cumulant) in terms of the previous moment (cumulants): Eq. (15) and Eq. (19).

These expressions contain a double integral, which for most models must be computed numerically but which also might supply some general information on M_n: ratio M_n/M_{n-1}, dependency on parameters. The concepts of drift $a(x)$ and dispersion $b(x)$ have a central position in derivation and results.

At this stage in the development of the theory, we want to draw attention to the fact that knowledge of the properties of a probabilistic variable X can be expressed in several complementary ways, which are (nearly always) unequivocally interrelated:

(a) probability density function: $f(x)$,

(b) characteristic function: $\check{f}(k)$,

(c) sequence of moments: $M_0, M_1, M_2, \ldots,$

(d) sequence of cumulants: $K_0, K_1, K_2, \ldots,$

(e) sequence of coefficients of orthogonal expansion: $C_0, C_1, C_2, \ldots$.

A summary of the relations between the different descriptions is given in the diagram of Fig. 5.

If the stochastic variable does only assume values between zero and infinity, Laplace instead of Fourier transformation can be used and an analogous diagram constructed.

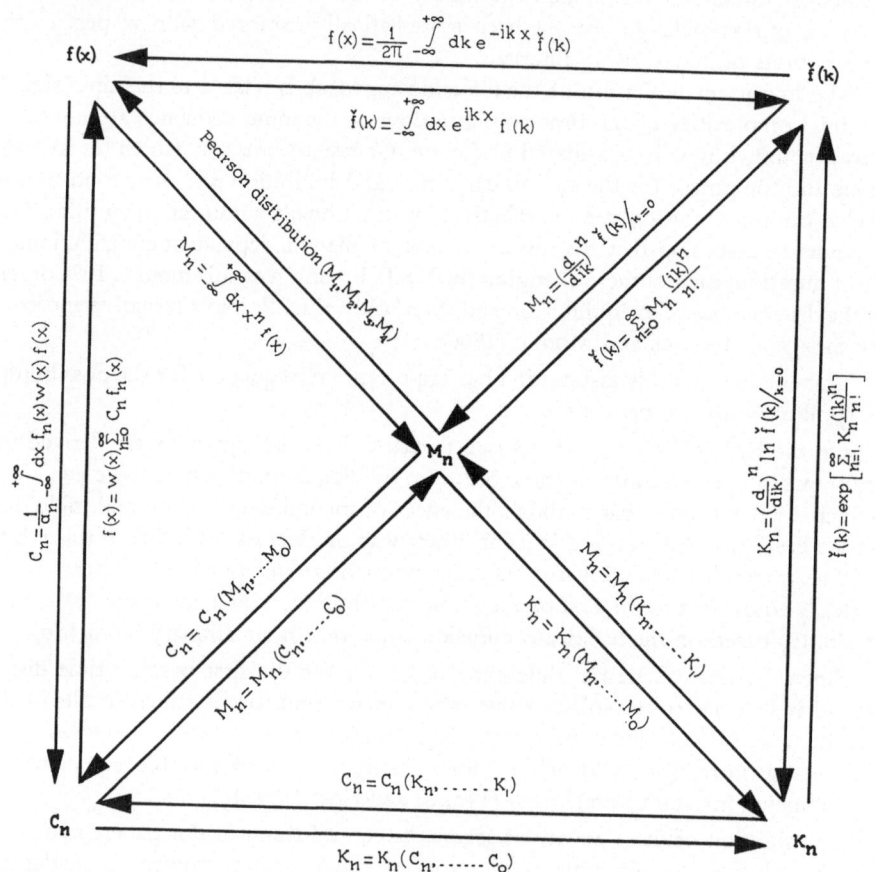

Fig. 5. Diagram of the relations between functions and sequences characterizing a stochastic variable

With the exception of the Pearson distribution, which is an approximation that takes only the first four moments into account, all representations give a complete description.

There are other ways of presenting partial knowledge, for instance: location of mode and quantiles or the fact that the stochastic variable is limited to positive values. These data are sometimes difficult to connect with some of the representations given in the diagram.

Usually we prefer to present our knowledge by the probability density $f(x)$, which can easily be compared qualitively with histograms resulting from experiments, though it is not always easy to fit parameters and to evaluate the goodness of fit.

However, there are stochastic variables which allow determination of moments or cumulants, but for which no closed expression for the probability density is known. Most of the stable distributions belong to this group (GERSTEIN and MANDELBROT, 1964) and we have the strong impression that this is also the case for many of the distributions of intervals between action potentials.

The representations in terms of moments, cumulants or orthogonal coefficients can easily be interchanged. The choice of the representation will depend on the purpose of the investigation. The cumulants have the benefit that they are closely connected with well known measures (mean, variance, skewness, excess); the coefficients of a Laguerre expansion may be better suited if the form of the interval histogram is the subject of interest. If the interval histogram is satisfactorily described by a gamma type probability density, the first three cumulants or the parameters p, α and β contain sufficient information. Advantages of moments and cumulants are also that there is much known about their sampling statistics, so that different values in successive experiments can be compared with respect to their probabilistic significance, and that the results of a number of experiments can be presented in one graph, which allows a better evaluation.

Though some of the conclusions of this paper are yet rather preliminary, they seem to argue in favour of a double presentation of experimental results for the stochastic activity of neurons under stationary conditions: to add to the usual presentation in the forms of histograms a complementary one in the form of a table with the values of the lower cumulants. If a digital computer is already used for the reduction of experimental data, this would increase the work by only a small amount.

Further investigations of the differences resulting from the use of the membrane equivalent circuit rather than the simple RC-circuit is needed before it is possible to decide whether or not it will justify the extra complications.

The theorem for the refractory properties gives a theoretically satisfactory solution, but may be unwieldy for applications.

Work on the numerical evaluation of the equations for the model with proportional decay is on the way; the outcome will be compared with results of simulation of the same model.

The limits of applicability and precision of the given approach are, apart from the assumptions already made, determined by two facts.

— The description of the timecourse of the P.S.P. combined with a threshold condition is a simplified one-variable model substituted for the four coupled nonlinear differential equations relating four variables needed for the description of the state of a neuron.

— First order Markov processes, as assumed in this paper, do not describe the decremental conduction of POISSON distributed incoming pulses through the dendrites. This process is non-Markovian and no ways of handling first passage times in this case are known; for an approximate description a Markov process of at least second order would be needed.

The methods and results set forth in this paper may be useful in connection with the following problems.

— Definition of and relation between input and output variables under stationary conditions.

— Interrelations between the cumulants of the interval histogram; in particular standard deviation as a function of mean.

— Interpretation of the experimental evidence indicating that for a given neuron, all interval distributions with the same mean have an identical shape, regardless of stimulus or other conditions [Hermann and Olsen (1967), Poggio and Viernstein (1964)].

Appendix A

Approximative description of a physical process by diffusion equations (see Cumming, 1967).

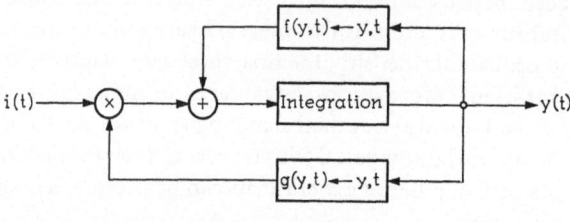

$$\frac{dy}{dt} = f(y,t) + g(y,t) \cdot i(t)$$

Fig. 6. Diagram of a general first order nonlinear system

We start from the equation

$$\frac{dy}{dt} = f(y, t) + g(y, t) i(t) \qquad (A\,1)$$

$i(t)$ is a strongly fluctuating signal, too complicated to know or predict its behaviour completely. Therefore we describe $i(t)$ as a stochastic quantity, of which only mean and correlation function are known:

$$m(t) \;\; = \langle i(t) \rangle,$$
$$R(t, \tau) = \langle j(t) \cdot j(t - \tau) \rangle, \qquad j(t) = i(t) - m(t),$$
$$= \text{autocorrelation function at time } t \text{ and with delay } \tau.$$

We write Eq. (A 1) now as

$$\frac{dy}{dt} = h(y, t) + g(y, t) j(t) \qquad (A\,2)$$

where: $h(y, t) = f(y, t) + g(y, t) m(t)$ represents the drift,
$\quad\quad\quad m(t) =$ average input signal,
$\quad\quad\quad g(y, t) =$ state- and time-dependent effectiveness of noise,
$\quad\quad\quad j(t) =$ zero mean noise with known autocorrelation function.

Conditions:

a) It is possible to define for the system a time constant τ_s,

b) there exists a correlation time τ_c for the noise-like input signal such that $R(t, \tau) \simeq 0$ for $\tau \gg \tau_c$,

c) correlation time of input small with respect to the time constant of the system: $\tau_c \ll \tau_s$.

Remarks:

ad a): τ_s is related with $\langle f(y, t)/y \rangle$ and/or with $\langle [\sqrt{R(t, 0)} \frac{\partial}{\partial y} yg(y, t)]^{-1} \rangle$.

ad b): this implies

$$\int_0^T d\tau \, R(t, \tau) \simeq \int_0^\infty d\tau \, R(t, \tau) \text{for } T \geq \tau_c .$$

Definitions:

$$S(t) = \int_0^\infty d\tau \, R(t, \tau) \qquad S^*(t) = \int_{-\infty}^0 d\tau \, R(t, \tau)$$

$$f(y, t \mid x, s) = \text{transition probability} = P[Y(t) = y \mid Y(s) = x] ;$$

$$A_n(y, t; \Delta t) = \frac{1}{\Delta t} \int_{-\infty}^\infty dz \, z^n f(y + z, t + \Delta t \mid y, t) .$$

Under the given conditions it is possible to show for $\Delta t \gg \tau_c$:

drift $\qquad\qquad a(y, t) = A_1(y, t; \Delta t) = h(y, t) + \frac{1}{2} S(t) \frac{\partial}{\partial y} [g(y, t)]^2 \qquad$ (A 3a)

and

dispersion $\qquad\quad b(y, t) = A_2(y, t; \Delta t) = [g(y, t)]^2 \cdot [S(t) + S^*(t)] \qquad$ (A 3b)

are both independent of Δt.

Now Eq. (A 2) can be replaced by

$$\Delta y = a(y, t) \Delta t + b(y, t) \Delta W(t), \qquad \text{for } \Delta t \gg \tau_c \qquad \text{(A 4)}$$

where $W(t)$ is integrated white noise.

Eqs. (A 4) and (A 2) result in the same drift and dispersion for $\Delta t \gg \tau_c$. The behaviour of the transition probability can then be described by Eq. (5a).

CUMMING reaches the conclusion:

The diffusion process is a "diffusion model of" or an "equivalent diffusion process for" the physical process in the following sense the solution of the Fokker-Planck equation [Eq. (5a)] gives approximate values for the transition probability density $f(y, t \mid x, s)$ of the physical process, for values of t sufficiently far removed from the "initial condition time" s so that $t - s \gg \tau_c$. The approximation is valid as long as the response time of the physical process τ_s is much greater than the memory time of the physical noise τ_c. Though CUMMING does not treat the backward equation, general physical considerations indicate that an analogous derivation, interchanging $S(t)$ and $S^*(t)$, should apply.

Appendix B

Because of the fundamental nature and the importance of Eqs. (5a, b) we make some remarks:

— They have several names: a) and b): Kolmogorov equations, diffusion equations; a): Fokker-Planck equation, forward (diffusion) equation; b): Chapman-Kolmogorov equation, backward (diffusion) equation.

— Derivation and treatment of these equations can be found in many of the books on stochastic processes.

— As a rule the forward equation is the most easy to derive, the backward sometimes the easiest to solve.

— Note the difference in position of the differentiation with respect to y in Eq. (5a)
and to x in Eq. (5b).

— They describe stochastic phenomena in several different situations: Brownian
motion, diffusion, heat conduction, thermal noise, population genetics.

— The theory of the Brownian motion is the most suitable for a physical interpretation of the equations: x and y are space coordinates of particle at time s and time t,
$a(y, t) = $ drift, average velocity, $b(y, t) = $ dispersion, variance of displacements
$f(y, t \mid x, s) = $ probability density for transition from x at time s to y at time t.
The Brownian motion language is used several times for explanation of mathematical operations.

— If in Eq. (5a) $a(y, t) = m - y/\tau$, $b(y, t) = s^2$ then this equation is identical with
Eq. (4).

— The diffusion equations give an approximate description for the neural model,
which is better as n_e and n_i are larger and e and i smaller; they are exact descriptions
in the limits: $n_e \to \infty$, $n_i \to \infty$ and $e \to 0$, $i \to 0$ where at the same time $m = n_e e + n_i i$
and $s^2 = n_e e^2 + n_e i$ remain constant.

— The assumption that there is only one size of excitatory (e) and one size of inhibitory input (i) is not necessary at all, we can take directly $m = $ average input,
$s^2 = $ variance of input.

— A rather different looking neural model, sometimes used in the literature, is given
in Fig. 7.

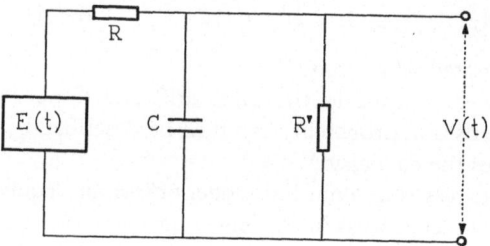

Fig. 7. The simple RC-model

$E(t)$ represents a voltage source and $E(t) = m + s n(t)$, where $n(t) = $ Gaussian
white noise and m and s are constants. The stochastic differential equation for $V(t)$

$$\tau \frac{dV}{dt} = - \alpha V + E(t), \quad \alpha = \frac{R + R'}{R'} \frac{1}{\tau}, \quad \tau = RC$$

leads, without any approximation to the diffusion Eq. (5) with: $a(y, t) = m - y/\tau$,
$b(y, t) = s^2$.

— The stochastic differential equation

$$\frac{dy}{dt} = \alpha(y, t) + \beta(y, t) n(t),$$

where $n(t) = $ Gaussian white noise, results in diffusion Eq. (5), with

drift $\qquad\qquad a(y, t) = \alpha(y, t) + \tfrac{1}{4} \frac{d}{dy} [\beta(y, t)]^2 ,$

dispersion $\qquad b(y, t) = [\beta(y, t)]^2 .$

Appendix C

A simpler derivation of the solvable equation for the moments [Eq. (13)] from the unsolvable equation for the first passage time distribution [Eq. (9)]. Starting from the last equation

$$\frac{\partial}{\partial t} g(t, x) = Q\left(x, \frac{\partial}{\partial x}\right) g(t, x) \tag{C 1}$$

— multiplication of both sides with t^n,
— integration of t from 0 to ∞

$$\int_0^\infty dt\, t^n \frac{\partial}{\partial t} g(t, x) = \int_0^\infty dt\, t^n Q\left(x, \frac{\partial}{\partial x}\right) g(t, x),$$

— partial integration of left hand side,

— use of $t^n\, g(t, x)\Big|_0^\infty = 0,$

— change of the order of operations in right hand side,

— use of $M_n(x) = \int_0^\infty dt\, t^n g(t, x),$

results in

$$Q\left(x, \frac{\partial}{\partial x}\right) m_n(x) = -\, n M_{n-1}(x), \tag{C 2}$$

the solvable equation for the moments.

Acknowledgement. The author wishes to express his gratitude to Prof. Dr. A. J. H. VENDRIK for his guidance and unlimited confidence, to Dr. B. McA. SAYERS for the kind hospitality enjoyed as a visitor to the section Engineering in Medicine, to Prof. Dr. J. D. COWAN for many stimulating discussions and expositions of inspiring perspectives in biophysics, to Mr. P. LYNN for his collaboration and friendship.

References

ABRAMOWITZ, M., and STEGUN (Ed.): Handbook of mathematical functions. Dover: 1965. London.

CHANDRASEKHAR, S.: Stochastic problems in physics and astronomy. In: WAX: Selected papers on noise and stochastic processes. Dover — New York.

COX, D. R., and H. A. MILLER: The theory of stochastic processes: Methuen 1965. London.

CUMMING, I. G.: Computing aspects of problems in non-linear prediction and filtering. Ph. D.-thesis, Imperial College, University of London 1967.

FELLER, W.: An introduction to probability theory and its applications, II: Wiley 1966. London.

FETZ, E. E., and C. L. GERSTEIN: An RC-model for spontaneous activity of single neurons. M.I.T., Quarterly Progress Rep. **71**, 249—256 (1963).

GERSTEIN, G. L., and B. MANDELBROT: Random walk model for the spike activity of a single neuron. Biophys. J. **4**, 41—68 (1964).

GLUSS, B.: A model for neuron firing with exponential decay of potential resulting in diffusion equations for probability density. Bull. Math. Biophysics. **29**, 233—243 (1967).

HERMANN, H. T., and R. E. OLSEN: Dynamic statistics of crayfish caudal photoreceptors. Biophys. J. **7**, 279—296 (1967).

TEN HOOPEN, M.: Probabilistic firing of neurons considered as a first passage problem. Biophys. J. **6**, 435—451 (1966).

Kendall, M. G., and A. Stuart: The advanced theory of statistics, Vol. I: Griffin 1963. London.

Kiang, N. Y.: Discharge patterns of single fibres in the cat's auditory nerve. M.I.T. Research Monograph No. 35 (1965).

Kimura, M.: Diffusion models in population genetics. Methuen's review series in applied probability, 1964. Lnndon.

Middleton, D.: An introduction to statistical communication theory: McGraw-Hill 1960. London.

Moore, G. P., D. H. Perkel, and J. P. Segundo: Statistical analysis and functional interpretation of neuronal spike data. Ann. Rev. Physiol. 28, 493—522 (1966).

Poggio, G. F., and L. J. Viernstein: Time series analysis of impulse sequences ot thalamic somatic sensory neurons. J. Neurophysiol. 27, 517—545 (1964).

Prabhu, N. U.: Stochastic processes: Basic theory and its applications: MacMillan, Mc Craw-Hill 1965. London.

Rall, W.: Theoretical significance of dendritic trees for neuronal input output relations. In: Reiss: Neural theory and modeling, 1964.

Segundo, J. P., D. H. Perkel, and G. P. Moore: Spike probability in neurons: Influence of temporal structure in the train of synaptic events. Kybernetik 3, 67—82 (1966).

Stein, R. B.: A theoretical analysis of neuronal variability. Biophys. J. 5, 173—194 (1965).

— Some models of neuronal variability. Biophys. J. 7, 37—68 (1967).

Stevens, C. F.: Letter to the editor. Biophys. J. 4, 417—419 (1964).

Stratonovich, R. L.: Topics in the theory of random noise, Vol. I: Gordon and Breach 1963. New York.

Statistical Approach to the Study of Neural Networks *

J.-Cl. Levy

Centre d'Etudes et de Recherches en Automation, 78, Velizy-Villaconblay, France

Introduction

We study here a model of the function of neural networks; our aim is not to obtain a faithful reproduction of the physiological properties of living neurons by means of mathematical analysis assisted by physiological experimentation, but rather a general theoretical approach to the study of neural phenomena. We are fully aware of its shortcomings deriving from the lack of experimental testing and exhaustive evidence.

We start with a model of the nerve cell and elaborate this model so as to realize the same elementary properties observed in the behaviour of organisms having nervous systems.

In the present state of the study, it is only possible to define some analogies to this behaviour, but some relevant theoretical results can already be obtained. This is apparent from the fact that the modification of certain parameters, defined at the level of the cell, causes characteristic modifications in the behaviour of the system. If such a correlation can be verified "in vivo" on living organisms, the present theory is well satisfied. Moreover, it is interesting that we find, even approximately, many properties analogous to those exhibited by the cells of biological systems.

The present work is not to be taken as a piece of pure mathematics, but rather as a set of ideas which may point the way to progressively deeper and more rigorous nvestigations and experimentations.

1. First Approach; von Neumann's Model of the Cell

Von Neumann's Boolean model is very elementary, but each microcell acts here only as a component of a macrocell, which will be, in turn, considered as a "population of cells" whose properties can be defined in a purely statistical manner.

We know that von Neumann's model is defined as follows: Being at the time t:

p the number of positive excitations which arrive on it,

n the number of negative or inhibitory excitations. The output signal at time $t + \theta$ is: $v = \gamma(p - n - \sigma)$, where γ is the Heaviside function step and σ is a threshold which is physiologically defined for the cell.

Now we consider a macrocell E formed by a number of microcells equal to r. This assembly receives P positive excitations and N negative excitations. We define reduced variables:

$$X = P/r \,,$$
$$Y = N/r \,.$$

---

* Research carried out under contract with the Direction des Recherches et Moyens d'Essais.

The distribution of these excitations on the r microcells is made according to the following principle: each connection carrying an excitation has an equal probability of attaining one or other of the r microcells. The theory is similar to that of ferromagnetism. It then gives the average value of the proportion F of cells which are excited at time $t + \theta$, when we know X and Y at time t. Let M be the total number of firing cells

$$F(X,Y) = m/r \leq 1$$

For a given value of Y, the function $F(X)$ has the classical shape of a ferromagnetic characteristic, or, in another sense, of the characteristic of a diode with cut-off linear shape and saturation.

Remarks. F is only the average value of a random function, but as soon as r rises to about a hundred, the dispersion is so weak that this function can be replaced by its average value and thus considered as an ordinary function.

From this point on, we shall consider only the macrocell, which in turn is the functional element representing a component of a larger system. Therefore, let us consider these levels of integration:

Microcells, indistinguishible among themselves. Each of them is only a member of a population.

Macrocells, composed of microcells. Each of them is only a functional element of the whole system.

The whole system, composed of macrocells or elements. Its "specificity" consists of the relations between elements.

Finally, we shall consider the fact that the connection between elements is to be defined only by means of a "density of connections", called "connectivity".

In the present stage of the work all the calculations have been performed by tabulating the characteristics which were statistically defined on an assembly of von Neumann cells.

2. Second Approach

Cells considered as being modulated by pulse density.
We suppose then an assembly of microcells, and we consider the total number of spikes arriving at that assembly:
spike density can be considered as a continuous function of time: $d(t)$.
The Cells emit in their turn, spikes whose density is also a function of time: $D(t)$.
As far as we can tell, no complete theory has yet been given which takes into account the hypothesis of statistical distributions of the spikes. But it is easy to foresee that the properties of such a system are comparable with those of the preceeding one.

$D(d)$ is comparable to $F(x)$.

We have a cut-off, if we remain below the threshold of the cells. We have a linear shape followed by saturation when each cell emits its maximum spike density according to the refractory periods. According to the available evidence, we can assume that, by the action of a negative feedback $D = d$ in steady condition, in practice, saturation does not occur.

Remarks. If we compare this hypothesis with the results of our calculations, we can see that in practice *saturation is never attained.*

We have then obtained results which are, in principle, compatible with real neural networks.

Moreover, the improvement of the characteristics of linearity can only favor the good operation of a system.

The system was then tested under conditions even more difficult than the actual ones.

Definition of delay

The principle of von Neumann's model is based on a constant synaptic delay θ.

Let $d(t)$ be the spike density received by a cell. Its synaptic potential is then given by the product of composition

$$\Phi(t) = \int_0^T \varphi(\tau)\, d(t - \tau)\, d\tau$$

$\varphi(\tau) =$ the average value of synaptic potential produced at the time t by a spike arriving at time 0.

T is the period in which $\varphi(\tau) > 0$.

Let us assume now that the function $d(t)$ is linear during the time from 0 to T and et us write it in the form

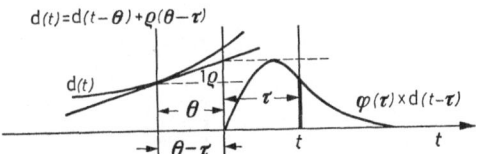

Fig. 1. Use of postsynaptic response curve

In fact the coefficient of P is

$$t - \tau - (t - \theta) = \theta - \tau$$

we have then

$$\Phi(t) = \int_0^T \varphi(\tau)\, [d(t - \theta) + \varrho(\theta - t)]\, d\tau$$

$$= d(t - \theta) \int_0^T \varphi(\tau)\, d\tau + \varrho \left[\theta \int_0^T \varphi(\tau)\, d\tau - \int_0^T \varphi(\tau)\, \tau\, d\tau \right].$$

We see that the coefficient of ϱ equals 0 if

$$\theta = \int_0^T \tau\varphi(\tau)\, d\tau \Big/ \int_0^T \varphi(\tau)\, d\tau.$$

Otherwise θ is the abscissa of the center of gravity of the curve $\varphi(\tau)$. Under these conditions $\Phi(t)$ is independent of the slope ϱ of the curve $d(t)$ and depends only on its value at time $t - \theta$.

Thus θ is a sampling period which is well-defined by physiological data. According to a hypothesis which is not very restrictive, the method of step-by-step calculation, established for von Neumann's model, is equally valid for a system composed

10*

of real neurons. Moreover, our calculations confirm this hypothesis with a 10% error approximation.

Remarks. A corrective term can easily be calculated using the curvature of the function $d(t)$.

3. Definition of a Non Self-Organizing System

The system is built from a certain number of elements. Each of these is defined by the characteristic $F(X, Y)$, which is the same for all elements, and by a synaptic delay θ which, according to the restrictions given above, can be considered the same for all elements.

Between the two elements, E_j and E_i, there exists a coupling coefficient A_{ij}.

Let $F_i(t)$ be at time t the output of E_i and X_j the input of E_j; we have

$$X_j(t) = \sum_i A_{ij} F_i(t) + S_j(t) .$$

S_i is a signal coming from outside.

The inhibition $Y(t)$ is the same for all elements and is determined by a regulating system which is described as follows:

At time t we calculate

$$SF(t) = \sum_i r_i F_i(t) .$$

This function corresponds to the total number of microcells which fired at time t.

We calculate now

$$Y(t) = B \cdot [SF(t)]^2 .$$

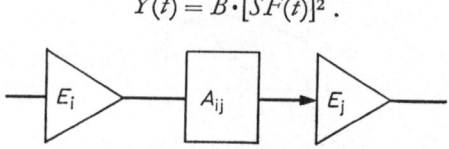

Fig. 2. Dynamic association

The evolution of the system is then calculated step by step. We name a step: iteration.

Remarks. The need for a quadratic law was evident by the first tests, since the linear law had no regulatory action.

In physiological systems this operation is performed by means of special circuits. This is in accordance with Professor Rall's lecture.

4. Utilization of the System

Each macrocell, or element, is specific for a component S, of the input signal, or of the signal given by the system response.

Each relation A_{ij} corresponds to a directive association from E_i to E_j, that is to say, the firing of E_i tends to cause the firing of E_j, and this with a time delay.

A coefficient A_{ij} is then the materialization of a temporal association.

The simplest example we can give is that of the syllables of a word, with association between consecutive syllables.

Each syllable is materialized by an element.

A purely special association is materialized by two coefficients.

Elements E_i and E_j, for example, materialize two simultaneous signals corresponding to two parts of the same picture.

Now let us come back to the first case. If we have materialized the syllables of a word, and if an input signal from outside is applied to the first elements, the system will find by itself the successive elements, thus completing the word from memory.

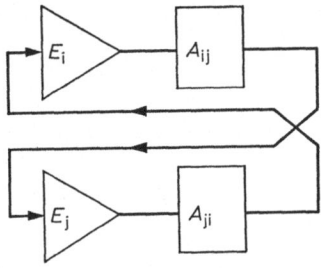

Fig. 3. Static association

This process will be described in more detail when we speak about self-organizing systems.

5. Self-Organizing Systems

The purpose of the operation is to build an associative memory: if an element E_j is fired after an element E_i, the system memorizes the temporal association $E_i - E_j$, that is to say, it learns that when E_i has fired, E_j will fire at the following iteration.

That means that the coefficient A_{ij} has to be increased. We use the following algorism:

$$A_{ij}(t + \theta) = A_{ij}(t) + \alpha r_i\, F_i(t) \cdot F_j(t + \theta)\, [1 - A_{ij}(t)/Am]\, .$$

Where r_i is the number of microcells contained in the element E_j.

α is a conditional probability establishing a new relation between two microcells, one belonging to E_j, the other to E_i A_m is a maximum value resulting from the number of connections it is possible to establish according to the anatomical configuration of the system.

This algorithm can be defined from Hebb's principle which corresponds to the "facilitation" of the transmission of synapses.

This algorithm is still valid even if $i = j$, when A_{ii} means a feedback.

This feedback acts when an element fires during consecutive iterations, and then it builds a memory by reverberating circuits.

Moreover, each microcell has its own memory. So an element E_i which fired at time t can fire at time $t + \theta$ even if it does not receive any input signal. Then it can build the feedback coefficient A_{ij}. This memory will be called dynamic memory.

6. Reproduction of a Dynamic Pattern

1. Recording

Let a system be built with a certain number of elements. A word is defined as an arrangement of elements, each corresponding to the choice of a syllable.

Let $S_1, S_2, \ldots S_i \ldots S_n$ be the syllables of a word. Let $E_1, E_2 \ldots E_i \ldots E_n$ be the specific elements of the syllables having the same index.

This means that the syllable S_i is identified, an input signal is injected into element E_i.

Let us now suppose that each signal S_i is applied to an iteration:
E_1 fires at iteration 1
E_2 fires at iteration 2.
The system builds coupling coefficients:

$$A_{1,2} \text{ thus } A_{2,3} \ldots A_{i g i+1} .$$

Now, according to the dynamic memory, E_1 has still a remaining output at time 2, as has E_2 at time 3.

$$A_{1,3} \text{ thus } A_{2,3} \ldots A_{i,i+2}$$

but $A_{1,3} < A_{1,2}$

We can also have relations like $A_{i,i+3}$ and so on, up to the time when the value of these coefficients is negligible.

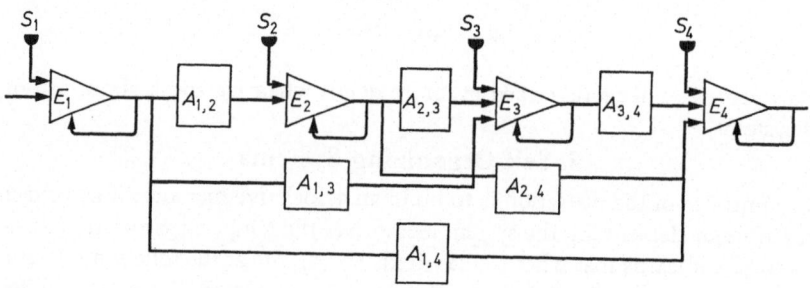

Fig. 4. Structure of a dynamic pattern

2. Interrogation-response

After recording an input sequential signal, we applied signals corresponding to the first components of the sequence. $S_1, S_2 \ldots S$ applied respectively to $E_1, E_2 \ldots E$.

Then the system generates a wave which at each iteration corresponds to the firing of consecutive elements.

Then we verify that this wave continues to propagate itself up to the elements E_i having $i > l$.

This propagation proceeds at a somewhat lower level and a slightly decreased speed (10—20%).

The system is then able to repeat from memory the end of a sequence whose beginning was given to it.

This operation has been performed by simulation on a digital computer.

3. Recognition of the Sequence

If we inject into the first element of a chain a powerful input signal, this can generate the firing of the other elements of the chain, one after the other successively.

Now inject into E_1 a signal which can only generate a weak output F_1 and so on. All the S_1 signals are equal to each other.

The input signal injected into E_2 will be

$$X_2(t) = S_2 + F_1(t) A_{1,2} > S_2 .$$

The input signal of E_3 will be

$$X_3(t + \theta) = S_3 + F_2(t + \theta) A_{2,3} + F_1(t + \theta) A_{1,3} > X_2(t)$$

and so on.

We can see the effect of accumulation, and the wave amplitude increases rapidly. At each step, the system has to verify the relation between the element E_j, which is fired by the memory, and the input signal S_j which is injected into it.

This is the process of dynamic pattern recognition

4. Redundancy

Now let us assume that some components of the input signal are missing, for example $S_i = 0$ and $F_i[t + (i + 1)\theta] = 0$

$$X_{i+1}[t + (i+1)\,\theta] = S_{i+1} + A_{i-1,\,i+1}\,F_{i-1}\,[t + (i+1)\,\theta] > S_{i+1}\,.$$

We can see that the integration of the signal can be achieved by means of the secondary relations, even if some components are missing.

5. Synchronisation

Let us assume that the interrogative signal $S_1, S_2 \ldots S$ be distributed at a velocity which is different from that of the recorded signal.

For example, with double velocity

iteration 1 input signal → S_1
iteration 2 input signal → S_3
iteration 3 input signal → S_5

or with half velocity

iteration 1 input signal → S_1
iteration 2 input signal → 0
iteration 3 input signal → S_2
iteration 4 input signal → 0
iteration 5 input signal → S_3

The wave is then synchronized on the signal, and identification of the signal can still be made.

6. Choice of the good Signal

We considered many other chains:

$$E_1^1, E_2^1 \ldots E_j^1 \ldots E_n^1$$
$$E_1^2, E_2^2 \ldots E_j^2 \ldots E_n^2\,.$$

Each chain was structured by means of a signal such as

$$S_1^1, S_2^2 \ldots S_j^1 \ldots S_n^1\,.$$

Now, we inject into the system an input signal such as

$$S_1^1, S_2^2 \ldots S_j^1 \ldots S_n^1\,.$$

The upper index is not always the same in each chain.

Each chain performs as well as possible the integration of a signal which is not in good accordance with it.

If, for one chain, the relation between S_j^a and E_j^a is the best, the integration of the signal will be better, and the wave propagation will increase faster than the waves of the other chains.

Now, the task of general inhibition is to allow only the firing of those elements which receive the greatest input signal.

The chain will remain the only one in function. *The system is then able to choose, among all the recorded signals, that which is closest to the unidentified input signal.*

The incoming signal is then classified, which means that the identification is made.

7. Mixed Signals

In what we have seen above, we have assumed the presence of one specific element for each syllable, as often as the syllable is included in a word. This involves an excessive complication of the system.

The first experiment concerns two chains having a common element:

$$E_2^1, E_2^1, E_3 \, E_4^1 \, E_5^1$$
$$E_1^2, E_2^2, E_3 \, E_4^2 \, E_5^1 \, .$$

The element E_3 without an upper index is the same for the two chains. This means that the interrogative signal is limited to the first three elements.

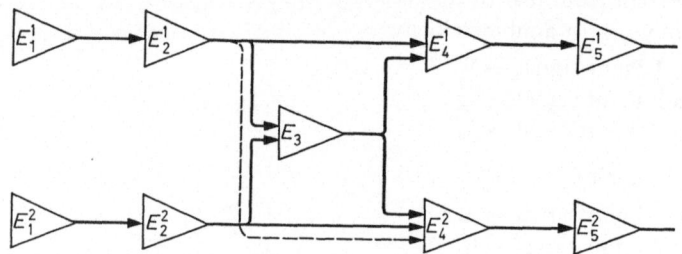

Fig. 5. Two signals having a common element

Assume that the input signal is injected into elements E_1^1, E_2^1, E_3. At the 4th interaction

$$F_2^1 \, (t + 3 \, \theta) = 0, \; F_2^2 \, (t + 3 \, \theta) = 0$$
$$X_4^1 \, (t + 3 \, \theta) = A_{3,4}^1 \, F_3(t + 3 \, \theta) + A_{2,4}^1 \, F_2^1(t + 3 \, \theta)$$
$$X_4^2 \, (t + 3 \, \theta) = A_{3,4}^1 \, F_3(t + 3 \, \theta)$$

Then $X_4^1 > X_4^2$.

General inhibition eliminates the outputs of elements E_4^2, E_5^2, and allows only the output of the end of the chain E_4^1, E_5^1.

To put it another way, by means of its dynamic memory, the system remembers having received before signal S_3, signal S_2^1 but not signal S_2^2.

It is then able to make the correct choice.

Remark 1. The information capacity of such a system is restricted because too many intersections can cause confusion.

Remark 2. The recording of two signals must be made progressively for the purpose of avoiding parasitic couplings, such as that represented in the dotted lines of the picture.

If this precaution is not taken, the response of the system will always be to the first recorded signal. *This property of the system was not foreseen and calls the behaviour of true biological systems.*

Remark 3. The system's capacity for treating information is improved by using multi-level lines, described in the following paragraph.

7. Multi-Level Lines

In the foregoing, all elements are considered as disjointed, i. e. none of the microcells which compose them can belong to two or more elements at one time.

Now consider that two elements E_1 and E_2 have a common factor $E_{1,2}$.

For example: the 2 syllables PEN and CIL correspond to the image of a pencil.

The system is now in the situation of a child learning to read from a picture book, but soon there is a question, at a very elementary level, of semantic association. In fact, the syllable PEN must be considered as the first syllable of the word PENCIL and characterized by a macrocell.

$$R_1 \equiv E_1 \, U \, E_{1,2}$$

and the syllable CIL by

$$R_2 \equiv E_2 \, U \, E_{1,2} .$$

The macrocells R_1 and R_2 are no longer disjointed, but they can be represented by 3 disjointed elements

$$E_1, E_2, \text{ and } E_{1,2} \equiv R_1 \cap R_2 .$$

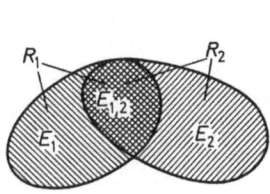

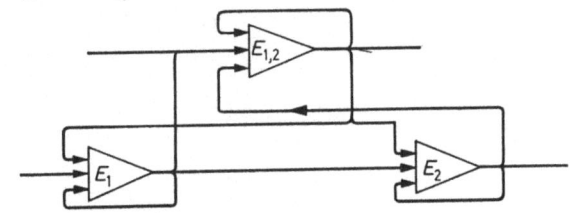

Fig. 6

Fig. 7

Fig. 6. Intersection of Networks

Fig. 7. Two Levels Structure

1. Recording the Signal

We inject the signal S into the elements having the same index

1st iteration $S_1, S_{1,2}$

2nd iteration $S_2, S_{1,2}$

The system then builds an assembly which is structured as shown in the figure.

Up to now we have realized only binary associations. A word with four syllables is represented by a 3-level structure such as that shown in the figure.

Relation between 1st + 3rd levels

not represented here)

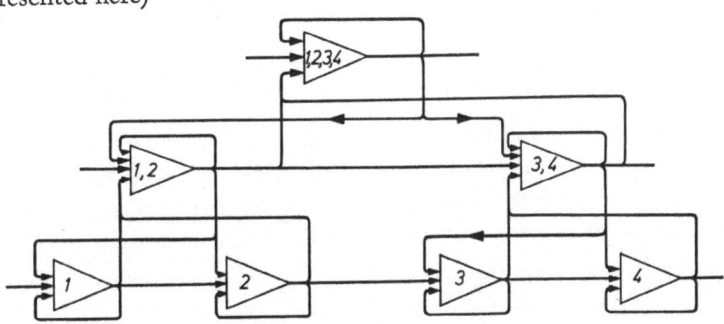

Fig. 8. Three Levels Structure

The upper level corresponds to a semantic association. The signal used for the recording is the following:

$$1^{st} \text{ iteration} \quad S_1, S_{1,1}, S_{1,2,3,4}$$
$$2^{nd} \text{ iteration} \quad S_2, S_{1,2}, S_{1,2,3,4}$$
$$3^{rd} \text{ iteration} \quad S_3, S_{3,4}, S_{1,2,3,4}$$
$$4^{rd} \text{ iteration} \quad S_4, S_{3,4}, S_{1,2,3,4}.$$

2. Mixed words

Consider now 2 words of S syllables each followed by a response of 3 syllables The 2 words have 2 syllables in common.

The interrogation signal is made by the 5 first syllables. The 3 syllables of the response are different for the 2 words.
The representation of the signals is

$$E_1, E_2^1, E_3, E_4^1, E_5, E_6^1, E_7^1, E_8^1$$
$$E_1, E_2^2, E_3, E_4^2, E_5, E_6^2, E_7^2, E_8^2.$$

For all the following syllables an element of syntactic association is foreseen. We do not need a third level.

The diagram is shown in the figure:

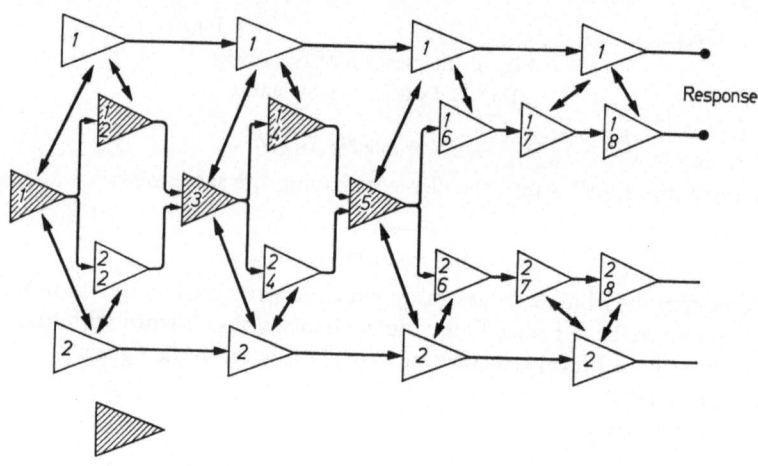

Fig. 9. Mixed Words. ▨ Element receiving the interrogation signal

The assembly is formed during the recording period by the method indicated in paragraph 7. This method is applied successively to each of the 2 signals.

For interrogation, we give only the elements of the first level which corresponds to the identification of syllables but without any syntactic indication.

The system then rebuilds the syntactic information of the word given to it: E_1, $E_2^1, E_3^1, E_3^1, E_4^1$, then it fires the elements E_6^1, E_7^1, E_8^1, the elements E_6^2, E_7^2, E_8^2 being inhibited.

3. Word Homonyms

Let 2 words of 4 syllables be identical but corresponding to different syntactic associations.

Let

$$E_1, E_2, E_3, E_4$$
$$E^1_{1,2} \; E^1_{3,4}$$

and

$$E_1, E_2, E_3, E_4$$
$$E^1_{1,2} \; E^2_{3,4}$$

these words are followed, each by 4 response elements

$$E^1_5, E^1_6, E^1_7, E^1_8,$$
$$E^2_5, E^2_6, E^2_7, E^2_8 \, .$$

The diagram is shown in the figure

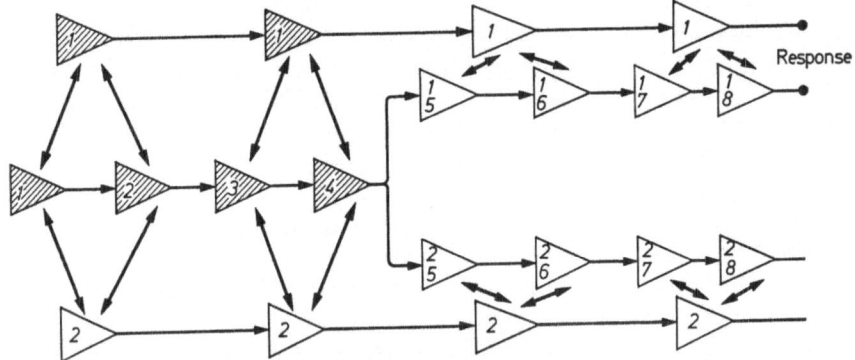

Fig. 10. Word Homonyms

By interrogation we can reproduce the word and one of the two possible syntactic interpretations.

Let

$$S_1, S_2, S_3, S_4$$

with

$$S^1_{1,2}, S^1_{3,4} \, .$$

The response of the system is then $E^1_5, E^1_6, E^1_7, E^1_8$; the elements whose upper index is 2 being inhibited and reciprocal.

That is to say, the system can, according to the context, respond in two different ways to the same input signal.

4. Propagation of the Signal

The signal always has a tendency to propagate from the lower to the upper levels.

In order for the lower levels to fire, they must receive input signals from the levels below.

The input of the upper levels serves only to direct the lower levels, by supplying them with just a small amount of stimulus for the purpose of a differentiating between different possible signals.

5. *Abstraction and Generalization*

If the upper levels continue to fire, the lower levels are inhibited. This means that the system retains the semantic information in its memory and forgets the particular form in which that information was given to it.

For example, it retains the notion of the identity of a person regardless whether he was seen full-face, in profile, recognized by the tone of his voice, etc.

The system is soon able to perform abstraction and generalizations.

8. Conclusions

The present theory is not the result of biological experiments. It comes mostly from intution and imagination: all that we can say now is that it does not contradict our actual knowledge.

It provides a synthesis permitting a relationship between the cell and some elementary properties of psychological behaviour.

We call "elementary properties" those which can be represented by a relatively simple model such as ours. For example, the following:

Short-time dynamic memory,

Long-time static memory,

Recognition of temporal patterns independent of their velocity,

Redundancy by comparison between recorded and unknown signals,

Improved of discrimination using syntactic or semantic information,

Possibility of abstraction and generalization,

Necessity of a progressive adaptation to prevent the system remembering only the first patterns recorded.

Finally, some correlations must be made between the physiological constants of the cell on the one hand and certain characteristics of the systems behaviour on the other, such as the velocity of the repetition of a temporal pattern.

In résumé, such a theory may be neither "true" nor "false", but it will be useful, it is hoped, for the understanding of phenomena which are inaccessible to direct experimentation on a macroscopic scale.

References

Brick, D. B.: Pattern recognition and self organisation using wieners canonical forms. Cybernetics of the nervous system. Elsevier publishing company 1965.

Broadbent, D. E.: Applications of information theory and decision theory to human preception and reaction. Cybernetics of the nervous system. Elsevier publishing company 1963.

Hebb: Organisation of behaviour, 6 eme ed. Juin 1961. London: John Wiley & Sons N.Y.; Traduit de l'anglais par M. King sous le titre Psycho-physiologie du comportement, P.U.F. Paris 1958.

Jenik, F.: An outline of the development of a neuron model. Cybernetics of the nervous systems. Elsevier publishing company 1965.

Kleene: Representation of events in nerve nets and finite automata. Automata Studies. Princeton (N.Y.): University Press 1956.

LEVY, J. C.: Theorie statistique des combinaisons discernables. CR Academie des Sciences, 25 Février 1963.
— Un modele de réseau figurant le systeme nerveux. Onde Electrique, Avril 1963.
— Etude statistique des réseaux nerveux, circuits a majorité relative. Rapport contrat D.R.M.E. 64/34 146.
— Systeme nerveux et reconnaissance des formes. Onde Electrique, Février 1966.
— Complément a la théotie statistique des combinaisons discernables. CR Academie des Sciences, 2 Mai 1966.
—, D. BERTAUX et J. GROLLEAU: Structuration par apprentissage d'une mémoire a association sémantique. Symposium sur la cybernétique médicale et les intelligences artificielles. Toulouse 7.—9. Mars 1967.
—, F. LIEGEOIS, M. CHACRON et G. BERTRAND: Etude des assemblages de réseaux nerveux par le calcul electronique. Rapport du contrat D.R.M.E. 136/67.
LIEGEOIS, F.: Note sur la distribution des connecteurs dans les systemes composés d'un grand nombre de cellules.
McCULLOCH, W., and W. PITTS: A logical calculus of the ideas immanent in nervus activity. Bulletin of Mathématical Biophysics 1943.
— —, LETTVIN, and MATURANA: What the frog's eye tells to the frog's brain. Pire Vol. 47, 1959.
VON NEUMANN, J.: Probabilistic logics. Automata studies. Princeton (N.Y.): University Press 1956.
ROSENBLATT: Principles of neuro dynamics. Spartan Books 1962.
SIMON, J. C.: Sur l'algebre des processus d'intelligence artificielle. Symposium sur la cybernetique médicale et les intelligences artificielles. Toulouse 7.—9. Mars 1967.
TAYLOR, W. K.: Pattern recognition by means of automatic analogic equipment. Proceedings of the IEE vol. 106 part B, Mars 1956.
— A model of learning mechanism in the brain. Cybernetics of the nervous system. Elsevier publishing company 1965.

A Fundamental Consideration on Pattern Recognizers

S. Noguchi, K. Nagasawa, and J. Oizumi

Research Institute of Electrical Communication, Tohoku University, Sendai, Japan

Introduction

Much research has been done in the field of the pattern recognition. It is generally classified into two types; 1. dynamic system and 2. static system. The typical model of the dynamic system is the one proposed by Caianiello [1].

In this system, every pattern is converted into dynamic reverberation in the networks. This model has many attractive features for pattern recognition problems, but there are still many problems which remain to be solved before this model can be utilized in pattern recognition.

From this standpoint, we discuss only the static model. The static model is chiefly composed of six parts; 1. sensory unit, 2. normalizing unit, 3. feature extracting unit, 4. associative unit, 5. decision unit and 6. response unit.

In this model, the signals flow only from left to right and the information is processed sequentially in each unit.

In order to design a powerful pattern recognizer, we should carry out basic research on the recognition system and utilize each unit in a synthetic way. But as the first stage of the research, it is important to obtain and analyze enough information about the characteristics of each unit.

As regards normalization and the feature extracting process, we have had some important theoretical research [2], and also some on the characteristics of a non-statistical classifier [3], but not as yet on the statistical one.

The statistical classifier has many important points from the practical point of view, as follows:

1. in this system, it is not necessary to consider the linear separability of input patterns as the system can organize the recognizer in optimal way, even when the patterns are not linearly separable,

2. organization of the system can be made quickly by the analogue technique.

From this standpoint, we made a fundamental consideration about the evaluation of the theory of the statistical classifier, this enables us to introduce the concept of information capacity as in the non-statistical case.

Statistical Classifier

In the following analysis, we set up the basic assumptions as follows:

1. The patterns are classified into two categories, ω_1 and ω_2.

2. Both categories have a member of m_l $(l = 1, 2)$ sample patterns respectively and the total number of patterns is M.

3. Each pattern is represented by an N-dimensional vector $\boldsymbol{X}^{(l)}$, and each $\boldsymbol{X}^{(l)}$ is distributed according to multivariate normal distribution $\boldsymbol{N}(\boldsymbol{\mu}_l, \Sigma)$ $(l = 1, 2)$ respectively.

As the basic statistical classifier, we pick up the following two typical cases; 1. Bayes' rule classifier and 2. the regression classifier.

In the following, we summarize the result of the recognition function based upon these two methods.

(i) Bayes' rule classifier

In this model, the fundamental principle is to find the min. Cx (i) when input pattern X is applied;

$$\text{where } Cx \text{ (i)} = \sum_{j=1}^{2} \lambda(i \mid j) P(X \mid j) P(i) \tag{1}$$

and $\lambda(i \mid j)$ is a loss function assigned to this system.

For simplicity, we assume $\lambda(i \mid j)$ as follows:

$$\lambda(i \mid j) = 1 - \delta_{i,j}. \tag{2}$$

In this case, the decision function $g(X)$ is summarized as follows;

$$g(X) = X^t \Sigma^{-1}(\mu_1 - \mu_2) - \tfrac{1}{2}(\mu_1 + \mu_2)^t \Sigma^{-1}(\mu_1 - \mu_2) \tag{3}$$

where t means transposition of the vector.

Because, μ_1, μ_2 and Σ are unknown, we replace these parameters by unbiased estimaters $\bar{X}^{(l)}$ and S in the following way:

$$\bar{X}^{(l)} = \frac{1}{m_l} \sum_{\alpha=1}^{m_l} X_{\alpha}^{(l)} (l = 1, 2) \tag{4}$$

$$S = \frac{1}{(m_1 + m_2 - 2)} \sum_{l=1}^{2} \sum_{\alpha=1}^{m_l} (X_{\alpha}^{(l)} - \bar{X}^{(l)})(X_{\alpha}^{(l)} - \bar{X}^{(l)})^t. \tag{5}$$

The final decision rule is made as follows:

$$X^t S^{-1}(\bar{X}^{(1)} - \bar{X}^{(2)}) - \tfrac{1}{2}(\bar{X}^{(1)} + \bar{X}^{(2)})^t S^{-1}(\bar{X}^{(1)} - \bar{X}^{(2)}) \geq 0; \quad x \in \omega; \quad < 0; x \in \omega_2 \tag{6}$$

where

$$\theta = \log \frac{m_2}{m_1}$$

(ii) Regression classifier

In the linear system, the output of this system $Z_{\alpha}^{(l)}$ form the quantity

$$Z_{\alpha}^{(l)} = W^t X_{\alpha}^{(l)} + W_0 \tag{7}$$

where W means the weight vector of input pattern and W_0 threshold.

In the regression classifier, we assigned to each pattern the desired output $Y_{\alpha}^{(l)}$ respectively (this corresponds to education), and considered the setting of variable parameter so as to minimize the following Q function:

$$Q = \sum_{l}^{1,2} \sum_{\alpha=1}^{m_l} \{Y_{\alpha}^{(l)} - W^t \cdot X_{\alpha}^{(l)} - W_0\}^2. \tag{8}$$

The optimum value of W_1 and W_0 which minimize Q function are obtained as follows:

$$\tilde{W} = V^{-1} U$$
$$W_0 = \bar{Y} - \tilde{W}^t \bar{X} \tag{9}$$

where

$$V = S + \frac{m_1 \cdot m_2}{M} \delta \delta^t \qquad U = \sum_{l}^{1,2} \sum_{\alpha=1}^{m_l} (Y_\alpha^{(l)} - \bar{Y}) (X_\alpha^{(l)} - \bar{X}) \qquad (10)$$

$$\bar{Y} = \frac{1}{M} \sum_{l}^{1,2} \sum_{\alpha=1}^{m_l} Y_\alpha^{(l)}, \quad \bar{X} = \frac{1}{M} \sum_{l=1}^{2} \sum_{\alpha=1}^{m_l} X_\alpha^{(l)}, \quad S = \frac{1}{(M-2)} \sum_{l}^{1,2} \sum_{\alpha=1}^{m_l} (X_\alpha^{(l)} - \bar{X}^{(l)}) (X_\alpha^{(l)} - \bar{X}^{(l)})^t$$

and

$$\delta = (\bar{X}^{(1)} - \bar{X}^{(2)}) .$$

In this model, the final decision rule are as follows:

$$\tilde{W}^t X + \tilde{W}_0 \geq 0 ; \qquad X \in \omega_1 ,$$
$$< 0 ; \qquad X \in \omega_2 . \qquad (11)$$

Characteristics of Classifier

For simplicity, we assume $m_1 = m_2$ in the following (there is no difficulty in the case where $m_1 \neq m_2$).

1. Bayes' rule classifier

By the assumption (3), the patterns applied to this classifier are approximately distributed according to uni-normal distribution $N(\mu l, v)$ where

$$\mu_1 = \tfrac{1}{2} \delta^t S^{-1} \delta, \mu_2 = - \tfrac{1}{2} \delta^t S^{-1} \delta \text{ and } v = \delta^t S^{-1} \delta . \qquad (12)$$

We define the new parameter d_b as follows:

$$d_b = \mu_1 - \mu_2 = \delta^t S^{-1} \delta . \qquad (13)$$

This parameter d_b expresses the measure of separation of two categories and is a random variable.

By this new parameter, we can calculate the correct classification probability R_b, if d_b is given, as follows:

$$R_b = \Phi(\tfrac{1}{2} \sqrt{d_b})$$

where

$$\Phi(x) = \frac{1}{\sqrt{2\pi}} \int_{-\infty}^{x} e^{-\frac{x^2}{2}} dx . \qquad (14)$$

The next important problem is the calculation of the distribution function of d_b.

We show here the final result in the following: $f(d_b)$, the probability density function of d_b is expressed in non-central F distribution as follows:

$$f(d_b) = \sum_{k=0}^{\infty} e^{-\lambda} \frac{\lambda^k}{4\,k!} \frac{\Gamma\left(\frac{\alpha+\beta}{2} + k\right)}{\Gamma\left(\frac{\alpha}{2} + k\right) \Gamma\left(\frac{\beta}{2}\right)} \left(\frac{d_b}{4}\right)^{\left(\frac{\alpha}{2} + k - 1\right)} \left(1 + \frac{d_b}{4}\right)^{-\left(\frac{\alpha+\beta}{2} + k\right)} \qquad (15)$$

where

$$\alpha = N, \beta = M - N - 1, \lambda = \tfrac{1}{2} V^t \Sigma^{-1} V$$

and

$$V = \sqrt{\frac{M}{4}} (\mu_1 - \mu_2) .$$

2. *Regression classifier*

We assume educational value $Y_\alpha^{(1)} = 1$, $Y_\alpha^{(2)} = -1$. It is proved theoretically that this strategy on average corresponds to the optimum.

In this case also, it is easily proved that the pattern applied according to assumption (3) is distributed according to uni-normal distribution

$$N(\mu_e^*, v^*) \qquad (l = 1, 2) ;$$

where

$$\mu_l^* = \frac{M}{2} (V^{-1}\delta)^t [\bar{X}^{(l)} - \bar{X}]$$

$$v^* = \tfrac{1}{4} \frac{M}{(M-2)} (V^{-1} \cdot \delta)^t S(V^{-1}\delta) . \qquad (16)$$

As in the case of Bayes' rule, we define the new parameter d_r as follows:

$$d_r = \mu_1^* - \mu_2^* = \frac{M}{2} \delta^t V^{-1} \delta \qquad (17)$$

where

$$V = (M-2) S + \frac{M}{4} \delta \delta^t .$$

Eq. (16) can be written in terms of d_r as follows:

$$\mu_1^* = \tfrac{1}{2} d_r , \qquad \mu_2^* = -\tfrac{1}{2} d_r, \qquad \text{and} \qquad v^* = \tfrac{1}{4} \frac{M}{(M-2)} d_r (2 - d_r)$$

respectively.

In the same way, if d_r is given, the probability of the correct classification R_r is obtained as follows:

$$R_r = \Phi\left(\sqrt{\frac{d_r}{2 - d_r}} \right) \qquad (18)$$

$f(d_r)$, the probability density function of d_r is expressed in a kind of beta distribution as follows:

$$f(d_r) = \sum_{k=0}^{\infty} \frac{e^{-\lambda} \cdot \lambda^k}{k!} \cdot \frac{2^{\left(1 - k - \frac{\alpha + \beta}{2}\right)}}{B\left(\frac{\alpha}{2} + k, \frac{\beta}{2}\right)} d_r^{\frac{\alpha}{2} + k - 1} (2 - d_r)^{\frac{\beta}{2} - 1}$$

$$(19)$$

where

$$B(\alpha, \beta) = \frac{\Gamma(\alpha) \Gamma(\beta)}{\Gamma(\alpha + \beta)} .$$

Classification Ability

Classification ability of each system has already obtained in Eq. (15) and (19). In order to see through the general feature, we consider the mean value $\bar{d}_b$ and $\bar{d}_r$. $\bar{d}_b$ and $\bar{d}_r$ are easily calculated by Eq. (15) and (19) as follows:

$$\bar{d}_b = 4 \left(\frac{N + 2\lambda}{M - N - 3} \right)$$

$$\bar{d}_r = 2 \sum_{k=1}^{\infty} \frac{\lambda^k e^{-\lambda}}{k!} \left(\frac{N + 2k}{M + 2k} \right) . \qquad (20)$$

We replace each distribution function by these mean values as a first stage approximation.

11   Neural Networks

By these parameters, we define mean recognition rates $\bar{R}_b$ and $\bar{R}_r$, replacing d_b and d_r by $\bar{d}_b$ and $\bar{d}_r$ in Eq. (14) and (18).

Next, we introduce two new concepts on pattern processing: pattern processing capacity I_n and α-% pattern processing capacity $I_n(\alpha$-%). These are defined as follows:

(1) $\qquad I_n^{(b)} = \left(\dfrac{M}{N}\right) \qquad$ when $\bar{R}_b = 1$,

(2) $\quad I_n^{(b)}(\alpha$-%) $= \left(\dfrac{M}{N}\right) \qquad$ when $\bar{R}_b = \alpha$-%,

$I_n^{(r)}$, and $I_n^{(r)}(\alpha$-%) are also defined in the same way.

As an example, we consider the ideal case where each component of vector pattern is independent and has the same mean value difference Δ between two categories, respectively.

In this case, λ given in Eq. (15), is calculated as follows:

$$\lambda = \frac{M}{8} N \Delta^2 .$$

In this case, we have

$$\bar{d}_b \simeq 4 \left(\frac{1 + \dfrac{M}{4}\Delta^2}{\dfrac{M}{N} - 1} \right)$$

$$\bar{d}_r \simeq \frac{2\left(1 + \dfrac{M}{4}\Delta^2\right)}{\left(\dfrac{M}{N} + \dfrac{M}{4}\Delta^2\right)} . \tag{21}$$

From these facts, it is proved that I_n and $I_n(\alpha$-%) coincide with each method and their information capacities are calculated as follows:

$$I_n = 1 , \qquad I_n(99\%) \simeq 1 + 0.184\left(1 + \frac{M}{4}\Delta^2\right) . \tag{22}$$

From these considerations, it is concluded that the two statistical classifiers, Baye's rule classifier and the regression classifier, show the same classification ability in the first stage approximation.

Computer Simulation

We show some typical results of computer simulation. Fig. 1 shows the variation of the $I_n(99\%)$ vs mean value difference Δ.

Figs. 2 and 3 show the average recognition rate vs M/N ratio for Bayes' rule and regression classification respectively.

In Figs. 2 and 3 the parameters are set up as follows:

$$\lambda = 0 , \quad \Sigma = I , \quad \text{and} \quad \mu_1 = \mu_2 = 0 .$$

In these figures, the curve shows the theoretical line and the points the experimental results, which show good agreement with the theoretical curves.

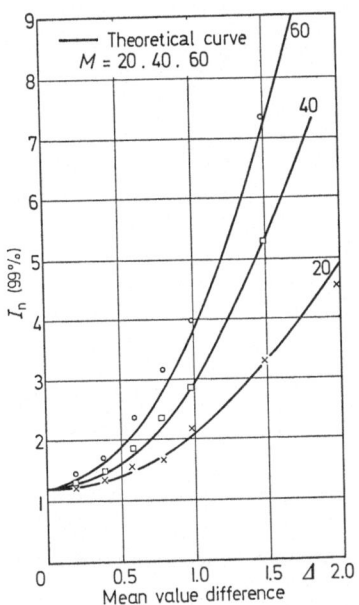

Fig. 1. Variation of I_n (99%) vs$\varDelta$

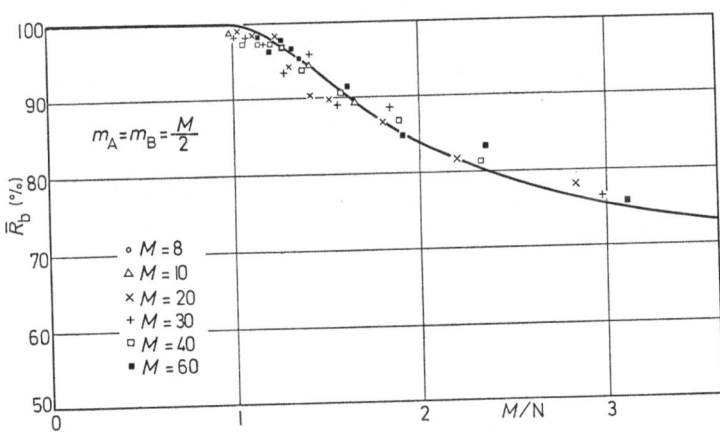

Fig. 2. The average recognition rate vs M/N for Bayes' rule classifier

We also made some simulations for the case when the pattern follows another distribution, such as a uniform distribution, and so on.

In these cases, the results of the computer simulation show the same tendency as the case of normal distribution.

Conclusion

In this paper, we evaluated the recognition ability of the two typical statistical classifiers, Bayes' rule classifier and the regression classifier. According to our analysis, these two methods show the same classification ability on average in the

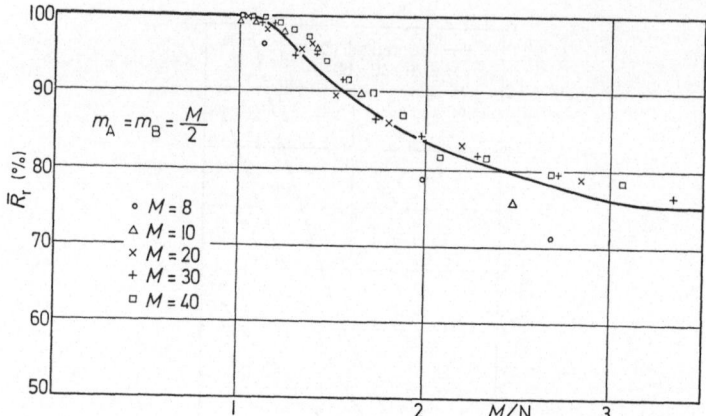

Fig. 3. The average recognition rate vs M/N for regression classifier

first stage approximation. if the input pattern is distributed according to a multi-variate normal distribution.

Next, we introduced the two new concepts, pattern processing capacity and α-% pattern processing capacity.

By this measure, we can evaluate the ability of the recognition processor. We made computer simulations, and these results agree well with our theoretical results.

References

1. Caianiello, E. R.: Outline of a theory of thought process and thinking machine. J. Theoret. Biol. 1, 2 (1961).
2. Iijima, T.: Theory of pattern recognition. J. Inst. Electr. Communication Engrs (Japan), 1963.
3. Cover, T. M.: Geometrical and statistical properties of linear threshold devices. Stanford Electronics Laboratories, Technical report 6107-1, May 1964.

Multilayer and Multilevel Control Structures

A. STRASZAK

Institute for Automatic Control, Polish Academy of Sciences, Warsaw, Poland

I. Introduction

Up to now it is difficult to speak exactly about the relation between the control problems and neuronic networks problems, however modern control problems and modern neuronic network problems have something in common. First of all high dimensionality and second the necessity to consider the data processing behaviour in modern control systems and in neuronic networks. From the anatomy of biological neuronic networks we know about the existence of the multilayer and multilevel structures; for here some special control problems we obtain the multi-layer and multi-level structures as a result of analytical solution of the control problem.

Therefore, I think that the presentation of these results may be interesting also for neuronic network research.

II. Statement of the Problem

Let us consider an optimal controller problem. From the theory of the optimal control problems [1, 4] we know that it is possible to find for some special optimal control problem the so-called "feedback" solution (Fig. 1)

$$u = c(x) ,$$

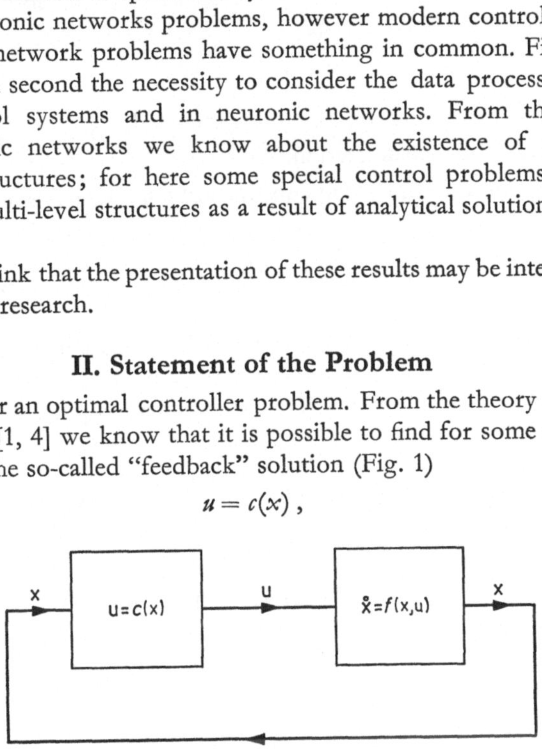

Fig. 1. Feedback control system

where u is an optimal control vector, which minimized the index of performance

$$I = \int_{t_0}^{t_1} \varphi(x, u) \, dt ,$$

x is a state vector of the controlled process $\dot{x} = f(x, u)$.

Let dim $u = n$, dim $x = n$.

The list of the data processing operation for realization of the optimal control law depends on the form c. For example if optimal controller is linear, than the full list of the data processing operation will be following:

a) $n \times n$ multiplications by constant values c_{ij},

b) n summations.

If the optimal controller is nonlinear, we have additionaly

a) multiplication variables by variables,

b) generation of the nonlinear function and so on.

Let us introduce the function over the list of data processing operation

$$Z = m_\alpha k_\alpha + m_\beta k_\beta + \ldots$$

where m_α = number of the data processing operation α,

m_β = number of the data processing operation β,

k_α = "cost" or "complexity" of the operation α,

k_β = "cost" or "complexity" of the operation β and so on.

For the linear optimal controller

$$Z = n^2 k_{c_{ij}} + n k_\Sigma,$$

where $k_{c_{ij}}$ = "cost" of the multiplication by constant c_{ij},

k_Σ = "cost" of the summation.

For the enough high dimension control problem, we have that

$$Z_C > Z_0,$$

where Z_0 = "complexity" or "cost" of the existing or available data processing devices.

Therefore the following problem arises. How to organize the data processing operation for control system such that quality of control (in sense of the index of performance) will be the same or will change as small as possible and

$$Z_{c*T_i} \leq Z_0 < Z_c,$$

where Z_{c*T_i} = "complexity" or "cost" of the modifing optimal or suboptimal controller.

III. Multilayer Control Structure

Let us consider the linear optimal controller problem and let us introduce the new variables (Fig. 2)

$$z_1 = T_1 x$$

$$z_2 = T_2 z_1 = T_2 T_1 x$$

$$z_k = T_k \ldots T_1 x.$$

The list of the data processing operation will change since we must introduce additional summation and multiplication by constants, however if some new con-

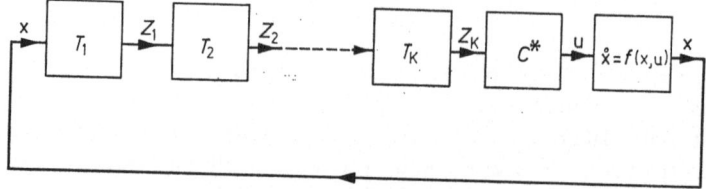

Fig. 2. Multilayer control system

stants will be equal zero, than the number of multiplication by constants may be reduced. If the reduction of the multiplication by constants will be very large we may expect that

$$Z_{(T_1, T_2, \ldots, T_k, C*)} \leq Z_0 \leq Z_C.$$

For optimal control it is neccessary that

$$C = T_1 T_2 \ldots T_k C*.$$

It was shown [7, 8] that for some optimal control matrixes C exist such linear transformation T_i. For example if optimal control matrix C has the rank $1 < n$, and that r leading principal minors of this matrix differ from zero, than we can find

$$
C* T = C =
\begin{Vmatrix}
c_{11}^* & 0 & \text{---------------} & 0 \\
\cdot & c_{22}^* & & \cdot \\
\cdot & & & \cdot \\
\cdot & & c_{11}^* & \cdot \\
\cdot & & 0 & \cdot \\
c_{n1}^* & \text{-------} & c_{n1}^* \ 0 & 0
\end{Vmatrix}
\begin{Vmatrix}
t_{11} & \text{----------} & t_{1n} \\
0 & t_{22} & \\
\cdot & & \\
\cdot & t_{11} & t_{1n} \\
0 & \text{-----------} & 0
\end{Vmatrix}
$$

where

$$
c_{ik}^* = \frac{c_{ik} - \sum\limits_{j=1}^{k-1} c_{ij}^* t_{jn}}{t_{kk}}
$$

$$i = 1, 2, \ldots, n \, ; \qquad i \geq k, \quad k = 1, 2, \ldots, 1$$

$$
t_{ik} = \frac{c_{ik} - \sum\limits_{j=1}^{i-1} c_{ij}^* t_{ik}}{c_{ii}^*}
$$

$$i = 1, 2, \ldots, 1 \, ; \qquad i \leq k, \quad k = 1, 2, \ldots, n \, .$$

The complexity function Z will be the following

$$Z_{C*T} = (n + l) \, k_\Sigma + 2 \left(nl - \frac{(l^2 - l)}{2} \right) k_{c_{ij}} \, .$$

If the optimal control matrix C is not singular, than by using the special grouping of the components of the state vector x, we can also obtain the new variable $z_1, z_2, \ldots, z_n$ such that

$$C* \, T_1 \, T_k = C$$

and

$$Z_{(C*T_1 \ldots T_k)} = k \, n \, k_\Sigma + k \sqrt[k]{n} \cdot n \, k_{c_{ij}} \, .$$

Therefore, in general, by using the multilayer structures we may economize the list of data processing operation for optimal control. However, from forms of functions $Z_{(C*T_1 \ldots T_k)}$ follows that we cannot obtain by this approach very large saving of the data processing operations.

IV. Multilevel Control Structure

Let us consider a property of the complexity function Z. Since Z is fast growing function of the dimension of the control problem, we have that

$$Z(n) \geqslant \sum_{i=1}^{k} Z_i(n_i) \, ,$$

where

$$\sum_{i=1}^{k} n_i = n \, .$$

It means that the decomposition of the original control problem into a set of less dimensional control subproblems may reduce the full list of the data processing

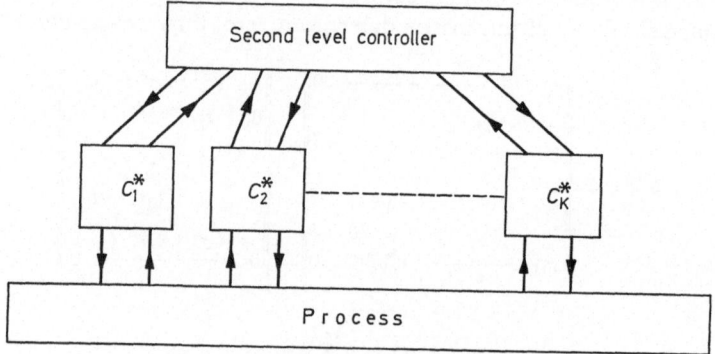

Fig. 3. Two-level control system

operation. However, in general, by the decomposition of the control problem we may loose the quality of the control. Therefore it is necessary to improve quality of control by introducing the second level (supervisory) controller which will compensate the influence subsystems or will allocate the resources between the sub-systems [5, 6, 8] (Fig. 3).

Of course, for second-level controller we need additional data processing operations.

Therefore, overall complexity function Z will be

$$Z = \sum_{i=1}^{k} Z_i(n_i + 1) + Z_s \, .$$

The second-level supervisory control problem can be decomposed into a new set of supervisory controllers. To improve the quality of supervisory control it may be neccesary to introduce the three-level control problem for which we need additional data processing operations (Fig. 4).

In general, we have that

$$Z = \sum_{i=j}^{k} Z_i(n_i + 1) + \sum_{j=2}^{b} \sum_{r=1}^{r_b} Z_{,jr}$$

where $k =$ number of local controller,

   $b =$ number of control levels.

The multilevel control structure approach is a much more powerfull method for reducing the overall list of the data processing operation than the multilayer approach.

However in this case it is necessary to introduce the set of the connected supervisory control problems. For example the global index performance Ig must be approximated by the modified index performance $Ig*$ [6, 8].

$$Ig = \int_{t_0}^{t_1} \varphi_g(x, u)\, dt \approx Ig* = \sum_{i=1}^{r} \int_{t_1}^{t_2} \varphi_i(x_i, u_i, \mu_i)\, dt .$$

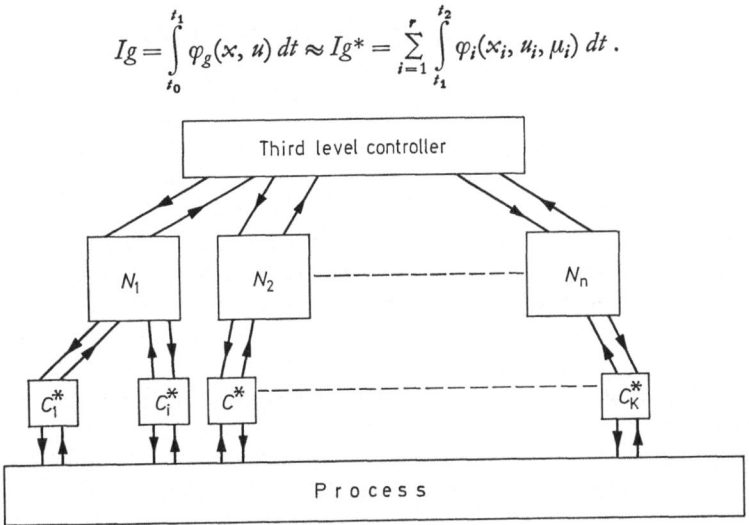

Fig. 4. Three-level control system

References

1. CHANG, A.: An optimal regulator problem. J. Siam. Ser. A Control 2, 220 (1964).
2. GOODWIN, B. C.: Temporal organization in cells. A dynamic theory of cellular control processes. New York 1963. Academic Press.
3. MESAROVIC, M. D.: Advances in multilevel control. IFAC Tokyo Symposium on System Engineering, Tokyo 1965.
4. PONTRIAGIN, L. S.: Mathematical theory of the optimal process. Moscow: Fizmatgiz 1961.
5. STRASZAK, A.: On the structure synthesis problem in multilevel control systems. Proc. IFAC Tokyo Symposium on System Engineering, Tokyo 1965.
6. — Suboptimal supervisory control. Functional analysis and optimization. New York: Academic Press 1966.
7. — Optimal and sub-optimal multivariable control systems with controller cost constraint. Proc. III IFAC Congress, London 1966.
8. — Control methods for largescale multivariable dynamic processes. Raport No. 60, Institut for Automatic Control, Warsaw 1967 (in Polish).

On the Mathematics of Model Building

R. E. KALMAN

Stanford University, Stanford, California (USA)

1. Background Remarks

The purpose of this talk is to present, in nontechnical language, an account of recent developments in mathematical system theory. They are related to the questions: What is a system? How can it be effectively described in mathematical terms? Is there a deductive way of passing from experiments to mathematical models? How much can be said about the internal structure of a system on the basis of experimental data? What is the minimal set of components from which a system with given characteristics can be built?

Of course, these questions are of considerable interest to the theoretical biologist. It is equally clear that any *direct* application to biology will take many, many more years. Still, the intellectual kinship between biology and modern system technology (we might call them the "natural" and "artificial" biologies) is undeniable. The ideas of modern control theory (especially *feedback* and *optimization*) have now invaded every corner of science, from biology to political science. Unfortunately, this "invasion" cannot be equated with "conquest", because of the low level of mathematical training outside the hard sciences, and, more importantly, because many questions are not yet settled even in mathematical system theory (= abstract artificial biology). For instance, the true significance of feedback is still not really understood. On the other hand, the new branch of mathematical system theory which might be called "theory of modeling" has undergone very rapid progress in recent years. My personal feeling is that the type of questions to be discussed here today will (if anything) contribute more to biology than vague thinking which utilizes undefined glamor words such as feedback.

2. Some Views about Mathematics vs. Science

As a mathematician, I want to show how mathematics and mathematical thinking can be directly relevant to science, that is, to the explication of natural phenomena. Since I mean this quite seriously, it is incumbent to admit also that in many respects mathematics has *not* been essential to science.

There are all sorts of romantic exaggerations about the "importance" of mathematics in physics. Many of them are so blatently false that the modern (pure) mathematician wants to learn nothing about physics, since such knowledge would not help him prove theorems. (At the John Hopkins University, undergraduates in mathematics were recently prohibited by their department from taking courses in physics, as detrimental to their professional preparation. On the other side, university rules forbid forcing a nonmathematics student to take more than two mathematics courses per semester, since any more could be interpreted, in the American legal lingo, as "cruel and unusual punishment".) POINCARE, in his lectures on probability theory, quotes an anecdote attributed to LINDEMANN, around 1900, about the status of the central limit theorem. When asked about it, LINDEMANN said everyone thinks the theorem is true: the mathematicians know it has not been (at that time) proved but they believe it is an experimental fact; the physicists know that it is not experimental fact but they believe it is a theorem. Such a situation is all too common even today.

In short, we must distinguish between "weak" and "strong" interactions between Mathematics and Science. The former category includes most of mathematical physics, especially that concerned with differential equations. Hard mathematical facts about ordinary and partial differential equations (for instance, sharp existence theorems) are of minor physical interest; hard physical questions (for instance, the search for explicit solutions) are for the mathematician either intractable or pedestrian exercises.

There are some, but *very few*, strong applications of mathematics where a hard theorem corresponds to a basic scientific fact. Example: Some economists assert that the law of supply and demand says nothing more (and nothing less) than the Brouwer fixed-point theorem.

In my own experience, system theory (= artificial biology) is *the* area where hard (or at least solid) mathematics interacts most fruitfully with applied problems. There are at least two main reasons for this:

1. The systems studied are not natural but man-made; that is, they do not even exist when we begin to be interested in them. The main purpose of the theory is the creation of new systems. This is the essence of modern engineering (automatic long-distance telephone, computers, missile defense systems, centralized accounting), and even extends to economics (government control of growth rate, competing economic systems).

2. The systems of real interest are exceedingly complex; only the sharp conceptual order of mathematics can provide insight and understanding. (Computer design problems are a good example.)

With these caveats, I hope the following discussion will convince you that in the area of model building mathematics *does* offer some sharp insights.

3. Conceptual Framework

Although not wholly accurate and safe, it may be helpful to define some current terminology in mathematical system theory in general biological terms (after all, the latter influenced the former).

By *input/output function* (of a system) we mean some description of a stimulus/response relationship. A *dynamical system* is any system possessing memory. By a *realization of an input/output function* we mean any dynamical system which, when subjected to the same stimuli, yields the same response as the experimental object. By a *minimal realization* we mean (in some agreed sense, dependent on the circumstances) that the realization is as simple as possible. In other words, our interest in the problem of realization is not merely to "explain" the experimental data in dynamical terms but also survey all possible explanations and select, in a mathematically deductive way, the simplest *possible* explanation. A great scientist, by definition, is a person who has excelled in such a task. We seek to understand the process of model building so that some of this can be done, via computers, in a routine way, without need for (people of) exceptional intelligence or intuition. It is rather surprising, to me, how much *can* be done.

The mathematical ideas involved are as simple as they are fundamental: We put mathematical structure on the experiment (by assuming certain properties of the input/output functions, such as linearity) and then *induce* new structures which will turn out to give us the desired realization.

The specific mathematical techniques we use have an algebraic flavor, in contrast to the traditional tools of mathematical physics which belong to analysis. The theory of modeling as it is emerging today was anticipated in a speculative way by NORBERT WIENER in the 1930's who stressed the role of group theory (and algebra in general) in connection with the Laplace transform and the solution of differential equations. Today Laplace transforms are very well known because every engineer is subjected to a pidgin-mathematics course in it; but unfortunately the depth of WIENER's overview has now been almost completely forgotten. It would be very sad if the sloppy treatment of Laplace transforms (good enough for conventional engineering but not good enough for science) were to be adopted by biologists for want of something better. The algebraic approach sketched here does everything which the standard Laplace transform formalism can or pretends to do; at the same time our formalism is much closer to (say, biological) intuition and its mathematical structure is clear and rich.

The main topics of realization theory at present are the following:

Question: Is it always possible to construct a realization? *Answer*: Yes. Surprisingly, this is very easy.

Question: Do minimal realizations exist and are they unique? *Answer*: Essentially, yes. This is far from trivial, and in many cases the answer is known only conjecturally, not precisely.

Question: What properties does the minimal realization have? *Answer*: In most cases, unknown.

Since we are dealing with a precise and sophisticated mathematical theory, one should not rush into translating the mathematical terminology into a naive, everyday sense (warning occasioned by discussions after the lecture). For instance, "uniqueness of minimal realizations" does not mean that there is only one model to explain the experiment. It does mean that minimal realizations are *abstractly* just one object. This single abstract object may be exhibited in several different forms, "essentially" equivalent forms; for instance, by changing the internal coordinate system. No input/output experiments on a black box can ever say exactly what is inside the black box; this can be done only by opening the box and examing minutely what is inside (or performing correspondingly refined experiments). However, the minimal realization can serve as a workable theory if it is sufficiently simple. Given a few more years of computer development, I think we may be able to claim that NEWTON's model of the solar system *could* have been discovered via our methods from the experimental data available to NEWTON.

4. Mathematical Formalism

It is quite impossible in the given space and time to set up a precise mathematical framework for the general ideas sketched above. In the case of linear, discrete-time systems this has been done at length in my paper for the Varenna summer school

2 weeks ago [1]. As long as linearity is retained, the theory is now fairly complete (see the forthcoming book [2], in which many references are given). In the nonlinear case, only fragmentary or very general results are available. See the work of KROHN and RHODES and their collaborators (referenced in [2]). In the specific case of multi-linear systems, some new results are given in [3]. An earlier version of the present lecture will appear in [4].

For our present purposes, the following explanations are intended to convey the essential flavor of the subject.

We idealize an input/output experiment in the following way. An *input space* is a collection Ω of all experiments in which the inputs last over a finite length of time and terminate at present. We visualize the elements of Ω as functions of time which are nonzero on a finite interval in the past and are zero in the distant past as well as in the future. The *output space* Γ is the collection of experimental results observed *after* the inputs are terminated. In other words, Γ consists of functions of time which are zero in the past and present and are generally nonzero in the future. An *input/output function* $f: \Omega \to \Gamma$ associates with an input ω the output γ resulting from ω after $t = 0$. (We do not consider outputs while inputs are still impinging upon the system; this is a handy notation convention which does not imply any loss of generality.)

We define the *memory* or *state* of a system as the collection (more precisely, equivalence class) of all inputs that result in the same output after $t = 0$. This is a critical idea. We express it as follows: the state x is given by

$$x = [\omega]_f,$$

where $[\omega]_f$ is the *equivalence class of all inputs under the equivalence relation*

$$\omega \underset{f}{\equiv} \omega' \quad \text{if and only if} \quad f(\omega) = f(\omega') \tag{1}$$

induced by f. Note that this definition of "state" coincides with the intuitive of idea "memory".

The input space Ω admits automatically a bit of mathematical structure, that of a *semigroup under concatenation.* This structure is available regardless of what level of abstraction we are at, because it expresses nothing more than the idea of time. The definition is this: $\omega \cdot \omega' =$ input ω shifted to the left and then followed by input ω'. (Draw picture: Assume the graph of ω is a triangle with base on the time axis and right-hand vertex at 0, and the graph of ω' is a half disk with base on the time axis and right-hand vertex at 0. Then $\omega \cdot \omega'$ is obtained by sliding the triangle along the time axis to the left, until the right-hand vertex of the triangle just touches the left-hand vertex of the half-disk.)

We can visualize dynamics by saying *the input acts on the state.* (The output then changes also because it depends on the state.) Recalling the definition of state, the abstract "equations of motion" are given by the map

$$[\omega]_f \xrightarrow{\omega'} [\omega \cdot \omega']_f.$$

The mathematical problems in the theory arise from trying to evaluate this map explicitly and to study its properties. But in a conceptual sense, the abstract definition given above is completely general (includes quantum mechanics, say).

Special case 1. For linear, discrete-time systems, we can make the preceding setup much more concrete, as follows: $\Omega =$ all polynomials; $f =$ linear map. More explicitly, we denote an input sequence

$$(\ldots, 0, 0, \omega_n, \omega_{n-1}, \ldots, \omega_0, 0, \ldots)$$

by means of a polynomial $\omega(z)$, given by

$$\omega(z) = \sum_{i=0}^{n} \omega_i z^i.$$

This means that the indeterminate z "encodes" time in the following sense: the coefficient of z^k is the input symbol received by the system at time $t = -k$. (The minus sign arises through a notation convention.) The map $f:\Omega \to \Gamma$ is to be interpreted as follows: $f(\omega)$ is an infinite sequence, in which the first term is the output symbol resulting from ω at $t = 1$, the second term is the output symbol at $t = 2$, etc.

Under these conditions (see [2, Chapter 10]) the equivalence class (2) can be evaluated quite explicitly as follows:

$$[\omega]_f = \omega \text{ modulo a polynomial } \chi,$$

where χ is the familiar *characteristic polynomial* of a linear system. We get a convenient representation of $[\omega]_f$ by picking one particular member of this equivalence class, namely the polynomial of least degree. In other words, we identify

$$[\omega]_f = \bar{\omega} = \text{remainder of } \omega \text{ after division by } \chi. \tag{3}$$

This means that a dynamical system may be regarded as a kind of "pattern recognition" machine: the input ω is "recognized" or "remembered" by the machine as the lower-degree polynomial $\bar{\omega}$.

Special case 2. A much more difficult problem is the following. We take a system with N input channels, each carrying the same signal as in the linear case. Then $\Omega =$ all polynomials in N variables. We can then deal with various types of non-linear systems; the simplest of these is the case where $f =$ multilinear. Then it follows that $[\omega]_f =$ complicated collection of polynomials in N variables; no simple characterization exists, in contrast to (3) above. This problem was studied by WIENER (early 1950's) using analytical methods, and by GABOR (early 1960's) using engineering methods. Both were unsuccessful. Major advances have been achieved recently (actually, after the presentation of the talk) by algebraic methods [3], but the results are much too complicated to be described here.

4. Examples

Let us return now to special case 1 above and give some specific illustrations. As is well known, in linear system theory everything depends mainly on the characteristic polynomial χ. We can illustrate this fact especially nicely within the framework of the present formalism.

Example 1. Let $\chi(z) = z^k$, $k =$ positive integer. Then (3) shows that the system retains from ω precisely the last k terms $\omega_{k-1} z^k + \ldots + \omega_0$, and remembers nothing else. In other words, this system has a memory of length k, in the most obvious sense of the word.

Example 2. Let $\chi(z) = z - 1$. To say that $\omega = \bar{\omega}$ modulo $z - 1$ (or to divide by $z - 1$ and keep the remainder) is the same as setting $z = 1$ and evaluating the polynomial ω at this value of z. Hence

$$\bar{\omega} = \omega(1) = \sum_{n}^{0} \omega_k \qquad (\text{degree } \omega = n);$$

in other words, this system acts as a summer or integrator by remembering nothing else but the sum of all past input values.

Example 3. $\chi(z) = z^k - 1$. Here "modulo $z^k - 1$" means, generalizing the previous example, "substitute 1 for z^k". After a little thought, we obtain the explicit formula

$$\bar{\omega}(z) = \sum_{i=0}^{k-1} (\sum_{j=0}^{n-1} \omega_{i+jk}) z^i \qquad (\text{degree } \omega < nk).$$

This system tends to recognize especially well periodic patterns of period k.

Example 4. $\chi(z) = z^k - \alpha$, $0 \leq \alpha < 1$. The same reasoning as in the preceding example gives the formula

$$\bar{\omega}(z) = \sum_{i=0}^{k-1} (\sum_{j=0}^{n-1} \omega_{i+jk} \alpha^j) z^i \qquad (\text{degree } \omega < nk).$$

We see that this system also tends to recognize periodic patterns of period k, but at the same time it "forgets" the distant past because of the "amnesia" factor α. The closer α is to 1 the more effect the distant past has on the state; if $\alpha = 0$, we are back to Example 1. In other words, this system works as a correlator of periodic patterns, in which α may be adjustable to lessen the difficulties due to the nonstationarity of the pattern.

The system given in Example 4 is already quite close to situations which have definite practical significance. A further nontrivial case is given below. It is surprising to me that problems of this sort have not been treated more often in the pattern recognition literature. (I am not aware of *any* specific analysis of this sort.)

Problem. Suppose we want to build a machine ($=$ dynamical system) whose task it is to detect an input signal φ as $\bar{\varphi}$ and an input signal ψ as $\bar{\psi} = 0$ (pattern discrimination problem). To build this machine, it is of course sufficient to specify χ. So, what is χ?

Solution. To say that $\bar{\psi} = 0$ means that $\psi = 0$ modulo χ, or that χ divides ψ. Similarly, if $\varphi, \bar{\varphi}$ are given, then $\varphi = \bar{\varphi}$ mod χ or χ divides $\varphi - \bar{\varphi}$. It may well be that these two divisibility requirements are incompatible so that no χ exists. Lesson: We must not insist on specifying $\bar{\varphi}$ and $\bar{\psi}$ too strictly. It is better to take any χ which divides ψ but does not divide φ, and then accept whatever $\bar{\varphi}$ we get in accordance with (3). In other words:

The problem has a solution (in the sense of being doable by a linear machine) if and only if ψ is not a factor of φ, in which case any factor of ψ which is not a factor of φ can be used as χ; then $\bar{\varphi}$ is uniquely determined by (3).

The reader is invited to design this little system by working out a numerical example. He will see that (usually) $\bar{\varphi}$ bears no obvious relationship whatever to φ. I think this example should warn all of us not to try to give overly simple explanations of what goes on in the brain of so-and-so when he sees or hears that-and-that.

6. New Structures from Old

The preceding discussion is based on the fact that the description of dynamics (the principle of causality) admits a certain mathematical structure. This is what enabled us to write down the abstract equations of motion as (2). The explicit evaluation of the equivalence relation induced by f depends of course also on linearity (we have not given the details).

It turns out that this process can be pushed much further. Time allows only one very simple example. Consider two (not necessarily finite-dimensional) vector spaces X, Y with respect to the field R of real numbers as scalars. Suppose that we are given a linear map $f: X \to Y$ (which we can view, on the basis of the preceding discussion, as basically the same as the input/output function of a linear dynamical system). Given the objects X, Y and f, we induce, that is "associate in a natural way", three new objects, X^*, Y^*, and a map $f^*: Y^* \to X^*$. Here X^* is the *dual space* of X, namely

$$X^* = \text{all linear functions } X \to R \; ;$$

Y^* is defined similarly; and f^* is the so-called *dual* (or adjoint) map of f. The definition of f^* is very instructive, because we see directly that it is "built" from f. Indeed,

$$f^*: y^* \to f^*(y^*) \, ,$$

where $f^*(y^*) \, \varepsilon \, X^*$ is a *function* on X. We define it by giving its values as

$$f^*(y^*) \, (x) = y^*(f(x)) \, , \; x \, \varepsilon \, X \, .$$

The important feature of the process of "natural induction" in mathematics, of which we have just given one of the simplest examples, is that the new objects (here X^*, Y^*, f^*) exist whether we like it or not; they are part of the picture (though they may be unknown at a given stage of mathematical knowledge) the moment we have given a specific definition of the primary object (X, Y, f). In this way, a realization can be viewed as a secondary mathematical object which is induced in a natural way from the primary object, which is the experimental data. One of the difficulties of the theory is of course the need to express the experimental data in a suitably idealized mathematical form so that we have indeed a well-defined primary object.

It is not at all obvious that the secondary objects have any direct relevance to a specific problem. This question is today rather unexplored (abstract research in modern mathematics has created a very large array of induced objects!). But there are enough examples to justify looking upon these secondary objects carefully; in fact, this is now a "hot" research area. Some further examples may be found in [1] and [2]. To be specific, the concept of a dual map as discussed here leads naturally to a formulation of the state-estimation problem (given the output, what is the state?). This leads to the development of the so-called Kalman-Bucy filter (the modern version of the Kolmogorov-Wiener filter), which is one of the major practical accomplishments of mathematical system theory today. The map f^* turns out to be essentially the input/output function of the Kalman-Bucy filter.

I have no doubt that many of the discoveries yet to be made in system theory will fit into patterns roughly sketched out here today.

References

1. Kalman, R. E.: Introduction to the algebraic theory of linear dynamical systems. Proceedings International Summer School on Mathematical System Theory and Economics, Varenna (Italy), June 1967 (To appear).
2. —, P. L. Falb, and A. M. Arbib: Topics in Mathematical System Theory (book). McGraw-Hill 1969. London.
3. — On the realization of multilinear machines. (To appear).
4. — New developments in system theory relevant to biology, Third Systems Symposium Case Institute of Technology, October 1966 (to appear).

A Statistical Clock

B. Touschek

Istituto di Fisica, Rome, *Italia*

In this note I want to present a mathematical model, which may be described as a statistical clock and which some years ago I constructed under the stimulus of a discussion with E. Caianiello and V. v. Braitenberg on cyclic recurrences in 'thinking machines'.

Apart from its possible significance as a model of what may happen in a neuronic network the statistical clock, also sheds some light on the connection between reversibility and the validity of the 2nd law of thermodynamics: there is none.

A statistical clock has N states, labelled $0, 1, \ldots N = 0$. It is capable of performing the cycle

$$0 \to 1 \to 2 \ldots \to N-1 \to 0 .$$

The inverse cycle is prohibited. The probability W_{mn} of a transition from a state n to a state m is different from zero only if $m = n + 1$, thus

$$W_{mn} = \delta_{m,n+1} \, v . \tag{1}$$

This system is irreversible, since the principle of detailed balancing would require $W_{mn} = W_{nm}$, which obviously is not the case. This does not surprise: the very meaning of the principle of detailed balancing is to exclude cyclical processes.

The master equation for this system has the form:

$$p_n = v(p_{n-1} - p_n) + [\textstyle\sum_s (v_s p_{n-s} - v_s p_n)] . \tag{2}$$

Here $p_n = p_n(t)$ is the probability of finding the system in the state n at time t. The addition of the second bracket on the right hand side makes the statistical clock imperfect. The second term allows detailed balancing provided that $v_s = v_{-s} \cdot v_s$ is the probability that the clock makes an unprogrammed jump of s states in the unit of time.

Eq. (2) can be solved by introducing normal modes:

$$p_n = \sum_k c_k \exp(-\lambda_k t - 2\pi i k n/N) . \tag{3}$$

The eigenvalues λ_k follow if one inserts from (3) into (2):

$$\lambda_k = v(1 - e^{2\pi i k/N}) + \textstyle\sum v_s(1 - e^{2\pi i k s/N}) . \tag{4}$$

The eigenvalues are generally complex. If there is detailed balancing ($v = 0, v_s = v_{-s}$) they are real. k is defined mod (N) and can assume exactly N values: $k = 0, \pm 1, \ldots$

Note that the mode with $k = 0$ has $\lambda = 0$. From the normalization $\sum p_n = 1$, which is compatible with (2) it follows that for the $k = 0$ mode one has

$$p_n = 1/N \text{ for } k = 0 . \tag{5}$$

This — constant — solution represents the state of equilibrium, which is invariably reached unless the clock is rewound.

The real part of λ_k corresponds to the damping of the normal mode k, if it is positive and to antidamping if it is negative. For $k \neq 0$ it is always positive:

$$\text{Re}(\lambda) = 2\,v \sin^2 (\pi k/N) + 2 \sum v_s \sin^2(\pi_{ks}/N) = 1/\tau_k \tag{6}$$

where τ_k is the damping period. The imaginary part of λ describes the period of the system:

$$|\,\text{Im}(\lambda)\,| = |-v\sin(2\pi k/N)| = 2\pi/T_k . \tag{7}$$

We have assumed detailed balancing for the bracket term in (2), which in this case makes no contribution to the frequency of the kth normal mode.

It is seen from (7) that the frequency is a monotonic increasing function of the mode index k. $k = 0$ corresponds to equilibrium (frequency 0), $k = 1$ to the frequency of a full cycle provided that $2\pi/N \ll 1$. If the second term in (2) is neglected or if only $v_1 \neq 0$, also the decay constants of the modes are monotonic increasing functions of k. Indeed one finds in this case and for large N

$$T_k/\tau_k = \frac{2\pi^2}{N} (1 + 2\,v_1/v) . \tag{8}$$

The left hand side represents the inverse of the 'quality' of the statistical clock excited in the normal mode k and it is seen that the quality is highest for the lowest modes.

It is exactly this property which allows us to consider the object defined by equation as a clock. Once wound, i.e. given the initial conditions $p_n(0)$, the higher modes disappear exponentially and after a sufficiently long interval of time only the lowest mode $k = \pm 1$ and — of course — the equilibrium mode $k = 0$ survive. The lowest mode dies when its amplitude disappears under the noise level.

It is important to note that the clock can tolerate a certain level of stochastic noise, its quality decreases by only a factor 3 if $v_1 = v$.

It is quite easy to show that the entropy of this clock defined by

$$S = - \sum p_n \log p_n \tag{9}$$

is a monotonic increasing function of t: $S > 0$, where the equality only holds for the equilibrium state defined by (5). The value for the entropy in this state is $\log N$ —an example of Boltzmann's relation.

The method of demonstration is quite general and not restricted to the special system (2). We illustrate it here for $v_5 = 0$. Indeed one has

$S = v \sum (p_n - p_{n-1})\log p_n$ [from (2) and using the normalization of the p_n] $= v \sum p_n$ $(\log p_n - \log p_{n+1})$ (after relabelling the indices in the 2nd term) $= v \sum [p_n (\log p_n$ $- \log p_{n+1}) - p_n + p_{n+1}]$ (the total contribution of the last two terms is 0 since $\sum p_n = \sum p_{n+1}$). The second theorem now follows by observing that the function

$$L(x, y) = y(\log x - \log y) - x + y$$

is positive or zero, zero only for $x = y$.

The example therefore shows that the periodic behaviour of the system is in no way contradictory to the 2nd law of thermodynamics.

The system described by the master equation (2) can be considered a statistical model of a damped oscillator and the question naturally arises of how such an oscillator can be excited by external action. It can be readily seen that it is not possible to add an external driving force to the right hand side of Eq. (2). Though it is possible to define a driving force in such a way that it preserves the validity of the condition $\sum p_n = 1$ — for this it is only necessary to subject the force to the condition $\sum f_n(t) = 0$ — it is not possible to maintain an essential property of the masterequation: that of ensuring that if the p_n are initially all contained within the interval $0 < p_n < 1$ they will always remain s_o.

Any excitation or feedback will therefore have to take the form of a 'frequency modulation' of the masterequation. Such a frequency modulation can be used to reset the clock by — for example — making $p- = 1$ at intervals dictated by the clock itself.

Statistical Mechanics of Nervous Nets*

J. D. Cowan

Committee on Mathematical Biology University of Chicago, Chicago, Ill.

Introduction

There are many deep and difficult problems to be solved before any adequate understanding is achieved, of the workings of the central nervous system. "Macro"-neurophysiology and neuroanatomy provide an image of the central nervous system as a system of ordered nets arranged in a multileveled hierarchy, with an immense number of circuits within and between nets. Feedback inhibition undoubtedly plays a very important role in maintaining the activity of such nets, which is controlled by internal and external signals, especially from nets in the lower levels of the hierarchy (the reticular systems), *and* by signals from the receptors. "Micro"-neurophysiology and anatomy fill in the details necessarily obscured by macroscopic analysis. The analysis of intercellular interactions and of the responses of cells to specific forms, has established that there is a specific organization of nets into functional columns maintained by nearest neighbor interactions, by spatial summation and by inhibition. There are topological maps between many nets and from receptive fields. There are differences between the responses of nets in anaesthetized and unanaesthetized animals. In unanaesthetized animals, cells may exhibit a maintained or "steady-state" reponse in addition to the transient response normally found in the cells of anaesthetized animals. How do these tonic and phasic responses influence each other? What is the role of the functional columns, and of the multileveled hierarchies? These are key questions that must be answered before any real understanding of neural coding and information processing can be expected.

Models of Nervous Activity

It is clear that the answers to these questions will entail some novel mathematical modeling and some novel experiments. Current approaches to the modeling of nervous function lean heavily on the *formal neuron* concept of McCulloch and Pitts (1943). However the formal neuron is a rather crude abstraction of neural behavior and the theory of formal neurons covers properties of nets that are not of immediate relevance to neurophysiology, such as the completeness and reliability of *atomistic* representations of behavior. The theory of formal neurons is actually a psychological theory concerned with elementary units of behavior or *psychons* (McCulloch and Pitts *op. cit.*), it was never designed for the analysis of the activity of large-scale nervous nets comprising thousands or millions of cells.

* This research has been sponsored in part by the Physics Branch, Office of Naval Research, Washington, D.C., under Contract No. F 61052 67C 0061.

Digital computer simulations of nervous nets (B. G. Farley, 1965; D. R. Smith, and C. H. Davidson, 1962) together with some analysis of their combinatorics (Smith and Davidson *op. cit.*, J. S. Griffith, 1963) have provided some indication of the type of activity to be found in nets of randomly interconnected formal neurons. If there are only excitatory synapses in the net, the only stable states of activity are either a large proportion of all the units in the net are active, or else the net is quiescent. This is the "switching-effect" discovered by many investigators. It has been suggested that a nervous net which acts as a switch might itself serve as a functional unit, and so correspond to one of McCulloch and Pitts' formal neurons or psychons. If there are also inhibitory synapses in a net, its activity is more complicated, and several intermediate stable levels of activity can exist. Farley has shown that even small nets of about 100 model neurons can exhibit quite complicated modes of activity reminiscent of the recruiting and augmenting responses, and the rhythmic responses of nervous tissue.

What is missing from these investigations however, are the concepts and mathematical results that would further the understanding of the activities of largescale nets. There has been one noteworthy and pioneering attempt to give such a mathematical treatment (R. L. Beurle, 1956). In this model neurons are assumed to be randomly distributed in the system with a given volume density. The cells have thresholds, synaptic delays, EPSPs and a membrane time-constant. The proportion of cells becoming excitable or *sensitive* per unit time is considered, and the proportion per unit time becoming refractory or *intensitive*. Although the mathematical treatment is not rigorous, the conclusions are essentially correct. The switching-effect is demonstrated and the conditions for distortion free propagation of plane waves of neural excitation are given. It is shown that the connection function which gives such propagation is similar to that one found empirically by D. A. Sholl (1956). Since only excitatory synapses are assumed to occur, such waves of excitation are unstable and depend critically on the stimulus, on cell properties, and on the local density of interconnections. However, excitation-waves are stabilized by "servo" control from external nets which act by firing off cells ahead of the wavefronts. Finally, cells thresholds are dependent on the activity. Such extensions of the randomly connected net are important. The servo idea is an attempt to treat net interactions, the control of one net by another; and threshold modification by activity changes the activity of a net according to past activity. So nets can "learn", given proper feedbacks, and can function as permanent stores of coded messages. Indeed all the properties of behavior that are found in McCulloch-Pitts nets and their extensions such as plasticity (A. M. Uttley, 1966; W. K. Taylor, 1964; F. Rosenblatt, 1962) and reliability (J. von Neumann, 1956; S. Winograd and J. D. Cowan, 1963), are to be found *ceteris paribus*, in such assemblies of randomly interconnected nets. However the scale has been changed, so to speak, in that nets play the role of functional units, not formal neurons, and so the net activity is itself an important aspect of the coding process.

It is quite possible that an answer to the questions of coding and information processing might result from an analysis based on Beurle's investigations. But there are a number of problems which must be solved before this approach can be made useful. As I have noted, Beurle's mathematical analysis has some defects: for example, the effects of refractoriness, of the finite size of the net, and of delays are not properly formulated. To some extent these defects are not too serious, and correct formulations of similar problems have been given by J. S. GRIFFITH (1963 b, 1965) and by M. TEN HOOPEN (1965). Their conclusions are similar to BEURLES concerning switching and stability, if somewhat less far-reaching in scope. However what is really lacking from the whole approach is that it does not make contact with the experimental variables of the neurophysiologist — electroencephalograms and electrocorticograms, interspike interval histograms and correlograms — and so it does not provide a series of testable and falsifiable models of coding and information processing in the central nervous system.

Statistical Neuromechanics

In an attempt towards a formulation that does make contact with experimental variables, I have recently developed a statistical mechanics of the activity of nervous nets. The "equations of motion" which I have obtained are nonlinear differential equations that represent the changes in nervous activity that result from interactions within and between assemblies of nervous nets. In a certain special case these equations represent neural oscillators, and can be transformed into the well-known Hamiltonian mechanics of the physicist. From this the transition to statistical mechanics is fairly standard. The utility of this approach is that the statistics that it generates are related to certain ensemble averages — formal analogues of temperature, energy, and entropy — which appear to give useful descriptions of the changes that occur in the activity of nets following interaction. There is some reason to believe that the mathematical model so constructed will predict some of the statistics associated with microelectrode data, and perhaps some of the statistical parameters of macroelectrode recordings from nervous tissue. An example may make this clearer. The equations of motion are as follows:

$$\frac{dX_r}{dT} = (\gamma_r + \beta_r^{-1} \sum_s \alpha_{sr} X_s) X_r (1 - X_r)$$

$$r = 1, \ldots, N: s = 1, \ldots, N. \tag{1}$$

X_r is dynamical variable measuring the sensitivity of the rth neuron in a net. It measures the fraction of time in a long time-interval during which the neuron is not refractory, and can be fired. γ_r is a growth coefficient, a function of the various electrical parameters of the neural membrane, as is β_r. However γ_r is also a function of control stimuli, i. e., the input to the neuron enters nonlinearly through γ_r. The coupling coefficient of the interaction between the rth and sth neurons, α_{sr}, is given by:

$$\alpha_{sr} = \begin{cases} r^{-1} (-E_m) \delta_e g_{sr} b_{sr}, & \text{excitatory synapse,} \\ r^{-1} (E_i - E_m) \delta_i g_{sr} b_{sr}, & \text{inhibitory synapse.} \end{cases} \tag{2}$$

The coefficient r is the refractory period of the neuron. E_m is the resting-potential of the cellmembrane, E_i the equilibrium potential for an IPSP, δ_e and δ_i are the operating times for synaptic transmission, g_{sr} is the conductance of the srth synapse, and b_{sr} is an attenuation factor that serves to represent electronic decrement in the flow of excitation from dendritic to somatic regions of the cell (W. RALL, 1959). The variable T is dimensionless, and is in secs. τ_{sr}^{-1}, where τ_{sr} is the mean intercellular

transit-time for neural activity[1]. Incorporated in τ_{sr} are delays due to axonal conduction, synaptic transmission, and passive electrotonic flow in dendrites.

These equations are obtained by combining ECCLES' equivalent circuit for neural
SD-membrane (J. C. ECCLES, 1957) with an approximation to RALL's equations for the
electrotonic spread of post-synaptic potentials from dendrites to soma (W. RALL,
1959), plus the assumption that the mean rate of neural spike emission is given by the
function $\varphi\,[x]$, where x is the mean current intensity built-up in the cell membrane.
The equations are only a heuristic step towards an exact treatment of the activity of
nets, and their validity can best be judged by the accuracy of the predictions which
can be deduced from them. For example the equations can be used in the following
fashion to model the activity supposedly generated in certain thalamo-cortical
circuits. Fig. 1 shows what is involved.

Thalamic neurons are assumed to act on the apical dendrites of pyramidal neurons in the upper layers of the cerebral cortex, by way of non-specific afferents. EPSPs
initiated by pre-synaptic activity in these afferents are assumed to travel down the
dendrites to the somas of these pyramidal cells and there summate to fire them. The
pyramidal neurons are in turn supposed to act back on the thalamic neurons by way
of corticifugal fibers, thus completing a closed cortico-thalamic circuit. The cortico-
thalamic synapses are all assumed to be inhibitory, and there is a continued bombardment of both sets of neurons from other nets. The consequences of such a 'vertical'
coupling are considered, on the assumption that there are no interactions between
neighboring cells within the same net.

Under these assumptions eqns. (1) readily transform into the equations:

$$\frac{dv_r}{dT} = \sum_s \lambda_{sr} \frac{\partial \mathcal{H}}{\partial v_r} \tag{3}$$

where

$$v_r = ln[(X_r/q_r)\,(1-X_r)^{-1}] \tag{4}$$

$$\lambda_{sr} = \alpha_{sr}/\beta_s\beta_r \tag{5}$$

and

$$\mathcal{H} = \sum_r \beta_r[(1+q_r \exp\,(v_r)) - q_r\,v_r]\,. \tag{6}$$

The variable q_r is the stationary-state of X_r, the state for which $dX_r/dT = 0$. By
suitable control of γ_r the background bombardment, and whenever

$$\alpha_{sr} = -\alpha_{rs},\, \alpha_{rr} = 0 [2] \tag{7}$$

---

[1] I should also mention a very important point. Although the range of X is (0,1), the
range of X_r and of X_s for which equations (1) are valid is not (0,1) but a disjoint subset of
(0,1). This occurs because equations (1) are actually approximations to the nonlinear
difference eqns.

$$X_r(t) = \varphi\,[\varepsilon_r + \beta_r^{-1} \sum_s \alpha_{sr}\, X_s\,(t-\tau_{sr})]$$

where φ is the function $\varphi\,[x] = e^x\,(1+e^x)^{-1}$, and ε_r is the growth coefficient that contains
the input. The net result is that all our results concerning ensemble averages are valid only
for disjoint strips on the interval (0,1).

[2] Eqn. (7) is a rather stringent condition on the αs. However it is only a sufficient
condition that shows up when vertical coupling alone is considered. More general coupling
would lead to conditions such as $\Sigma \alpha = 0$ round multi-element loops. The question of
whether these stationary-states lie in the correct subjects of (0,1) for which equations (1) and
(3) are valid is a delicate one which will not be considered in this abstract.

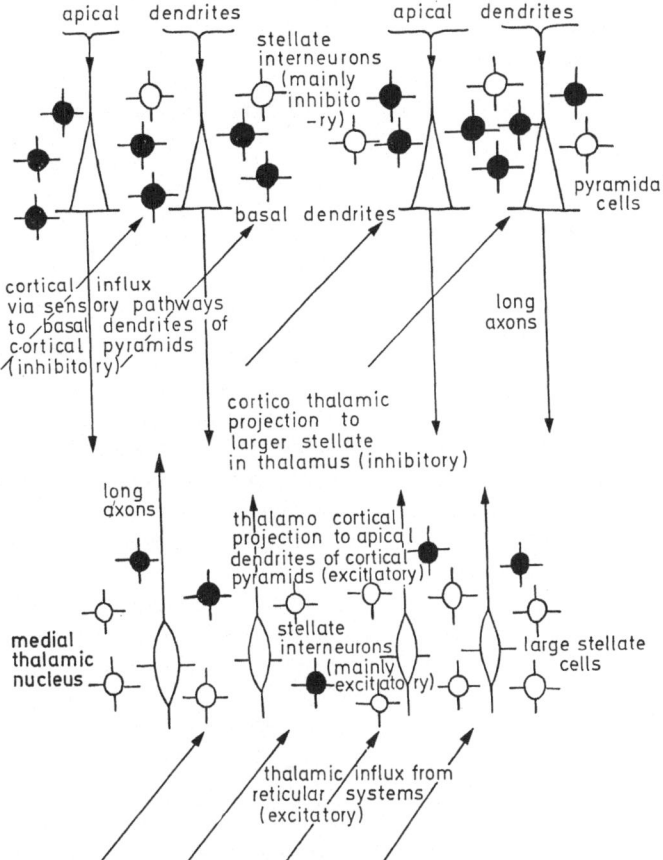

Fig. 1. Cortico-thalamic circuits

there are stationary states in the interval (0,1). It is noteworthy that the background bombardment controlling the γs must lie within the ranges $(0, -\alpha_{rs})$ and $(-\alpha_{sr}, 0)$, for the sth and rth cells respectively. Since α_{rs} is negative and α_{sr} positive, the controlling bombardment to the sth (thalamic) cell must lie within the first (positive) range, that to the rth (cortical) cell within the second (negative) range. It is tempting to suppose that the cortical inhibition is provided by stellate cells which are known to be in close proximity to the cell bodies of the cortical cells that are being modelled. Under such an assumption a major component of the cortical influx controlling the activity in the cortico-thalamic circuits would be sensory inputs (see J. C. ECCLES, 1966).

In such a case $\mathscr{H}$ is a positive constant of the motion of a system of neural *oscillators*, the *Hamiltonian*, and can be rewritten in the variables X_r, as:

$$\mathscr{H} = \sum \beta_r(-q_r \ln X_r - (1-q_r) \ln (1-X_r) + q_r \ln q_r) . \tag{8}$$

Thus the Hamiltonian is a function of certain logarithms of (essentially) the probabilities of spike emission of neurons in the net. Given such a Hamiltonian we can develop by standard methods a statistical mechanics of nets. In passing, it is not without interest that N. Wiener and W. Pitts in the late 1940's appear to have been working along similar lines, but nothing noteable was published by them on this topic. All there is, is the following remark of Wiener:

The anatomical picture of the cortex suggests that we may usefully employ statistical methods in the study of its function. This work has been taken up brilliantly by Walter Pitts. He finds that under many conditions, the approximation to the activity of the cortex should not be made on a basis of rest and the zero basal activity. Proceeding from this he has developed the wave equations of the cortex. These promise to give an interpretation of the electrocorticogram. He has also suggested the exploration of the connections between different parts of the cortex by suitable stimulation of regions and the observance of the frequency response at several points.

N. Wiener 1948

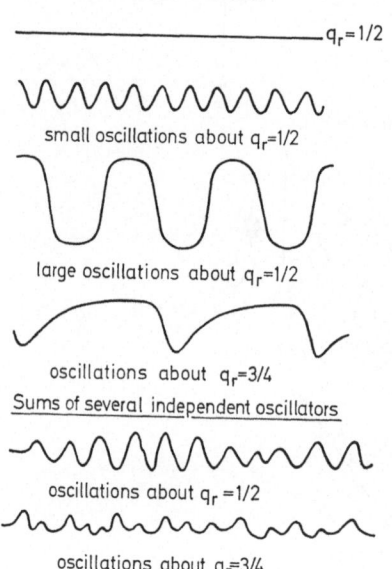

Fig. 2. Sensitivity oscillations

Wiener's remarks were actually made at a 1946 conference. In my view it is remarkable that in the 20 years since, with the exception of Wiener's own rather abstract work on Hamiltonians and neuronmechanics (N. Wiener, 1965), there is no trace of Hamiltonians and Statistical Mechanics in the field.

Before outlining the development of the statistical mechanics it is of interest to examine the behavior of the oscillators. When $X_r = q_r$, $dX_r/dt = 0$, so that activity is constant. The stationary states q_r correspond to neurons firing at constant rates. Whenever $X_r \neq q_r$, $dX_r/dt \neq 0$, and the result is oscillations of X_r about q_r corresponding to periodic variations in the mean neuronal firing rates.

Fig. 2 shows some examples of these oscillations. If one now considers a single oscillator to be continually bombarded by other circuits one is led to the point of view of statistical mechanics in which the individual oscillatior loses its identity and the average behavior of the oscillator can be viewed as if it were a member of a very large assembly whose dynamics is of the type outlined.

To first order there is an invariant measure of the form:

$$\frac{\exp\left(-\alpha\mathcal{H}\right)}{\displaystyle\prod_r \int_{-\infty}^{+\infty} \exp\left(-\alpha\mathcal{H}_r\right) dv_r}$$

so that there is a probability measure available for the computation of ensemble averages. It is easily shown that this measure is equivalent to:

$$\prod_r \frac{X_r^{\alpha\beta_r q_r}(1-X_r)^{\alpha\beta_r(1-q_r)}}{B[\alpha\beta_r\, q_r;\, \alpha\beta_r\,(1-q_r)]} \tag{9}$$

where $B[x, y]$ is EULER's *Beta* function. So in this case the well-known canonical distribution of statistical physics is the equally well-known *beta*-distribution of mathematical statistics, usually written in the form:

$$p(X)\,dX = \frac{X^{p-1}(1-X)^{q-1}}{B[p, q]}\,dX \tag{10}$$

$$(p, q > 0)$$

By simple transformations one can obtain the interval distributions of neural firing patterns, and the amplitude distributions for membrane potential fluctuations. Thus for the interspike-intervals τ_r:

$$X_r = 1 - r/\tau_r \tag{11}$$

and

$$p(\tau_r)\,d\tau_r = \frac{r^{-1}(1 - r/\tau_r)^{p-1}(r/\tau_r)^{q+1}d\tau_r}{B[p,q]} \tag{12}$$

where

$$p + q = \alpha\beta_r.$$

These distributions have enough free parameters (r, $q_{..}$, and $\alpha\beta_r$) for them to fit many of the histograms recently obtained from experimental data, for which a variety of stochastic process models have been constructed (cf.: G. L. GERSTEIN and B. MANDELBROT, 1964; R. B. STEIN, 1965; and M. TEN HOOPEN, 1966). The indications are that the model I have outlined, *mutatus mutandis*, will fit the expectation densities and interval histograms obtained from cells in somatic relay nuclei (G. F. POGGIO and L. J. VIERNCSTEIN, 1964), and thus serve as an alternative to the compound stochastic process models recently investigated (D. R. SMITH and G. K. SMITH, 1965; E. A. C. THOMAS, 1966; M. TEN HOOPEN and H. REUVER, 1967). One can also compute the excepted value of the rate at which the sensitivity X_r of a given cell crosses a fixed value X. In the simplest case of two interacting cells, 1 and 2, the formula is:

$$\omega[X_1 - X] = \langle\, |\dot{X}_1|\,\delta\,(X_1 - X)\rangle$$
$$= X(1 - X)\,p(X_1 = X)\,q_2(1 - q_2)\,p(X_2 = q_2)\,|\lambda_{21}|\cdot 2\alpha^{-1} \tag{13}$$

where the density function $p(.)$ is given by eqn. (10). Other formulas of interest are those for the coupling coefficient λ_{sr}:

$$\lambda_{sr} = \frac{\left\langle \frac{d}{dT}[X_r(1 - X_r)^{-1}])\,(X_s - q_s)\right\rangle}{\langle(X_s - q_s)^2\rangle} \tag{14}$$

and for $\alpha\beta_r$:

$$\alpha\beta_r = \frac{1 - [(q_r(1 - q_r))^{-1}\langle(X_r - q_r)^2\rangle]}{(q_r(1 - q_r))^{-1}\langle(X_r - q_r)^2\rangle} \tag{15}$$

Eqns. (14) and (15) are of interest in that they give the microscopic coupling parameters of the net, α_{sr} in terms of the first two moments of the activity, for it is easy to show that $q_r = \langle X_r \rangle$.

Concluding Remarks

The statistical mechanics that I have outlined evidently provides a method for estimating important parameters of neural nets. Of course the particular Hamiltonian that I have exhibited, $\mathscr{H} = \mathscr{H}_r$ is very simple, in that it is a sumfunction, so that thn variables in the net, the X_r, are effectively uncoupled, and may be said to be the *quasi-particles* of the net (D. TER HAAR, 1958). This follows from the nature of the postulated interactions between cells. More realistic interaction assumptions would generate more complicated Hamiltonians. The predictions obtained so far with the simple formulation do appear to fit experimental data however. The next step is to introduce thermodynamic functions and to investigate the resulting statistical *thermo*-neurodynamics. The constant α^{-1} in the canonical distribution is of course the formal analogue of the thermodynamical variable *temperature*. Eqn. (15) indicates that this temperature, θ, is in fact a function of the first two central moments of the distribution of neural sensitivities, $\langle X_r \rangle = q_r$, and $\langle (X_r - \langle X_r \rangle)^2 \rangle = \langle (X_r - q_r)^2 \rangle$. Therefore θ is a function of the mean and variance of the rate of neural spike emission. Following KERNER (1957), who investigated a statistical mechanics of interacting species closely related to the statistical mechanics I have outlined, I have called θ the *amplitude of fluctuation* of neural activity, reserving the term *neural activity* or simply *activity*, for the function $\mathscr{H}$, which is of course the formal analog of energy.

References

ECCLES, J. C.: The physiology of nerve cells. Baltimore: Johns Hopkins Press 1957.
— Brain and conscious experience, 24—58. Ed. J. C. ECCLES 1966.
FARLEY, B. G.: Computers in biomedical research 2, Academic Press 1965.
GERSTEIN, G. L., and B. MANDELBROT: Biophys. J. 4, 1 (1964).
GRIFFITH, J. S.: Biophys. J. 3, 299—308 (1963).
— Bull. Math. Biophys. 25, 111—120 (1963); 27, 187—195 (1965).
TER HAAR, D.: Introduction to the physics of manybody systems. Interscience (N.Y.) 1958.
TEN HOOPEN, M.: Cybernetics of neural processes. Ed. E. R. CAIANIELLO, CNR, Rome 1965.
— Biophys. J. 6, 435—451 (1966).
—, and H. A. REUVER: Selective interaction of two recurrent processes. J. Appl. Prob. 2, 286—292 (1965).
McCULLOCH, W. S., and W. PITTS: Bull. Math. Biophys. 5, 115—133 (1943).
VON NEUMANN, J.: Automata studies, 43—98, Eds. C. SHANNON, and J. McCARTHY, P.U.P., 1956.
POGGIO, G. F., and L. J. VIERNSTEIN: J. Neurophysiol. 1964, 6.
RALL, W.: Exp. Neurol. 1, 491—527 (1959).
ROSENBLATT, F.: Principles of neurodynamics. Spartan Books 1962.
SHOLL, D. A.: The organization of the cerebral cortex. London: Methuen 1956.
SMITH, D. R., and C. H. DAVIDSON: J. Amer. Med. Ass. 9, 268—279 (1962).
—, and G. K. SMITH: Biophys. J. 5, 1 σ(1965).
STEIN, R. B.: Biophys. J. 5, 2 (1965).
TAYLOR, W. K.: Proc. Roy. Soc. B. 159, 466—4678 (1964).
THOMAS, E. A. C.: Brit. J. Statist. Psychol. 1966 (in press).
UTTLEY, A. M.: Brain Res. 2, 21—50 (1966).
WIENER, N.: Ann. N.Y. Acad. Sci. 50, 4 187—278 (1948).
— Prog. in Brain Res. 17, 398—415 (1965).
WINOGRAD, S., and J. D. COWAN: Reliable computation in the presence of noise. M.I.T. Press 1963.

Subject Index